Professor
Reinhold Niebuhr

———

Edited by Ronald H. Stone
Theology of Peace, by Paul Tillich

Professor Reinhold Niebuhr

A MENTOR TO THE TWENTIETH CENTURY

RONALD H. STONE

Westminster/John Knox Press
Louisville, Kentucky

Unless otherwise noted, scripture quotations are from the King James Version of the Bible.

Scripture quotations marked RSV are from the Revised Standard Version of the Bible, copyright 1946, 1952, © 1971, 1973 by the Division of Christian Education of the National Council of the Churches of Christ in the U.S.A., and are used by permission.

Certain material in this work originally appeared as "The Contribution of Reinhold Niebuhr to the Late Twentieth Century," in Charles W. Kegley, ed., *Reinhold Niebuhr: His Religious, Social, and Political Thought* (New York: Pilgrim Press, 1984), and is reprinted by permission of Pilgrim Press.

Book design by Publishers' WorkGroup

First edition

This book is printed on acid-free paper that meets the American National Standards Institute Z39.48 standard. ∞

Published by Westminster/John Knox Press
Louisville, Kentucky

PRINTED IN THE UNITED STATES OF AMERICA

2   4   6   8   9   7   5   3   1

Library of Congress Cataloging-in-Publication Data

Stone, Ronald H.
   Professor Reinhold Niebuhr : a mentor to the twentieth century / Ronald H. Stone. — 1st ed.
     p.   cm.
   Includes bibliographical references and index.
   ISBN 0-664-25390-3 (alk. paper)

   1. Niebuhr, Reinhold, 1892–1971.   2. Theologians—United States—Biography.   I. Title.
BX4827.N5S73 1992
230'.092—dc20   91-47155

To the students of
Christian Social Ethics,
Pittsburgh Theological Seminary,
1969–1992

Contents

Preface

REINHOLD NIEBUHR (1892–1971) is regarded by many as the dominant North American theologian and political philosopher of the twentieth century. In the decades of the 1930s, 1940s, and 1950s his thought was paramount in informing the American learned-Protestant establishment. His influence continued to grow after his stroke in 1952, as the cumulative importance of earlier work was augmented by the late writings. His work was always criticized and opposed. He was controversial. In the late 1960s increasing radicalness in religious circles diminished his influence in the circles of reforming religious leadership. The influence of his thought in political places continued to grow into the 1980s. By the late 1980s, with both neoconservatives and liberals pulling at the mantle of his legacy, something of a revival occurred, with more and more dissertations being written on aspects of his thought. New books of interpretations kept appearing.[1] His widow, Ursula M. Niebuhr, provided two new books of original source material.[2] *Life* magazine chose him in 1990 as one of the most important Americans of the twentieth century.[3] Shortly before his death, eighteen of his books were still in print,[4] his aphorisms were widely quoted, and a whole generation of scholars, preachers, and policymakers was deeply affected by those who used much of his conceptual apparatus.

This book appears for the centenary of his birth. Written from within his tradition of liberal-Protestant Christian social ethics, it is an attempt to share an understanding of this brilliant and powerful man with a generation of readers who did not know him personally and whose times are different from his times.

Previous studies, including my own,[5] have failed to locate Niebuhr in the context of his vocation. He was not primarily a pastor or a preacher. He was not primarily an adviser to public figures. He was not primarily an author of immense productivity. He was first and foremost a professor of Protestant social ethics in the context of Protestant theological education. He was a professor who, for his entire adult life, taught in one theological seminary. Offers came from Harvard, Yale, and elsewhere to move him from Union Theological Seminary, but he stayed and, from September through May for thirty-two years, taught Protestant social ethics. This was his vocation. It was his life project. The evidence surveyed in this book will, I hope, force the studies that follow it to recognize this context. Charles Brown, with whom I have corresponded and discussed Niebuhr for two decades, also emphasizes the educational role in his new biography, *Niebuhr and His Age*.[6] Brown's careful study, which he has shared with me, emphasizes the contours of American history more than does this book. It does not go into the detail of the class lectures, as this book does, and in Brown's own interpretation, his work is more descriptive and less analytical. This book's emphasis on Niebuhr as professor is becoming an aspect of current interpretation of his work. This is demonstrated in the Union Theological Seminary and the Society of Christian Ethics Centenary observances focusing on that role.

My research includes the published works, the archives of Bethel Evangelical Church, the Niebuhr papers and other records at the Burke Library of Union Theological Seminary, the Niebuhr papers of the Library of Congress, the FBI file on Niebuhr, my personal collection of letters and manuscripts, and the secondary sources. Sources for this study that are largely unused by other studies are his class lectures, combining those of the Library of Congress, Niebuhr's students, and, for 1964–1968, my own class notes. Finally, with the kind assistance of Matthew Peterson, Hargie Likins, and Barry Jackson, a questionnaire was sent to 320 randomly chosen Union graduates, ten from each year of his full-time teaching, and to 80 selected Union graduates. The results of over one hundred replies are now in the Clifford E. Barbour Library of Pittsburgh Theological Seminary. (See the Appendix for a copy of the survey instrument.)

This study deals with the public Niebuhr, as did my first book. My refusal to share personal revelations in that book was based on my hope that he would remain alive to look at it. His death in 1971 disappointed that hope. The attempt to probe the inner life of Reinhold Niebuhr undertaken by Richard Fox is in my opinion largely a failure.[7] It is simply not possible to find that powerful, original, acute mind in the trail of short letters and remembrances of those of Niebuhr's acquaintances whom Fox could interview. Fox did not know Niebuhr, and the ambitious, scheming, frightened figure he shows us, shaped by Freudian family conflicts, is inaccurate and largely irrelevant. For those of us who counted Niebuhr among our closest friends, the picture of Niebuhr as unable to sustain a friendship is laughable; such a portrait is denied by the very letters Fox read from Niebuhr to John C. Bennett, Will Scarlett, and Felix Frankfurter. I have tried to stress Reinhold Niebuhr's brilliance, originality, and persuasiveness while avoiding psychoanalytic speculation.

This study does not include a chapter evaluating the Niebuhr legacy. That task is a book in itself. I do discuss other interpretations of Niebuhr in this work and elsewhere.[8] This book returns to the subject of international relations only occasionally, as that was the theme of my earlier book, but it was impossible to exclude the subject. As I have been writing on Niebuhr for thirty years, I have found myself including some newly edited revisions of that material in this book. Sections of *Reinhold Niebuhr: Prophet to Politicians* (Nashville: Abingdon Press, 1972) are reworked and reprinted in this study. Another major difference from my earlier study is that I do not distinguish the late Niebuhr from the middle Niebuhr so sharply. By the end of World War II he was what he would remain, an Augustinian liberal; it required an examination of his class lectures for me to see that. Others who knew him at Union in the 1950s probably understood: Roger Shinn, for example.

If Niebuhr's perspective was limited, so is mine. Niebuhr presented an affirmation and a critique of the reforming-Protestant liberal social ethic in which I stand. My origins were in Iowa, his in Illinois. He was my teacher, and I was his last teaching assistant. Our perspectives are finite—other interpretations will emerge—but Reinhold Niebuhr was the most brilliant professor I ever met. I hope this book, whatever its limitations, shows him as that professor.

My thanks for assistance are extended to John C. Bennett; Charles

Brown; Matthew Peterson; Roger L. Shinn; the graduates of Union Theological Seminary who shared their remembrances with me; Robina Leeper, who typed the manuscript from handwritten pages; and the staffs of Pittsburgh Theological Seminary and Union Theological Seminary, who helped me along the way.

NOTES

1. Susan Nelson Dunfee, *Beyond Servanthood: Christianity and the Liberation of Women* (Lanham, Md.: University Press of America, 1989); Kenneth Durkin, *Reinhold Niebuhr* (Wilton, Conn.: Morehouse Publishing Co., 1989); Richard Fox, *Reinhold Niebuhr: A Biography* (New York: Pantheon Books, 1985); Richard Harries, ed., *Reinhold Niebuhr and the Issues of Our Time* (Grand Rapids: Wm. B. Eerdmans Publishing Co., 1986); Dennis P. McCann, *Christian Realism and Liberation Theology* (Maryknoll, N.Y.: Orbis Books, 1981); Paul Merkley, *Reinhold Niebuhr: A Political Account* (Montreal: McGill-Queens University Press, 1975); Richard J. Neuhaus, *Reinhold Niebuhr Today* (Grand Rapids: Wm. B. Eerdmans Publishing Co., 1989); Judith Plaskow, *Sex, Sin, and Grace: Women's Experience and the Theologies of Reinhold Niebuhr and Paul Tillich* (Lanham, Md.: University Press of America, 1980).

2. Ursula M. Niebuhr, ed., *Reinhold Niebuhr: Justice and Mercy* (1974) and *Remembering Reinhold Niebuhr: Letters of Reinhold and Ursula M. Niebuhr* (1991).

3. *Life* (Fall 1990), p. 12. The only other figure from the world of religion was Billy Graham.

4. *Books in Print, 1968*, vol. 1 (New York: R. R. Bowker Co., 1968), p. 1130.

5. Ronald H. Stone, *Reinhold Niebuhr: Prophet to Politicians* (Nashville: Abingdon Press, 1972); reprinted (Lanham, Md.: University Press of America, 1981); out of print.

6. Charles Brown, *Niebuhr and His Age: Reinhold Niebuhr's Prophetic Role in the Twentieth Century* (Philadelphia: Trinity Press International, 1992).

7. Richard Fox, *Reinhold Niebuhr*.

8. See Ronald H. Stone, *Realism and Hope* (Lanham, Md.: University Press of America, 1976, 1977); "The Realists and Their Critics," *Worldview* 16 (June 1973), 19–23.

1

Origins

THE STORY of a social ethics professor is a history of society and self. Karl Paul Reinhold Niebuhr was born on June 21, 1892, in Wright City, Missouri. He grew up in small towns in Missouri and Illinois in the center of an expanding American empire. His was the land of flat fields and glorious sunsets. The rivalries were between farm kids and town kids in those days of relative innocence. Between Wright City, Missouri, and the town of Lincoln in Illinois flowed the Mississippi. Growing up on both sides of the Mississippi centers a person in America. Mark Twain's tales are not far wide of the mark in describing life in the Midwest near the Mississippi. *Huckleberry Finn* (1884) was set only 80 miles from both Wright City and St. Charles, Missouri, Niebuhr's childhood homes, and 130 miles from Lincoln, Illinois.

Half the nation's population still lived on farms, but the transformation toward an urban civilization had begun. African Americans had been subdued by Reconstruction, and their festering wounds had not yet translated into migration northward. Women were still a third of a century away from gaining voting rights and full citizenship. Immigration from Europe provided workers for expanding industries. Attempts at unionization failed before the courts and the terror of the industrialists' violence. In Pittsburgh in 1892 it took both an army of Pinkerton men and the state militia to secure Henry C. Frick and Andrew Carnegie's steel company from the threat of unionization.

In 1892, McKinley was defeated by the resurgent Grover Cleveland,

1

the only Democrat to win the presidency in the post–Civil War nineteenth century. The panic of 1893 in some ways was the worst recession of the century, and the government allowed it to run its course. Issues of employment and welfare led to the invasion of Washington, D.C., by Cox's Army in 1894. Issues such as the gold standard and tariffs reflected basic divisions in the country, with reformers favoring the losing cause of silver and low tariffs. Reformers in the Midwest struggled against the economy's domination by growing monopolies and eastern banks. By 1900, 10 percent of the population controlled 90 percent of the wealth. Yet a child of the Midwest knew only the rough equality that characterized midwestern small-town life.

Before Reinhold Niebuhr reached his teens, the United States became an empire with offshore colonies. The Spanish-American War of 1898 left the United States controlling Cuba, Puerto Rico, Guam, and the Philippines. Hawaii was added in 1898 and Samoa in 1899. Forces were sent to China in 1900. Theodore Roosevelt intervened in Colombia in 1903 to take Panama, in the Dominican Republic in 1905, and in Cuba in 1906. In 1907 he sent the Great White Fleet around the world to show the flag. The legacies of these armed projections of U.S. power in Niebuhr's youth were to occupy the social ethicist for his whole career.

In New York in 1892 an intellectual drama was taking place that would also affect the maturing Niebuhr. When Charles A. Briggs applied the new historical-critical scholarship to the Bible in his teaching at Union Theological Seminary, the General Assembly of the Presbyterian Church in the United States of America vetoed his appointment as professor. Union Seminary supported its professor and his scholarship. Briggs was cleared of heresy in two subsequent trials, but on a later appeal of the decision, he was dismissed from Presbyterian ministry. This action, spread over four trials, from Portland, Oregon, to New York City, attracted national and international attention. The outcome led Union Theological Seminary to separate itself from the Presbyterian Church and to develop as an ecumenical seminary, without institutional dependence on state, church, or university. So the seminary went with modernist trends in scholarship to defend its academic freedom. Almost forty years later this action and Reinhold Niebuhr would intersect.

Family

Gustav and Lydia Niebuhr gave the church three theologians, two sons and a daughter—a large proportion of the religious genius of the twentieth century. Reinhold's family provided him with a background of piety and trust. It also gave him an introduction to liberal German theological scholarship in the context of a devout household. This was provided within the authoritarian family structure of progressive German immigrants, tempered by midwestern America's principles of equality and freedom. Many testimonies add immense energy and strength as family inheritances. The biographical evidence suggests successful resolution of the various crises of life-cycle development. One other factor was significant. The greatness of German theological scholarship at the beginning of the twentieth century is widely acknowledged, but it coexisted with a disastrous social situation. The freeing of this theology from its negative social context could not happen in Germany. It could be freed in Switzerland or America, but in Switzerland it took on a certain neutralism, parochialism, and intraecclesiastical confinement. In the United States the liberal German inheritance had a different opportunity, for here, freed from the German social disaster, it had a chance to blossom along with an American social philosophy of equality and liberty. This of course could happen only in bilingual persons who were really comfortable with their heritage as Americans. Reinhold's German family gave him the gift of being free to be an American.

Previous interpretations of Reinhold Niebuhr have stressed his father's role in shaping his vocation.[1] This is a natural outcome of viewing his origins in a patriarchal period, given the expressive personality of his father, Gustav. However, the truth requires a more balanced picture. Niebuhr's mother, Lydia, was as central to his development as his more famous father.

Gustav Niebuhr, born in 1863, emigrated from Hardissen, Lippe-Detmold, Germany, as an eighteen-year-old. He brought with him only a few possessions, but he had the traditions of Germany in his nearly completed studies of the *Gymnasium*. He also had the Christian traditions of pietism and the Lutheran-Reformed theology of the Heidelberg Catechism as a confirmed member of the church.[2]

Gustav received a ready welcome on the farm of his cousin, Karoline Luettman Hummermeier, in Eleroy, Illinois. Her husband, William, encouraged Gustav to consider the ministry after the young Niebuhr was moved by the preaching of Ernst Nolting at the Salem Church.[3] Nolting, also from Lippe-Detmold, had been educated in the denominational seminary at Marthasville, Missouri, which eventually developed into Eden Seminary.[4]

Gustav entered this seminary of the Evangelical Synod of North America in 1883 as its building in North St. Louis was being built. The building was dedicated with the expectation of growth in an expanding church in a developing land. It began its fall classes with three instructors for seventy-eight students.[5] Two of the three faculty were educated in Germany, and the traditions of Berlin were thus transmitted to the students in Missouri.

Gustav was ordained in 1885 and by that summer had moved west to San Francisco to serve German immigrants in that expanding city. He founded a church, St. John's, and turned a second mission project over to a colleague. On May 8, 1887, he married Lydia Hosto, the daughter of a pastor who was also planting Evangelical Synod churches in San Francisco, Oregon, and Washington. Lydia, who worked as an assistant in her father's ministry, plunged into her duties as a pastor's wife. Her own deep religious life and organizational skills contributed first to Gustav's ministry and then for nearly twenty years to Reinhold's work, culminating in an association with her daughter Hulda's vocation as a religious educator and professor at McCormick Theological Seminary in Chicago for more than twenty-five years.

Lydia became influential as a practical organizer of the church and as a religious educator. William G. Chrystal, who pioneered in the study of the Niebuhr family, diminished her importance when he credited Reinhold with following his father and Hulda with following Lydia's leadership. Lydia also deeply affected the lives of her two younger sons, for they too became religious educators. All three children, after various other services to the church, found their vocations as seminary professors. The role of the seminary teacher is to the Sunday school as the professor in a graduate school of education is to the public school classroom. Lydia's piety and emphasis on religious education shaped Reinhold and propelled him toward his vocation.

From his father, Reinhold inherited a willingness to found institutions for church service and a commitment to persuasion through journalism. Gustav wrote often for the denominational paper *Der Friedensbote* and was a founder and director of a home for epileptics, Emmaus Home. His ministry was characterized by bold energy. He became the fund-raiser for the Emmaus Home, resigning his pastorate for this risky undertaking. When he succeeded, he plunged into founding churches in Utah, while advocating a program of mission to the suffering. His writings show a dedication to the relief of suffering through direct institutional work with the poor, reflecting the inner-mission strategies of the German churches.

Social action was just part of the environment in which the Niebuhr children grew up. The Christian life was witnessed to by the good work that flowed from it. Gustav, of course, drew his emphasis upon practical consequences of faith from the Christian tradition generally. But it also came from William Becker, a seminary professor who was still teaching at Eden Seminary when Reinhold attended theology classes there. In Reinhold's writings, this teaching would echo like a refrain. Becker had taught both men that "the foremost and final proof of Christianity will be found in the influence which the Christian faith has exerted upon life."[6]

In 1902, the news that Gustav was being considered for a professorship at Eden reached Utah. Although he left Utah for Missouri, the call went instead to a professor trained in Germany at Königsberg. Reinhold recorded that his father discussed the opportunity with him. William G. Chrystal reports that several years later, when the professor appointed in place of Gustav resigned from Eden because of student protest, Reinhold was among the student leaders.[7]

Gustav moved on to Lincoln, Illinois, reuniting the family from whom his work had frequently distanced him. There he managed and energized the deaconess movement, directed a hospital, taught in the church school, pastored St. John's Church, and wrote, becoming a leader of his denomination.

At Reinhold's ordination, his father's friend William Theodore Jungk could say, "We are about to lay the mantle of a father upon the son."[8] The reference to the mantle is to Elisha taking up the mantle of Elijah and the promise of a "double portion" of his spirit (2 Kings 2:9–14). It was a weighty saying at an ordination, especially when the father had been buried for only two months. Indeed, all the children took up parts of the mantle, with Reinhold being only the most obvious as he literally followed in his father's pulpit. Hulda became a religious educator. Helmut Richard followed, first as academic leader in the denominational educational institutions of Elmhurst and Eden and later from Yale in developing the study of Christian ethics. Reinhold most actively demonstrated the political dimensions of the prophetic ministry. As with Elisha, conflict with rulers went with the mantle.

Reinhold's older brother, Walter, went into the field of journalism and was an unsuccessful candidate for the Democratic nomination for

Congress in 1912 as a Wilsonian liberal. Walter's contacts with Carl Vrooman, whom he supported for the seat, would later lead to an offer to Reinhold to accept political appointment. The Niebuhr brothers seemed to be supporting the reforming side in a reforming age. Their father had supported Theodore Roosevelt's progressivism and the boys followed, but on the democratic side of the political conflict.

The split in the Republican party between Roosevelt and Taft allowed Democrat Woodrow Wilson to win the presidency in 1912. The idealism of Wilson suited the age and the Niebuhr boys well. Conservation issues, free trade, regulation of commerce, prohibition, and women's suffrage were all moving ahead as reforming issues in 1912. Wilson combined academic distinction with the virtues of the Presbyterian manse in which he had grown up. His tendency toward pacifism was reinforced by his youth in a Yankee-despoiled Georgia. His policies of New Freedoms were pushed through Congress during his first eighteen months in office.

The reforms included treaties of conciliation negotiated by William Jennings Bryan. Tariffs were reduced, the banking system was rationalized by the Federal Reserve Act, business was tempered a little by the Clayton Antitrust Act, and workers received some breaks through the Workmen's Compensation Act of 1916, the Adamson Act of 1916, and the Seamen's Act of 1915. Enough was accomplished for the worker for Wilson to receive the condemnation of the business elite.

Despite his proclaimed anti-imperialist ideals, Wilson found himself engaging the marines in armed interventions in Nicaragua, which the United States took over again, and in Haiti, the Dominican Republic, and Mexico. Later interventions in 1917 involved Cuba and the purchase of the Virgin Islands. The Caribbean virtually became a U.S. lake, guarded from native aspirants to power by the U.S. Marines. Idealism gave way to force, but Wilson tried to exercise national self-restraint. He managed to avoid a major war with Mexico, but his policies did drive President Victoriano Huerta from office and into exile.

Reinhold's writing at Yale on international relations and his invitation from the Illinois reform politician Carl Vrooman to join the Wilson administration give a picture of young Niebuhr as a Wilsonian.[9] Despite his later denunciations of moralistic idealism in politics, the major outlines of Reinhold Niebuhr's politics of domestic political reform and the restrained exercise of power abroad seemed marked by Wilson's actual policies.

Church

Before leaving Eden Seminary for Yale University, Reinhold Niebuhr was ordained as a minister of the German Evangelical Synod of North America. The Evangelical Synod had grown from a frontier union of independent German (Lutheran/Reformed) congregations in 1840 into a solid denomination by 1915.[10] Though founded as a new society under American conditions it reflected the evangelical church of Prussia, which had merged Lutheran and Reformed traditions under King Frederick William III in 1817. As heir to both Reformed and Lutheran traditions, its theological founders included Luther, Melanchthon, Zwingli, and Calvin. The union in Prussia reflected the theological tendencies of Schleiermacher for unity as well as the practical political agenda of the king. Niebuhr's family, being from Lippe-Detmold, had a little more of the Reformed tendency than some of the others in the denomination, since that section of Germany had stronger Calvinist or Reformed tendencies than did much of Prussia. The immigrants from the Palatine (southern Germany, centered around Heidelberg) also represented the Reformed tendencies among the more heavily Lutheran denomination. By the time of Reinhold's ordination, the denomination thought of itself as American but still held services in German.

The union tradition was generous in allowing differences in theological judgments, and this open-mindedness made it suspect in the eyes of German Christians who considered themselves Lutherans rather than unionists. The union tendency also emphasized the ecumenical and uniting spirit of the denomination. A third characteristic was the early recognition of the social character and social reforming nature of Christian faith. The denomination was an early supporter of the Federal Council of Churches, adopting its social creed in 1913, and later it helped found the World Council of Churches. Another characteristic that distinguished it from some new denominations was a commitment to an educated ministry and, as far as possible, an educated laity. The early theologians at the denominational seminary at Eden were all German-university trained, and pastors were busy founding and administering parochial schools until the Sunday schools, in alliance with public school education, were seen as a replacement.

Reinhold Niebuhr grew up in this German-speaking denomination within the American culture, attending mostly parochial schools, with a year of public high school before Elmhurst College. Though the denomination had its share of immigrants who hung on stubbornly to what they thought they had learned in Germany, the leadership of the denomination was Americanized under the influence of World War I. By 1925 it had dropped the name "German," and the transition to English services and instruction was well under way. By 1934 the Evangelical Synod merged with the German Reformed Church, a more Calvinist immigrant church stronger in Pennsylvania and the eastern United States, to create the Evangelical and Reformed Church. Reinhold Niebuhr had urged such a union, and H. Richard Niebuhr served on the union committee in its early work; their teacher, Samuel Press, was influential in the merger, and his brother Paul was president of the Evangelical Synod at the time. Samuel Press was to continue his ecumenical push and, with the encouragement of the Niebuhr brothers, support the Evangelical and Reformed Church into union in 1957 with the Congregational Christian Church, the major American heir to the Calvinist Puritans.

The Niebuhr parents supported their church's liberal tendencies—toleration of theological differences, learned ministry, ecumenical spirit, and commitment to social engagement—and Reinhold's close identification with his parents set many of the directions of his own ministry. Another characteristic of the Evangelical Synod at its best was an informed piety. The pietist movement in Germany inspired the missionary society of Basel, which sent many ministers to the Midwest. Pietism can run counter to scholarship, and there was some tension over the direction it would take in the Evangelical Synod. But the German-educated pietists were able to hold their positions intellectually with the non-Christian rationalists of the nineteenth century and strengthened the church in the Midwest, so that it never split into opposing camps. The general recognition by Christian audiences that Reinhold spoke "with authority" is a witness to this inner piety, part of the socially communicated inheritance from his parents' church that formed his character. The decision of a youth such as Niebuhr to be confirmed in the Evangelical Synod was more the result of an internalized conviction of the persuasiveness of the catechism classes than it was any emotional decision. Young people from Christian homes grew into the Evangelical Synod through education in the classical symbols, principles, and teaching of the church. Between his confirmation and his ordination, Reinhold experienced two institutions of the church beyond his parents' parish.

Elmhurst and Eden

At the time Reinhold and H. Richard Niebuhr attended it, Elmhurst College was a church institution for pre-seminary education, in preparation for ministry. It also prepared teachers for parochial schools, but it did not grant regular A.B. degrees until H. Richard's first year as president of the institution in 1924. Reinhold described Elmhurst as "little more than a high school," and he was literally correct. Reflecting its German origins, Elmhurst had some of the characteristics of a *Gymnasium*, designed to prepare the way for further study.

The Niebuhr brothers attended Elmhurst during the Irion era, the long (thirty-two-year) presidency of Daniel Irion. The Reverend Mr. Irion taught Bible, catechism, and Greek and administered the institution in detail. He made the rounds at 5:30 A.M. to be sure the boys were responding to the wake-up bell, and he stayed with them from morning chapel to evening devotions. The faculty grew from six to eight teachers during Irion's tenure.[11] Reinhold later described Elmhurst as "strong in the classics and weak in everything else."[12] He felt adequately prepared in Greek, Latin, and ancient history, but deficient in modern history, science, and English. A letter of Reinhold's to his Eden professor Samuel Press in 1914 is uncharacteristically bitter as he reflects upon his Elmhurst years. Aside from his critique of Elmhurst, the interesting note is the reference to his own passion for ministerial education. Photographs and reminiscences concerning Reinhold at Elmhurst reveal a young man growing, enjoying life, acting in plays, participating in the band, and managing the baseball team. His ability to quote Shakespeare spontaneously in his later years must have owed something to his many roles in the dramatic productions of the school, and his later stage presence shows that those roles reinforced his developing self-confidence.

In 1910, Reinhold moved on from Elmhurst to Eden College in North St. Louis, prepared, as the Evangelical Synod intended him to be, to begin seminary work. Niebuhr's academic interests were awakened at Eden by Samuel Press. Press was the first American-born professor at the seminary and the first to teach all his courses in English. He himself had been educated at Elmhurst and Eden and after serving churches, at the Friedrich Wilhelm University in Berlin. Niebuhr would refer to Press's theological position as evangelical liberalism, since it combined the warm piety of the Evangelical Synod with German academic liberalism.

Press introduced the students to American theological traditions as well as German ones. His study of the inner-mission movement in the German church led him, like Reinhold's father, to found a social welfare institution. Under Press's direction, Reinhold was involved in social research to determine the needs for social welfare institutions in St. Louis.[13] Press's course on Amos involved both exegesis and the practical application of Amos's standards of justice. The choice of Amos and Paul as central biblical pillars for Niebuhr depended in part upon his teacher's choice of these sources. Reinhold later would serve on the Board of Directors of the renamed Eden Seminary for the duration of Press's "Americanization" of the seminary as president. For part of that time H. Richard Niebuhr served as dean of the seminary.

Reinhold distinguished himself at Eden as a leader in extracurricular activities, particularly as a debater and editor of the student journal and also as valedictorian. Thanks to William G. Chrystal's work, two of Reinhold's essays from student days at Eden are now published.[14]

The *Keryx* (Messenger) was first published in 1911 at Press's urging, and Reinhold was a founding member of the staff, later serving as editor.[15] The significance that founding and editing journals held for Niebuhr's practical theology has often been missed by his interpreters.[16] From his student days, Niebuhr took church journalism seriously, as part of the task of the learned minister, which involves teaching and persuading the church to a deeper understanding of its faith and the consequences of that faith. He learned first from his father and then from his teacher that church journalism was part of his vocation, and he practiced it for sixty years.

Niebuhr's first essay in *Keryx* has a very high doctrine of church, combined with reservations about the church's direct role in guiding public morals.[17] The church is of divine origin and a source of contact for humanity with the divine. Of course, the church must support morality, but Niebuhr wanted the church to emphasize the gospel, not public morality. The real task of the church, the eighteen-year-old wrote, was to make all people Christians and to make Christians better. Rushing into the fray of struggles about civic virtue would divert the church from its central task. The public moral problems he mentioned included the weakening of the family, low business standards, alcohol, and a growing gap between rich and poor. He repeated the view that morality comes from within, and only Jesus Christ can change hearts full of sin. Present-day moralists, he wrote, are tempted by Pharisaism and are in danger of losing the depth of their faith.[18] The essay shows no hint of the Social Gospel influence, except perhaps in opposing it. German Lutheran separation from society rather than Calvinist engagement with it characterizes the essay, which is also innocent of the knowledge of human factors shaping the church. It is the work of a young ministerial student who has not yet studied sociology or dealt with the church practically.

The second essay, written two years later as he left Eden, was on the merits of revival methods versus educational methods for the development of Christian life.[19] Reinhold found little of worth in the revival method, while regarding education as a major method of strengthening church life. He preferred one-on-one evangelism, but he recognized that sometimes, if revival were not abused, it could be useful in winning people's allegiance. For him, preaching and education were the most effective means of contributing to Christian life. His commitment to education as the means of preserving, advancing, and deepening the church is clear by the time he graduated from seminary.

Reinhold's mentor, Samuel Press, had inspired Reinhold to seek further education. After weeks of negotiating with the Evangelical Synod, he was granted permission to do graduate study, provided he would return to ministry in the Midwest. He sorted through various university catalogs and, with his father's encouragement, chose Yale. His father died in April 1913, and Reinhold filled the pulpit until he took the train to New Haven in September.

Yale University

The School of Religion at Yale was being revitalized under the leadership of Dean Charles R. Brown. New professors were installed, and efforts to expand student enrollment involved Dean Brown's own recruitment trips to the Midwest and other sections of the country. Financial arrangements with the rest of the university were strengthened, permitting further development. From Dean Brown's tenure to the present the school, returning to its name of Yale Divinity School in 1920, has remained a major force in the preparation of Protestant clergy.

Writing from Yale in 1914 for the Eden Seminary *Keryx,* now under the editorship of his younger brother, Reinhold focused on two of the three themes that Roland H. Bainton has ascribed to the Divinity School. Bainton emphasized the New England tradition of Yale as the Reformation emphasis on faith in God's role in history and the enlightenment emphasis on learning and pietism, with its emphasis on the emotions.[20] Niebuhr, furthermore, emphasized the devotional life reinforcing the piety and the demands for rigorous learning.[21] The theme of God's action in history did not attract his attention as he reflected on Yale in 1914. His writing for those back in Eden stressed the exciting intellectual challenge he found and the presence of piety, including regular chapel. His reflections also indicated a lingering insecurity about his German midwestern origins in the midst of an eastern ecclesiastical establishment, but it is easy to exaggerate the meaning of those reflections. Midwestern small-town boys often like to speak as if they are just off the farm while taking the better grades and scholarships at eastern universities. Reinhold was insecure the first semester, but by the second year he was joined by three more students from Eden, and he was on his way to winning a lucrative essay contest, completing his M.A. thesis, and being asked to undertake doctoral studies.

Reinhold's German background represented both gains and losses. He was not as secure in his English written construction as he wanted to be, but his knowledge of German helped to keep him ahead of his peers for years. German scholarship was dominant and he could easily read what they either waited for in translation or laboriously translated for themselves.

Elmhurst and Eden had not given Niebuhr the degrees of Bachelor of Arts and Bachelor of Divinity that Yale expected for graduate work in theology. He gained the B.D. degree at Yale by adding one year of Bachelor of Divinity curriculum and a thesis to his preparation at Eden. He skipped the B.A. degree and went on to receive his Master of Arts with the completion of a year in Yale University's graduate school and a second thesis. The previous impact of Eden was focused in the contribution of a single teacher, Press.

> The seminary was influential in my life primarily because of the creative effect upon me of the life of a very remarkable man, Dr. S. D. Press, who combined a childlike innocency with a rigorous scholarship in biblical and systematic subjects. This proved the point that an educational institution needs only to have Mark Hopkins on one end of a log and a student on the other.[22]

Niebuhr's correspondence with Professor Press reveals his growing development as a young scholar. At Yale, he became involved with a large university and the world of European scholarship. He was also freed from the limitations of a single denomination. Yale's academic life thrilled him; he rejoiced in the written assignments and in the quality of instruction he received. Professors Douglas C. Macintosh in philosophical theology and Frank C. Porter and Benjamin W. Bacon in New Testament studies particularly impressed him. He wrote to Press about his plans on his B.D. thesis on "The Validity of Religious Experience and the Certainty of Religious Knowledge."[23]

This Bachelor of Divinity thesis was the young Reinhold's response to his studies in philosophy and an attempt to answer the big questions. He approached his task of validating religious ideas with characteristic energy and hard work. But no matter how bright a twenty-one-year-old may be, he can hardly do justice to a title like "The Validity and Certainty of Religious Knowledge" in thirty-eight pages. The extant copy of the thesis in the Library of Congress may be only a rough draft, for it is full of typing and spelling errors, and there is no documentation of the dozen philosophers chosen as authorities. But it was no small accomplishment for Niebuhr to move from his primary academic language of German to a Yale thesis in English. Some of the sentences and paragraphs remain quite awkward, as if he were still striving for mastery of English rather than being comfortable with it. But Macintosh must have been impressed with the paper's power and boldness, even though many of the arguments were Macintosh's own views.

The thesis is in four parts. Chapter 1, entitled "The Decadence of Authority Religion," is intended to show the decay or waning of authoritarian religion. Niebuhr saw traditional arguments for the authority of scripture overcome by historical criticism. The rejection of the metaphysical claims of early church Christology weakened the authority claimed for Christ. Revelation itself could no longer be regarded as authoritative. The rise of evolutionary thinking also discredited traditional claims for religious authority. Still, people believed in "supernatural religion." How could such claims be true? Here the young Niebuhr found himself as a persuaded Christian studying philosophy and wondering how his faith could be verified.

Chapter 2, "The Inadequacy of Naturalism," is the shortest part of the thesis, and it suggested that various philosophies of naturalism do not explain the moral realities of life. The thesis did not consider a fundamental paradigm shift in consciousness. It argued rather that, within traditional Western expectations, naturalism new or ancient does not fulfill the metaphysical needs for understanding the accepted moral order. This section of the thesis began to signal the conclusion of the thesis that, because a moral order is a necessary precondition of human existence, there must be "a God who insures the moral order."[24] Also, the reality of human personality implies a God.[25]

Chapter 3, "Metaphysics and Supernaturalism," examined idealistic philosophies. This survey concluded that the God of idealism was too close to pantheism to be acceptable for the religious needs for a transcendent God. The transcendent God who permitted freedom and real moral struggle corresponded to the vital needs of the religious life, thought the young Niebuhr. He had rejected authoritarian religion in the first chapter, naturalism in the second, and here "as we reject idealism and turn to realism," the turn was toward pluralism, empiricism, and the "tough-minded" thought of William James.[26] Already, argumentation of Niebuhr's mature philosophy emerges—the creation of ideal types, their comparative rejection, and then the presentation of a preferred alternative, usually in terms of some kind of religious realism. In this case Niebuhr chose the preliminary use of William James's pragmatism. The final chapter, maintaining that supernatural religion was at least not defeated by pragmatism, could move on to what James called "over beliefs." Also prominent in allowing for religious belief were the arguments of Henri Bergson. Niebuhr's appreciation for Bergson's God of "superconsciousness" prefigures his later sympathy for Alfred North Whitehead's perspective of a somewhat limited God who permits human freedom.

The young Niebuhr thought he had secured the foundations of religious certainty by arguing that some metaphysics, including the ones he preferred, were favorable toward supernaturalism. The final chapter, "The Validity of Religious Ideas," combines several forms of religious apologetics to defend a religion of theism, immortality, freedom, and human ability to reason correctly in matters of religion. The strongest argument seems to be Kant's: Religious ideas are necessary if the moral order is to make sense.[27] He also appreciatively comments on Ritschl's formulation of this tradition: "It is to this view that we commit ourselves as most satisfactory."[28]

The young thinker accepted as postulates of his reasoning the existence of the human soul, the truth of morality, and the value of personality. Given these assumptions, religious beliefs supporting those assumptions seemed valid. He also needed to assume what he called "the dogma" of optimism that our minds could reach truth, that logic was able to reach reality.

It is hard to know how much he convinced either himself or Professor Macintosh. Both already believed in the Christian perspective liberally conceived. Their arguments were arguments from belief about belief. How much did they want to prove? At most, Niebuhr followed Kant in arguing for God, immortality, freedom, and responsibility. However, the title implied all religious ideas were being validated. Contradictory religious ideas on fundamental human moral questions, as for example marriage, might prove more about different religious taboos arising from different communities than they do about the "truth" of religious ideas. But that was a degree of relativity to be faced later. At this point, although the issue of moral relativity arose, the whole discussion presupposed the validity of Western, Christian, liberal morality.

After completing the year required for the B.D., Niebuhr applied to the graduate school. At first, his inquiries concerning graduate work were rebuffed, but the dean, a German scholar, went back to Germany in the summer of 1914 and got caught up in the events of World War I. A second interview, with the new dean, Wilbur Cross (later to become governor of Connecticut), was more fruitful. Cross admitted Niebuhr as a special student with accession to degree status after he had maintained a straight A average.

Niebuhr wrote his M.A. thesis and attended classes while serving a small congregation in Derby, Connecticut. His academic work was mainly under the supervision of Douglas Macintosh, and he threw himself into philosophical studies with a purpose that was new to him. Professor Macintosh lent him books from his study and encouraged him to pursue doctoral studies. Nearly forty years later, Niebuhr reflected on his Yale years, saying of Macintosh, "He persuaded me to work for a higher degree in order to teach theology. I didn't actually achieve that for years until I came to New York."[29]

Two other incidents while Niebuhr was at Yale throw light on his future career and development. First, he won the Church Peace Union's essay contest on the subject of needed developments or initiatives toward world peace, and the monetary prize was quite welcome to a student with growing debts. Second, he turned down a job.

Between Niebuhr's two years at Yale, Carl Vrooman, an Assistant Secretary of Agriculture under Woodrow Wilson visiting in Lincoln, Illinois, asked him to be his secretary. The young student, whose political leanings had thus been recognized, was also tempted by the salary, which was more than he had any chance of attaining through advancement within the Evangelical ministry, but he returned to Yale and his commitment to religion, despite his strong interest in politics.

Niebuhr was deeply influenced by the liberal thought and theology of Yale University. Although the impact of teachers upon many graduate students is immense, it may be more direct on divinity students and students in the humanities who are explicitly dealing with questions of personality and human value. Niebuhr came to have deep disagreements with Professor Macintosh,[30] but he never was ungrateful. He was proud, even as an elderly gentleman, that he had not in his writing misrepresented Douglas Macintosh's thought, and he remembered Macintosh as a supportive friend.

The major work by Niebuhr from his two years at Yale is "The Contribution of Christianity to the Doctrine of Immortality," his 1915 M.A. thesis. It reveals the extent to which the young Niebuhr was a product of the early twentieth-century liberal theology. The thesis argued that the idea of the immortality of the soul was enriched by Christianity, and that the idea of immortality could be maintained after claims for the physical resurrection of Jesus were abandoned. The thesis does not fall neatly into either New Testament studies or philosophy of religion. As a borderline study, it illustrates the influence of Professors Bacon and Porter in New Testament as well as of Macintosh in philosophy of religion.

The claim of the physical resurrection was, according to Niebuhr, a product of historical development. The evidence for a physical resurrection of Jesus was not credible to moderns. In any case, a general truth could not be proved by an isolated fact, and the argument from the resurrection of Jesus to eternal life for other people was fallacious. The resurrection, if true, could be used only as evidence for the eventual bodily resurrection of others and not as evidence for the immortality of the soul. The resurrection proved too much if it proved anything. "It [the resurrection] is the fossil remnant of a different [world of thought] than that of the present day and has therefore outlived its usefulness."[31]

On the other hand, the immortality of the soul seemed reasonable from the perspective of both moral and religious life. The doctrine of immortality was justified by the "will to believe" argument of William James and by an insistence upon the rights of personality. The Christian contribution to the Platonic notion of immortality, according to the thesis, was to personalize it and to make it more convincing by heightening the value of personality, which would be negated by a denial of immortality.

16

As Holtzmann says, though Christ was not resurrected it is entirely possible to believe that he was worthy to be. And by this unique value of his personality he has added just so much to the value of human personality, or at least to its appreciation, and therefore he made more plausible if not more possible the conviction that death does not end its life.[32]

The longing for immortality was increased by the greater value placed on the individual personality. The inherent optimism of faith prevailed in meeting the need for a doctrine of immortality. Niebuhr did not glibly assume every need was met, but following William James he thought it not improper to trust that a demand as strong as immortality of the soul would be fulfilled if there were no contradictory evidence.

By exalting the personal life of Jesus, Christianity contributed a radicalization of the claims for the survival of personal consciousness. In its doctrine of immortality, Christianity blended Greek and Hebrew elements, dropping Plato's conception of the transmigration of souls and the miraculous elements of the Jewish claim for resurrection. The Hebrew elements of moral judgment and fulfillment in community were maintained, but on the basis of the Greek form of argument from certain imperishable values in man.

The thesis gives no hint of its author's future contribution as a social philosopher. It is important in understanding Niebuhr because it establishes his early complete acceptance of the historical-critical method without following the more conservative biblical critics. It makes clear beyond any reasonable doubt that as a young man he shared the liberal temper of his time in rejecting traditional Christian claims as incredible to the sophisticated mind of his day. It reveals his own positive evaluation of religious optimism. Individualism was stressed in the thesis; social solidarity was relatively unimportant, although it later became basic to his understanding of the resurrection.

The thesis also indicates Niebuhr's awareness of the threat of death, which was later to become a major source of his emphasis upon human finitude and humanity's claims for itself. In his short thesis he answered affirmatively the query, "Can we still hold to the 'sublime idea' though we are forced to give up the 'sublime event'?"[33] Fifty years later he was still answering the query positively, though many suspected him of betraying his "orthodox" theology by admitting the contingency of religious symbols.

Niebuhr's realistic pragmatism, which was apparent in both theses, was dependent on William James and especially on Professor Macintosh. Macintosh found himself able to support the validity of religious beliefs if they were not proved false and if they had beneficial practical results. In *The Pilgrimage of Faith* he made clear his own conviction that a religious idea was true if it was considered practically satisfying. Macintosh would even conclude "the independent reality" of religiously posited realities on this basis. Also, by assuming "moral optimism" as valid in the universe and by defining God as a being "great and good enough" to justify an attitude of moral optimism on our part, he tried to reason to a conclusion of God's existence.[34] Niebuhr followed his teacher into this dubious bit of metaphysical reasoning in his B.D. thesis, which depended on the hypothesis and the definition. His later tendency was to ground religious belief on supposed practical consequences, as his professors at Eden had done and as Macintosh then did at Yale. Pragmatism, the use of the term "realism," and argument by virtue of the moral usefulness of the idea remained in Reinhold's mind, but he turned away sharply from much of Macintosh's argumentation. His contribution to the Macintosh Festschrift of 1937[35] showed a radical turn away from Macintosh's method.

Another point at which the influence of Yale may be seen is in Reinhold Niebuhr's involvement in World War I. He went to Yale a month after the war began. By the time of the U.S. entry, he was a pastor. The whole School of Religion faculty supported the purposes of the U.S. involvement in the war,[36] and so did the young pastor.

The support of the Yale School of Religion for the war effort was typical of liberal Protestantism. In New York, Harry Emerson Fosdick's pro-war rhetoric thrilled audiences in winning their support. Professors at Union Theological Seminary in New York also supported war with two exceptions. Julius Bewer, German born, dissented from the war and found himself criticized, but his classes in Old Testament continued.[37] A professor of Christian ethics, however, did not adjust so quietly. Thomas C. Hall, a tenured professor who had been on the faculty since 1899, favored American neutrality. During 1915–16 he was freed from classroom duties to minister to prisoners of war in Germany. After war broke out between the United States and Germany, he was dismissed from the seminary. Because of war conditions Hall never received his letter of dismissal. Furthermore, there were no hearings on the issue with Hall, who was in Germany. After the war, on his return to the United States, Hall protested, but to no avail; he went back to Germany and taught at Göttingen. His protest to the

Union Board of Directors was published as a pamphlet: "Union Theological Seminary and Christian Ethics: An Open Letter, Thomas C. Hall to William Kingsley."[38] The Board of Directors had abandoned its own procedures and standards in the midst of war enthusiasm. In the context of a destructive war, the dismissal of a tenured professor seems unimportant, but it showed the limits of tolerance of a liberal seminary. Hall had been Union's first professor of Christian ethics. He was replaced in 1918 by Harry F. Ward, Niebuhr's predecessor and sometime colleague, who would in his own way involve Union Theological Seminary with controversy over his social ethics.

At Yale, the professor of religion and social work, William B. Bailey, was not a dominant personality on the faculty. Dean Brown represented the influence of the social gospel, as did other members of the faculty, but it did not affect Reinhold greatly. In his writing from Yale the perspective of the social gospel is more missing than present. The arrival of deep social passions would await, as for many seminarians today, the service in the local church.

Professor Hershey Sneath, who taught Christian ethics, was probably past his best years by the time Reinhold took his course. Sneath introduced Reinhold to issues of the ethics of non-Christian religions. An unusual feature of Niebuhr's major course in the history of ethics years later was non-Christian ethics as the subject of the first semester. Sneath's book and several of the authorities in his edited volume *The Evolution of Ethics* also appear in Reinhold's course. Evidently, although Niebuhr emphasized biblical studies and philosophical theology at Yale, what he learned in ethics stayed with him when he took up the responsibilities of teaching that course.

Niebuhr was delighted and a little surprised to receive his M.A. degree in 1915. He had not quite maintained the grade average of "A," and others who wrote theses did not receive the degree. Apparently Professor Macintosh had been pleased with Niebuhr's work even if he was not to have the young man as a Ph.D. candidate. After Niebuhr's two years at Yale, the leaders of the Evangelical Synod pressured him to assume his duties as pastor. Hopes for preparation for teaching theology were shelved; his church called. Church leaders knew that leaving young midwestern students in eastern universities sometimes turned them away from the pastoral calling. Niebuhr would later reflect that he was becoming bored with some of the philosophical classifications that interested Macintosh, and he was not sure of pursuing a doctoral program in that direction. Furthermore, the family finances were shaky, and he felt he needed to assume the responsibility of providing an income and a home for his widowed mother. So he left Yale in the spring of 1915 for Lincoln, Illinois, to await the decision of the church elders about his placement.

NOTES

1. William G. Chrystal, *A Father's Mantle* (New York: Pilgrim Press, 1982); Ronald H. Stone, *Reinhold Niebuhr: Prophet to Politicians* (Nashville: Abingdon Press, 1972); Paul Merkley, *Reinhold Niebuhr: A Political Account* (Montreal: McGill-Queens University Press, 1975); Richard Fox, *Reinhold Niebuhr: A Biography* (New York: Pantheon Books, 1985).

2. Chrystal, *A Father's Mantle.*

3. Ibid., p. 12.

4. Ibid.

5. Ibid., p. 18.

6. William Becker, *Evangelical Theology* (New York: United Church of Christ, 1959), p. 1.

7. Chrystal, *A Father's Mantle*, pp. 74–75.

8. Ibid., pp. 111–112.

9. See Fox, *Reinhold Niebuhr*, for detailed discussion of Niebuhr's writing on international peace at Yale, pp. 35–36, and for discussion of Carl Vrooman, pp. 33, 39. See Thomas A. Bailey, *The American Pageant: A History of the Republic* (Boston: D. C. Heath & Co., 1956), pp. 670–705, for a description of the mood of reform.

10. David Dunn et al., *A History of the Evangelical and Reformed Church* (Philadelphia: Christian Education Press, 1961); Julius H. Horstmann and Herbert H. Wernecke, *Through Four Centuries* (St. Louis: Eden Publishing House, 1938).

11. Dunn, *A History*, pp. 252–258.

12. From "Reinhold Niebuhr letter to S. D. Press, March 3, 1914," quoted in William G. Chrystal, ed., *Young Reinhold Niebuhr: His Early Writings—1911–1931* (1977), p. 28.

13. William G. Chrystal, "Samuel D. Press: Teacher of the Niebuhrs," *Church History* 4 (1984), 504–521.

14. Chrystal, *Young Reinhold Niebuhr*, pp. 41–52.

15. Ibid., p. 41.

16. For example, Dennis McCann in his lengthy study of Niebuhr's practical theology fails to understand how central the role of church publications are to the shape and meaning of Niebuhr's practical theology. Dennis P. McCann, *Christian Realism and Liberation Theology* (Maryknoll, N.Y.: Orbis Books, 1981).

17. Chrystal, *Young Reinhold Niebuhr*, p. 41.

18. Ibid., p. 45.

19. Ibid., pp. 46–52.

20. Roland H. Bainton, *Yale and the Ministry* (New York: Harper & Brothers, 1957), p. 226.

21. "Yale-Eden" in Chrystal, *Young Reinhold Niebuhr*, pp. 53–58.

22. Charles W. Kegley, ed., *Reinhold Niebuhr: His Religious, Social, and Political Thought* (New York: Pilgrim Press, 1984), pp. 3–4.

23. Letter to Samuel Press in the June Bingham correspondence in Reinhold Niebuhr Papers (MSS in the Library of Congress, Washington, D.C.), Container 25, presented under the title "The Validity and Certainty of Religious Knowledge." The discussion of this thesis is edited from my book *Reinhold Niebuhr: Prophet to Politicians* (Nashville: Abingdon Press, 1972).

24. "The Validity and Certainty of Religious Knowledge," Niebuhr Papers, Container 17.

25. Ibid., pp. 12–13.

26. Ibid., pp. 21–22.

27. Ibid., p. 31.

28. Ibid., p. 28.

29. "The Reminiscences of Reinhold Niebuhr" (Oral History Research Office of Columbia University), microfiche, p. 8.

30. The debate is recorded in Reinhold Niebuhr's essay, "The Truth in Myths," which was published in a volume of essays honoring Douglas C. Macintosh: J. S. Bixler, ed., *The Nature of Religious Experience* (New York: Harper & Brothers, 1937), pp. 117–135. D. C. Macintosh replied in an article, "Is Theology Reducible to Mythology?" *Review of Religion* 4 (Jan. 1940), 140–158.

31. Reinhold Niebuhr, "The Contribution of Christianity to the Doctrine of Immortality" (unpublished master's thesis, Yale University, New Haven, Conn., 1915), p. 8.

32. Ibid., p. 31.

33. Ibid., p. 7.

34. Douglas C. Macintosh, *The Pilgrimage of Faith in the World of Modern Thought* (Calcutta: University of Calcutta, 1931), p. 200.

35. Bixler, ed., *The Nature of Religious Experience*.

36. E. Hershey Sneath, *Religion and the War* (New Haven, Conn.: Yale University Press, 1918).

37. Robert T. Handy, *A History of Union Theological Seminary in New York* (New York: Columbia University Press, 1987), p. 140.

38. Ibid., pp. 141–143; note on p. 358.

2

Bethel Evangelical Church
1915–1928

IN HIS OLD AGE, Niebuhr reflected that he finished his liberal education during the years of liberalism's decline. As he completed his M.A.
at Yale University in 1915, Europe at war was destroying the promises
of liberal society and the self-satisfaction of liberal theology. His own
life was wrenched from the liberal atmosphere of Yale into family and
church responsibilities in the Midwest. Thoughts of pursuing a doctor-
ate were surrendered to taking up the responsibility of family support.
His elder brother's newspaper career had failed, and Reinhold's intentions to journey to Europe as a war correspondent collapsed. He spent
the summer in Lincoln, Illinois, negotiating with synod officials and
Bethel Church, preaching in his late father's pulpit, consulting about
his brother's debts, and preparing to move.

Though unable to secure the salary he desired, he moved to Bethel
Evangelical Church in Detroit in the late summer and prepared for his
mother to join him in 1916. Bethel was a small neighborhood German
congregation. It had been founded only a few years earlier, and, as a
mission congregation of about eighteen families, it was very insecure
about its future. Detroit's ongoing industrial expansion and Niebuhr's
own growth led to the church's rapid development. Niebuhr's early
practice was to preach Sunday morning in both German and English;
in 1919, the congregation would abandon all German language services.

Niebuhr's education was a mixed blessing to the conservative congregation. The young Yale graduate arrived in 1915 in a city in which the automobile industry was maturing. Henry Ford had displayed the process of mass production at the Panama-Pacific Exposition in San Francisco on February 20, 1915. The process of focusing on Ford's seven principles—power, accuracy, economy, continuity, system, speed, and repetition—in the manufacturing process was changing the industrial landscape. With 46.6 percent of total automobile production, Ford Motor Company dominated the industry that was rapidly altering Detroit and promising to revolutionize transportation nationwide. The United States was piling technological-industrial advance upon advance. The Panama Canal was opened in 1914; transcontinental telephone lines were connected in January 1915; by 1915 the country's industrial production equaled the combined product of Germany and Britain.[1]

If culturally the United States was still immature and most trendsetters were European, industrially the country had come into the strength of early adulthood and its material accomplishments were impressive. The strengths of the country—vast resources, adaptable and skillful workers, brilliant engineers, the world's leading toolproducing plants, and bold resourceful entrepreneurs—were concentrated in Detroit and other growing industrial cities.

Detroit was in flux. The pressures of urban life combined with the new pressures of mass production to strain all who participated in the city's life. The city itself is best caught metaphorically in Allan Nevins's description of a Ford manufacturing plant:

> A kinetic plant!—moving, moving, moving; every segment—presses, furnaces, welders, stamps, drills, paint-baths, lathes—in use every minute; not an ounce of metal or a degree of heat avoidably wasted; and the economy in time and labor matching the economy in materials. Fascinating in its intricate intermeshing of activities, it meant a new era.[2]

Reinhold Niebuhr's years in Detroit were full of the social activism and the wrestling with issues of theology that were to characterize his later life. However, in Detroit he was first a pastor. He had left Yale University to come to the Bethel Evangelical Church with some reluctance, under the prodding of ecclesiastical superiors. Thirteen years in Detroit made him fond of the pastorate and, when he left for New York in 1928 to join the faculty of Union Theological Seminary, he was sorry to leave the people of his congregation.

Niebuhr criticized the failures of both the churches and the ministry, but, upon leaving the parish in 1928, he wrote glowingly of the opportunities available to the minister; no other profession had as many opportunities to serve in different areas. He enumerated particularly the chance to influence the lives of children and young people, the opportunity to engage in significant social action, the challenges of race relations in a polyglot city, and the provision of a message of hope to men and women who needed guidance in finding goals worthy of devotion. He took up the task of helping people to separate hope from dreams so that religious faith would not perish with the shattering of illusions. It was a responsibility no one could completely fulfill, requiring, as it did, the talents of a social scientist, poet, executive, and philosopher in one person.[3]

Pages from his diary for the years 1915–1928 were edited and published in 1929 under the title *Leaves from the Notebook of a Tamed Cynic*. The pages testify to the happiness Niebuhr knew as a pastor and point toward problems he would wrestle with at a later date. The slender volume, which reveals the young student turned pastor finding his Christian liberalism and innocence challenged by Detroit in the period of its pre-Depression expansion, deserves to be read by all persons contemplating a career in Christian ministry.

The young minister was surprised to find on his first Sunday in the pulpit that his small chapel was filled. He thought to himself, Well, this isn't a bad congregation, except that the composition is a little curious. Actually, the churchgoers were either very elderly or very young. After the church service, it was explained to him that only twenty members of the congregation actually belonged to the church; the others were guests from the Home for Orphans and Old People.

Bethel Evangelical Church, originally assisted financially from the central denominational offices, soon began to prosper under the new leadership. By the end of Niebuhr's pastorate, the membership had increased tenfold, from 65 to 656, and the benevolence budget from $75 to $3,889.[4] As the congregation grew, a new church was built. Though the minister was very active in Detroit industrial conflicts and race relations, the church membership was largely middle class, with some workers and a few very wealthy patrons.

In reflecting upon his preaching, Niebuhr contrasted the temper of his preaching with his work in the study. "Why is it that when I arise in the pulpit I try to be imaginative and am sometimes possessed by a kind of madness which makes my utterances extravagant and dogmatic?"[5] In his preaching he desired to proclaim a message and to move his audience. He was not averse to exaggerating a point to reach an essential truth. As he preached twice a week, once on Sunday morning and again on Sunday evening, he tried to maintain a balance by seeking to provide inspiration in the morning and education in the evening.[6] His preaching attracted attention, and increasingly he was asked to address college audiences and conferences across the country. His mother, once she had moved from Lincoln to Detroit, assumed some of the chores of administration. Starting in the fall of 1923, he was given assistant pastors to carry part of the ministerial responsibilities as he became more and more in demand as a lecturer.

In Detroit Niebuhr discovered, as have many pastors, that nuances of doctrine are less important in the pastor's relationship to his congregation than the attitudes of the pastor toward the people of his church. Though his theology was liberal and his people, particularly the older members at the beginning of his pastorate, were quite conservative, they did not attempt to make life difficult for him. The notes in his diary reveal again and again his deep affection for the members of his congregation. Niebuhr had a tendency to announce his affirmation boldly and to leave it to his detractors to find the weaknesses of his position if they could. This tendency, which reflects his training as a preacher, was articulated in his diary:

> If preachers get into trouble in pursuance of their task of reinterpreting religious affirmations in the light of modern knowledge I think it must be partly because they beat their drums too loudly when they make their retreats from untenable positions of ancient orthodoxy. The correct strategy is to advance at the center with beating drums and let your retreats at the wings follow as a matter of course and in the interest of the central strategy. You must be honest, of course, but you might just as well straighten and shorten your lines without mock heroics and a fanfare of trumpets.[7]

Preaching his affirmation boldly sometimes confused both admirers and critics, who regarded Niebuhr as more conservative in theology than he actually was. Most of the sharp conflicts in which he found himself in Detroit were due to his social liberalism rather than his theological liberalism. Because he held that religion was in large part a matter of poetic vision, and theology was the attempt to organize symbols so they would express the religious needs of humanity, he could preach creatively to his congregation even without sharing many of the more outdated aspects of their worldview.

The Great War

The importance of World War I to Reinhold Niebuhr's thought can hardly be overestimated. It is the first and most important example of Niebuhr's adjusting his thought so it could more adequately interpret current events in international politics.

Before the entry of the United States, Niebuhr regarded the war as a result of the economic egoism of the European nations. It revealed their political blindness and contained no promise of renewal for the European political situation.[8] The Great War was being fought over petty issues, requiring disproportionate sacrifices from ill-led peoples.

Niebuhr's position changed with the entry of the United States into the conflict. His political liberalism and his American nationalism combined to elicit his support for the war.

The young Niebuhr was enthusiastically in favor of Wilson's liberal foreign policy. Wilson had entered the war reluctantly, but once in the conflict he viewed it as a crusade for a new political order. Wilson's Fourteen Points, and particularly his emphases upon freedom of the seas, a league of nations, disarmament, the abolition of secret diplomacy, and respect for the consent of the governed, appealed to Niebuhr and helped him shed his reservations about the war. Given the fact of U.S. participation, Niebuhr fixed his attention on the proclaimed goals of the war and repressed earlier insights concerning the petty economic and political motivations behind the struggle.

Nationalism was the second major factor that prompted Niebuhr's support of the war. Self-consciously regarding himself as a member of an immigrant minority, he judged that the United States as a young nation was entitled to protect its unity. He saw many German-Americans harboring sentiments of resentment toward the United States and romanticizing the Kaiser; Niebuhr sharply attacked what he regarded as reluctant citizenship on the part of the German-American community. He deplored the conservatism of most German-Americans, attributing it partly to their peasant-class origins (which had excluded them from German universities) and partly to the fact that they had emigrated before the rise of progressive Germany. He argued that German-Americans had served America well only where the interests of the country coincided with their personal interests, particularly in business. The great moral, political, and religious questions had aroused no great interest on their part.[9] Niebuhr contrasted the Jewish contribution to progressive social reform with the failure of the German-Americans. The one activity that German-Americans had undertaken as a community was opposing prohibition.[10] His strong resentment of the provincialisms of his immigrant group, coupled with his deep sense of patriotism, made it impossible for someone with his German background to define himself in opposition to the United States. He felt that opposition to a country's war efforts should be expressed only on the "basis of an unmistakably higher loyalty." He regarded most German dissent as showing baser motives, and he could not associate himself with the dissenters. His attack upon those German-Americans who hid their German nationalism under the cloak of pietistic pacifism gave indications of his later polemics against using religious beliefs to cover political programs. The tension between his hatred of war and the peculiar position in which he found himself was expressed poignantly in his diary.

> Out at Funston I watched a bayonet practice. It was enough to make me feel like a brazen hypocrite for being in this thing, even in a rather indirect way. Yet I cannot bring myself to associate with the pacifists. Perhaps if I were not of German blood I could.[11]

William G. Chrystal revealed the full extent of Reinhold Niebuhr's role in World War I through his exploration of the Eden Archives of the Evangelical and Reformed Historical Society at Eden Theological Seminary.[12] Shortly after America's entry into the war, the young Niebuhr was appointed to the seven-person War Welfare Commission of the synod. Reluctantly he accepted the position of Executive Secretary, which was responsible for guiding the synod's war-related work. Provisions were made so that his responsibilities at Bethel Church were reduced for the duration of the war. Sister Hulda and mother Lydia picked up many of the responsibilities, and Reinhold continued with mainly Sunday duties and a few weekday ones.[13]

Niebuhr started visiting training camps, advising pastors near camps of soldiers' needs, developing and distributing synod publications to soldiers, and advising congregations on to how to keep in touch with their boys in uniform. His duties involved crisscrossing the country on speaking and organizational tours. He spent most of November and December in military camps in the South. He returned in January and, exhausted, fell ill and missed most of his local church responsibilities for the month.

Soon his work and his own patriotic commitments brought him into conflict with elements in his German church that seemed to be hedging their loyalty to their country in this war against their former Fatherland.[14] Gradually, the work of representing his church in its war activities weighed upon him. In 1918 he offered to resign from the War Welfare Commission to join the active military chaplaincy, but the president of the church, John Baltzer, prevailed upon him to remain in his office. Embarrassment at being free from physical peril and representing a church whose national loyalty was questioned both prompted him to try to resign, but Baltzer's insistence kept him in office until the end of the war.[15]

Niebuhr's office in the church required that he support the war effort uncritically and not give any reasons to cause the loyalty of the German Evangelical Synod to be doubted. His own sense of the righteousness of the war allowed him to urge the church to support Wilson's war aims, finding in them the high moral purpose of striving to create a peaceful international order. Niebuhr's role as a second-generation German pastor trying to make the German Evangelical Synod into an American denomination dovetailed with his Wilsonian idealism and his assigned position as a spokesperson for the synod's position to allow him to speak strongly. He could even permit his rhetoric to call the war a crusade.[16]

The Versailles Conference shook Niebuhr's liberal hopes for a better order, and he came to regard Wilson as a typical manse product who trusted too much in the power of words. In 1919 it appeared to him that Lloyd George and Clemenceau were determining the peace settlement, restricting Wilson's contribution to an ideological one. Still he hoped that the ideals being announced would eventually mold reality, even if at present they were being used cynically as ideology.

The hopes of 1919 went unfulfilled, and by 1923 Niebuhr was disillusioned with Wilsonian diplomacy. He regarded the war as a contest for power dependent on economic interest and the caprice of statesmen. He regretted his defense of the war effort on the basis of Wilson's reforming principles. His cynicism about the lofty ideals with which he had justified World War I was completed by observations in 1923 of the French vengeance on the Germans. While in Germany that year he resolved to have nothing to do with "the war business" and associated himself with the pacifists. His position is not surprising in view of the fact that, once hostilities ceased, the major factors that had evoked his support of the war dissolved. After the war even a German-American could be a pacifist without seeming disloyal to the United States. Niebuhr's disillusionment with Wilsonian idealism deprived his military policies of moral support. These two developments facilitated Niebuhr's return to pacifism.

Niebuhr's declaration of pacifism reflected his growing interest in emphasizing the conflict between the gospel and the world. Loyalty to the gospel meant a break with the world's values. In his view the "easy optimism" of his youth and of the nineteenth century was discredited. In 1923, the perfectionist Christian and the cynical observer of the political scene were united in Niebuhr the pacifist. One of the great evils of the moral obfuscation of World War I, he thought, was the enthusiasm with which the church had supported the slaughter.

Henry Ford and His Workers

Despite Henry Ford's pacifism, his plants had been turned to war production. After the war his plants returned to domestic production and the postwar boom in auto production. Henry Ford, through struggle, gained solitary control of the corporation that became one of the two or three largest manufacturing enterprises of history. Ford combined insight, engineering, and management skills to become a dominant force in Detroit and in the nation. His lack of sociological knowledge and his political naïveté reinforced the difficulties of labor in early American industrialization. Niebuhr regarded Ford as a symbol of America's technical genius—and of social ineptitude.[17] There had been a period in which Henry Ford's five-dollar-a-day minimum wage had been an improvement in the salaries paid to industrial workers. By the time Niebuhr left Detroit, the relative income of the Ford worker had declined vis-à-vis General Motors workers and also in relationship to the earlier period in which the minimum wage was an innovation.

Ford's reputation as a fair employer and a great benefactor of the working man had outlived the facts, and Niebuhr set out to confront the myth of Ford with financial data.[18] Other clergymen, writers, and journalists undertook the same task. It was not an easy cause to join if one wished to continue in Detroit in any capacity related to the automobile industry. One of Henry Ford's most ardent critics was Samuel S. Marquis, an Episcopalian clergyman who had been Dean of the Cathedral before being asked to head up Ford Motor Company's sociological department. Marquis accepted the position as head of the department in 1915 and held it for five years, when the department was phased out by Henry Ford for unknown reasons. The sociological department was itself a result of Ford's paternalistic humanitarian side. It was designed

29

to help workers find homes and to provide them with minimal welfare services. It also collected data on the personal lives of the workers and attempted to force middle-class mores upon the laboring class. Marquis himself regarded the demise of the department as a sign of the lessening in importance of humanitarian motives in the company. Niebuhr met Marquis in 1917 and knew him well for years. After his retirement, Marquis published a volume that focused on the ambivalence of Ford's character, detailing both his humanitarian and heartless sides. He accused Ford of a series of brutal actions and his lieutenants in the industry of worse. Marquis's book was taken out of the Detroit libraries and disappeared from bookstores soon after its publication.[19]

Niebuhr's sharpest polemic against the pretensions of Henry Ford appeared in *The Christian Century* in 1926. His name had appeared as an editor on the February 12, 1925, issue, and the magazine had won a reputation in Detroit motor company circles for being anti-Ford.

Niebuhr first accused Henry Ford of not supporting the various philanthropic organizations that met the needs of Ford workers. He said Ford's pretensions of serving justice rather than charity by paying an adequate wage would have earned him the reputation of humanitarian that his public relations men fostered *if* the claims had been true. Niebuhr documented his charges that in 1926 the actual wage was considerably lower for the average Ford worker than it had been in 1913.[20] He criticized the company for providing no unemployment insurance and for policies of frequent short, erratic work shifts.

The practice of speeding up the production lines also came under criticism for its tendency to work men so hard they were physical wrecks before they were fifty years old. He countered Ford's claim to relieve delinquency by hiring young workers with the argument that Ford plants had no place for the older men they had worn out.

Niebuhr joined in the speculation that characterized Detroit about Henry Ford's motives.

> It is difficult to determine whether Mr. Ford is simply a shrewd exploiter of a gullible public in his humanitarian pretensions or whether he suffers from self-deception. My own guess is that he is at least as naïve as he is shrewd, that he does not think profoundly on the social implications of his industrial policies, and that in some of his avowed humanitarian motives he is actually deceived.[21]

Even though Ford might in some cases have innocent intentions, his practices wreaked havoc among the workers, and many of his personnel policies among the higher executives of the corporation revealed a stark delight in destroying men's careers.

Ernest Liebold, Henry Ford's private secretary, wrote to one of the millionaires in Niebuhr's congregation who had, in the past, manufactured parts as a subcontractor for Ford automobiles. Liebold pressed the retired manufacturer to obtain a retraction from the young, well-intentioned, but of course misguided minister. Years later, Niebuhr was amused that Liebold apparently suffered under the impression that the traditionally anti-Ford *Christian Century* had beguiled the young minister into deep water. The fact was that Niebuhr's earlier, unsigned editorials were in large part responsible for the reputation of the journal that was now represented as ensnaring the young minister. Reflecting on the incident decades later, Niebuhr mused:

> The letter, as I remember it, said: "We want to protest against the wholly untrue article on Ford wage policy, written by the pastor of your church. He is no doubt an honest person, but he has fallen in the clutches of the worst anti-Ford journal in the country, *The Christian Century.*" Since the charge involved, in part at least, the similarity between the anonymous *Century* correspondence and my article, he was, in effect, accusing me of corrupting myself.[22]

The manufacturer, William J. Hartwig, stood firmly behind his minister, as many other laymen had been unable to do when Ford Motor Company attacked their ministers, and replied that he was sure the minister of his church would retract any item in the article that could be proven untrue. Earlier, Hartwig had donated the plot on West Grant Boulevard for the new building erected in 1921.

The membership of Bethel Evangelical Church also stood behind Niebuhr when he was one of the two ministers in the city who resisted Chamber of Commerce pressure to deny the Sunday evening pulpit to a representative of the American Federation of Labor in 1926. The pressure brought on the ministers of Detroit drew the attention of the *New York World,* and Walter Lippmann gave the incident national attention in his column. Members of the Chamber of Commerce in Niebuhr's church respected the freedom of the pulpit even when they disagreed with the AFL, and they did not really believe their minister would surrender to pressure from the Chamber of Commerce in any case. The AFL did not prove able to organize the auto workers, and Niebuhr's hopes for unionization and a guaranteed annual wage for the workers were years from fulfillment when he left Detroit.

Niebuhr had seen severe economic distress in Detroit in 1921 when the Ford plants were shut down for months of retooling after the Model T was no longer competitive. His identification with the workers' plight drove him into the mild socialism of the Social Gospel by 1926, but his deep involvement with Marxist theory did not occur, or at least appear in his writing, until after his move to New York in 1928. A small group including Bishop Charles Williams, the Jewish lawyer Fred M. Butzel, and Niebuhr pushed for an annual guaranteed wage and protection against the wishes of Detroit management. In 1926, in a debate with a famous English preacher and noted World War I chaplain named G. A. Studdert Kennedy at a student conference, Niebuhr advocated socialist answers to the problems of modern industry and argued that an entity the size of Ford Motor Company was in fact a public corporation and should no longer be privately owned. His writing dealt both with the structural aspects of industrial society and with the individual decision-makers, which were inadequate to regulate society in the 1920s. By the time of the 1929 crash, he had moved to an academic environment in New York, and his reaction to the deepening industrial crisis is part of the story of his life as a professor.

Race Relations in Detroit

Racial conflict broke out in the streets of Detroit in 1925. Immigration from the South had increased the African American population from ten thousand at the end of World War I to eighty thousand in 1925, and massive migrations still lay ahead.

Niebuhr accepted the chairmanship of the Mayor's Race Committee despite the complaint from some of his fellow pastors that a Christian minister should not cooperate with a mayor with such a shady political record. The vice-chairman of the group was Bishop William T. Vernon of the African Methodist Episcopal Church. Other members of the committee included lawyers, representatives from Ford Motor Company, physicians, and other leaders in Detroit. Fred Butzel provided much of the leadership of the committee and became a lifelong friend. Niebuhr often used Butzel as an example of the vitalities of prophetic Judaism.

The work of the committee was not crowned with success. It will be remembered in the history of Detroit as one of many twentieth-century race relations committees that failed to translate its findings into needed reforms. The committee did, however, base its recommendations on a study by the Detroit Bureau of Governmental Research, and its findings in 1926 seem quite farsighted, given the situation today. The report called for the creation of a permanent race commission to combat prejudice through education and through the exercise of control over public agencies relevant to racial discrimination. It also called for several immediate changes in the practices of municipal government, business, education, welfare agencies, recreational opportunities, and real estate.

The committee found a drop in real estate values in integrating neighborhoods to be the result of fear and not a necessary consequence of integration. Recommendations were made to encourage integrative tendencies in the real estate business and in the financing of house purchases. The need for city agencies to provide equitable services in African American neighborhoods was recognized. The report of the committee reveals at places a note of paternalism; it recommends a plan of education to help African Americans keep their neighborhoods in attractive condition. Someone on the committee even got that recommendation followed by a sentence that violates the organization of the paragraph: "A similar emphasis upon the personal appearance and demeanor of colored people and their children is equally desirable."[23] It is strange to see those words in the report of a committee Niebuhr chaired. (On the other hand, attitudes toward race have changed abruptly in the last few years, and some of Niebuhr's own writing on race is badly dated. In a 1944 book he suggested the need to give African Americans full credit for their native abilities and specifically mentioned only "artistic gifts."[24]) The report also put much of the blame for the failure to maintain their areas upon African American groups who were supposedly neglecting the upkeeep of their property; it failed to wrestle significantly with white ownership of slum housing.

The committee faced forthrightly the racism in the police department and called for the immediate transfer from African American neighborhoods of prejudiced officers and for intensive efforts to hire more African American police.[25] The inequity in the administration of justice was noted, but the committee felt it impossible to agree as to the causes of the unfairness. Most of the public services to African Americans were found to be inadequate, and recommendations for changes were made.[26]

In industry, discrimination on the part of both employers and unions was reported, but the committee trusted to the success of nondiscriminatory employers and to the unions for the promotion of change. Employers were urged to hire more minorities and to promote them, but the lead sentence of that section of the report set the tone: "The progress of the Negro in the industrial life of the city, following the large migrations since the war, has been most creditable."[27] The possibility of the committee's saying anything very critical was probably greatly reduced by the presence on the committee of the employment officer of Ford Motor Company and the president of Vulcan Manufacturing Company.

In both education and medical services the committee reported discrimination, and it found no African Americans in important posts in the institutions. Mild recommendations for change were recorded.

The committee studied the churches and recommended several actions. The changes recommended were: (1) the African American churches should organize an interdenominational organization; (2) the interdenominational agency should combat "irresponsible religious organizations which enjoy a mushroom growth in the city";[28] (3) white churches should help African American churches financially. The report seemed to accept, or at least did not question, the division of the churches into African American and white organizations. This section of the report bears the unmistakable mark of having been written by an African American whose interests lay in the ecclesiastical structure of the African American churches. The report gave no hint of the churches' role in combating segregation. The recommendations of the report on the churches were confined to bureaucratic intramural details of only incidental significance to Detroit.

By today's standards, the report was very mild and innocuous. It did, however, put an official voice of criticism against most of the structures of Detroit. Its proposals for reform, though perhaps inadequate, were stronger than Detroit in 1926 was willing to put into effect. The report was a composite of recommendations of many individuals, and it reveals the mind of a representative group of the establishment of Detroit more clearly than the particular convictions of its chairman.

Niebuhr's work on race relations continued as he spoke on the subject at Elmhurst College.[29] Later in the 1920s, he spoke at other conferences, and he included the subject in his address at the General Conference of the Evangelical Synod of North America in 1929.[30] These early years in Detroit provided him with experiences that would emerge again and again in his public speaking, fund-raising, writing, and organizing. The general pattern was to stress Christianity as having an ethic of love and justice and an ideal of universal community (called, in the 1920s, brotherhood). The overcoming of personal social prejudice and racism between groups was seen as extremely difficult. He used the evil of race relations to prove the brutality of human beings in group life. Though he appreciated the achievements of the past generation of church leadership, their failures in race relations received his criticism. Generally, racial bigotry had characterized their lives.[31] Already Niebuhr recognized that though the race problem was a particularly intractable problem, government pressure to promote justice was necessary. He began 1927 with his own series of four sermons on the race problem. Drawing upon the research of the committee on race relations, he announced the four topics for January: (1) "Race Relations in Detroit," (2) "What About Negro Crime?" (3) "Where Shall the Negro Live?" and (4) "The Christian Conscience and the Race Problem."[32]

Christian Education

The Bethel Church experience was literally between Reinhold's seminary years. It occupied a considerable part of his young life, from age twenty-three to thirty-six, and was a very formative period. It would be a mistake to distinguish his pastoral work as separate from his life as an educator. His vision of ministry never strayed far from the designation that Presbyterians, in times past, used for their ministers, that of a "teaching elder."

Preaching involved the moving of both the intellect and the will. In one of the first essays he had published while still a student, he had argued that the church grew by both education and revival. Both were present in the sermon.[33] He thought his German background lent itself more to serious instruction in the sermon than it did to moving religious emotions. While recognizing the possible value of revival methods, the young theology student was more impressed by personal conversation and most of all by education for strengthening the church.

The primary means of education for Bethel Church was the Sunday school. Religious education in the public schools was neither possible nor desirable in the American situation. While inadequate, the Sunday school was the best institution the church had. Though he had been educated in parochial schools, Niebuhr never exhibited any enthusiasm for them. He wrote and spoke often about Christian education and its two major forms for the Evangelical Synod of North America: the Sunday school and the confirmation class. He taught both in Detroit, and his reflections on both returned to the need to discuss practical life problems in the light of the Christian faith. His own experience of teaching teenage boys, as well as his passion for practical Christianity, led him away from separating faith and practical issues in instruction.

New in his congregation, he wrote in his denomination's teachers journal about the dangers of separating knowledge of the Bible from practical moral lessons. He used the term "Scylla and Charybdis" that readers of the late Niebuhr will recognize as a typical phrase for describing the need for moderation in political choices. Here it was used to describe the dangers of Christian education.

> There is a Scylla and Charybdis in almost every understanding, two opposite dangers, two extremes, between which one must sail and both of which one must avoid if the undertaking is to be successful.[34]

The dangers were the teaching of too much biblical history and building resentment against more detail than was necessary versus the drawing and teaching of moral lessons without the dramatic impact of the biblical stories. Sunday school, he argued, needed to capture the moral imagination of its students with the biblical drama.

After his service for the denomination's War Welfare Commission, he was asked to speak on educational issues at denominational meetings. He brought a deep commitment to the task of arguing for modernizing the church school. He pleaded with the German-language church to give up German in the Sunday schools, arguing that the children no longer thought in German. He joined the movement for relating less to the textual materials and more to the abilities of the pupils. He was arguing for the churches to move to graded classes with materials appropriate to specific age groups. His writing for church school teachers chose the modernist side of the debate as he tried to haul a conservative denomination into the modern (1919) American world.[35] His critique of learning the catechism through memorization was particularly blistering.

> Anyone versed in modern developments of pedagogy must admit that our catechism is a pedagogical monstrosity. Children are asked to learn meaningless definitions and, except if constant influence is exerted to the contrary, to look upon confirmation instruction as gymnastics in the art of learning by rote.[36]

His speeches before conventions of Evangelical Sunday schools and his essays in *The Evangelical Teacher* reflect the modernist, reformist agenda. However, he expected church educational institutions to inculcate the basic precepts and traditions of the church. He believed thought began with presuppositions, and he frequently criticized the idea that anyone should grow up without presuppositions or tradition. Much of his recommendation for church education was the relevant teaching of the church's own tradition. The wisdom of the previous generation needed to be learned by the present generation and then modified to its needs.

His growing reputation as a speaker and a writer permitted him to take long-standing concerns to broader audiences. In East St. Louis in the fall of 1924, he carried his oft-repeated criticism of the Evangelical Synod's educational institutions to the Fifth National Convention of the Evangelical Brotherhood. No longer confining his critique to the school journal, *Keryx,* he thundered that the Evangelical Synod had no educational program worthy of the name. He chided the denomination for its failure to build colleges and for the low status of Elmhurst. He begged the assembled leaders to found a women's college and to give finances to start other institutions. The argument was not only on behalf of the church, it was in his perspective on behalf of civilization. The union of religious inspiration, or the works of love, with intelligence was necessary if Spengler's decline of the West was to be avoided.[37] Of course, he was not just talking; he worked hard on behalf of Elmhurst, raising funds and serving on the denomination's commission of higher education. Some of the hopes for college education, renewing civilization, seem in retrospect more optimistically hopeful than he would be later in the Depression. However, the basic argument, that religion needed education and that education needed love to keep it from brutality, endured. He also caught in a couple of sentences a large part of the illness of Christendom: "Too many men have not the mind of Christ. Many people have a Christian heart, but not a Christian mind. They do not think in a Christian way."[38] His writing on the seminaries almost forecast his own vocational trajectory. His commitment to ecumenical Christianity and the search for academic excellence drew him toward the large, liberal, ecumenical schools.

Early in his ministry, he challenged the denomination to improve its seminary, Eden. He said that spiritually it was fine, but that it lacked academic standing. It was not properly accredited and it was more like a theological college than a seminary. He felt while the practical instruction for ministry was adequate, the students were usually unprepared in basic disciplines of many kinds. The graduates lacked the knowledge "to understand the 'signs of the times.'"[39]

Four years later, he returned to the theme of education for ministry. His essay argued, against the views of faculty members from Elmhurst and Eden, that ministers need a college education as well as a seminary education. Under the title "Shall a Minister Have an Education?" he fought against keeping education for ministry in the German language. The cultural issue of the Americanization of the Evangelical Synod was caught up in his arguments for more education. In a spirited polemic, he wrote, "The cause of higher education seems well nigh hopeless in our denomination."[40] Other constraints within the parish ministry were inclining him to think of a vocation in higher education. These denominational struggles would incline him to favor interdenominational theological education.

Three years later, in 1924, his essay on theological education was full of praise for the ecumenical theological schools. The short piece "On Academic Vagabondage" exhibits a note of humor, but beneath the humor is a very serious message. Niebuhr admits his provincialism, but he pleads that Evangelical Synod ministers fight against their German midwestern provincialism by studying theology elsewhere. The European universities are held out as destinations for theological education, but the schools the article really recommends are Chicago, Yale, Harvard, and Union. Among these, Union is his clear preference. He notes that no school has all the best faculty; each school has its strong departments. But then, in his fantasy, he populates his ideal faculty. ·

> An ideal school from the theological student's viewpoint would have on its faculty Harvard's philosophers and historians of religion, Yale's theologians, Union and Columbia Teachers' historians, practical theologians and specialists in religious education, New Testament, and social Christianity, and a Chicagoan or two to add spice.[41]

Mentally he had a direction that was clear by 1924. It would take several historical contingencies for that possible direction to become a reality.

The years 1924–1928 were the glory years of Bethel as the congregation grew to 656 and filled its new sanctuary and education rooms on West Grand Boulevard. The church bulletin carried the picture of the new building on its front page well into 1927. Niebuhr himself recorded the numbers in attendance and urged his members to bring others. The church set goals both for Sunday school members and for new church members and hustled to meet them.

The pastor participated in the decisions of the church council, and his energy in starting new programs and furnishing direction for ongoing programs is obvious in the minutes of the council and in the church bulletins from those years. He turned aside offers of teaching and other pulpits while nurturing Bethel and expanding his preaching and lecturing around the country. Often his younger brother, Richard, would fill the pulpit while Reinhold was on tour. As the demand for his speaking elsewhere grew, Bethel responded by permitting Sundays away from its own pulpit and eventually, in 1924, granting him two-month summer leaves. His speaking schedule testifies to his relentless drive. An entry for 1928 records that while he was absent from Bethel for ten days, he spoke at convocations of the universities of Kansas and of Iowa, attended a meeting at the University of Missouri, and conducted a student leadership conference in Kansas City.

The Sunday evening sermon was followed by a forum discussion. The forum drew international speakers, American ministers, philosophers, peace activists, social reformers, and labor representatives, but Niebuhr himself usually held forth on a variety of topics. A series of five talks on biography covered Francis of Assisi, Lord Shaftesbury, David Livingstone, R. L. Stevenson, and William Penn. Lectures on St. Joan, Abraham Lincoln, and Woodrow Wilson were given later. He often spoke on social problems and on topics of international relations. A series of poetry reveals an interest presented in his sermons but not in his essays or books. He spoke in January 1924 on "The Miracle of Regeneration," reflecting on "The Everlasting Mercy" by John Masefield. The following week the sermon title was "Is There Adventure in Religion?" and the poem was "The Bell Buoy" by Rudyard Kipling. "The Whole of Life" sermon was based on "Rabbi Ben Ezra" by Robert Browning. The final sermon, "The Inevitable Surrender," was from "The Hound of Heaven" by Francis Thompson. Moving on into February, his evening topics included themes later readers would find in his political writings of pessimism and optimism, the hero and the common person, and the wheat and the tares. In late March and early April, guest speakers would take morning services and evening services while he was off to speaking and preaching engagements in Chicago and Buffalo.

Niebuhr's winsome personality, brilliance, and driving energy made him a hard preacher to follow. Many who had joined out of loyalty to him faded from Bethel Evangelical Church on his departure. The terms of the two pastors who followed him were cut short by conflicts, but in a few years the congregation recovered. Niebuhr, who had been pastor for thirteen of the congregation's first sixteen years, returned to the twenty-fifth anniversary celebration of the congregation and remarked, "As I look back upon those years I am more than ever convinced that building a Christian church in a great metropolitan center can be a more challenging adventure than any to which one might set one's hands."[42]

A particularly interesting note was set by the printed title for the farewell dinner of his departure in 1928. The announcement read, *A Farewell to Rev. Niebuhr and His Mother.* Lydia had been the Sunday school superintendent and she assisted Reinhold, as she had her father and her husband, in the practical details of parish life. This assistance freed him for wider fields. Others of the family also were involved from time to time: Hulda taught Sunday school in the early years, Walter gave an illustrated lecture recorded in the church council minutes, and Richard often preached. The whole family served Bethel, though Lydia's was the continuous presence.

Does Civilization Need Religion?

Niebuhr's growing awareness in the 1920s of a gulf separating Christianity and civilization was not shared by all social reforming Christians. The mood of the liberal Protestant churches in the years following the war was generally one of confidence in the union of righteousness and power.[43] Churchmen had urged the war in moral terms, and successful prosecution of the war seemed to vindicate their preaching. A sense of victory at the armistice, a victory in the struggle for prohibition, and the great success of Protestant fund-raising programs patterned on the wartime bond drives buoyed Christian reformers' hopes for the appearance of a new social order.

The irrelevance of the church to the industrial order of Detroit[44] combined in Niebuhr's thinking with the vindictive peace of Versailles to encourage the apprehension of a disjuncture between Christianity and civilization. Power and righteousness were not simply united. Niebuhr's 1927 volume *Does Civilization Need Religion?* reflected this developing polarization of might and right in his thought.

Does Civilization Need Religion? represents an intermediate stage in the development of Niebuhr's political philosophy. It is not as thoroughly realistic as his mature writings, nor does it reflect the mastery of political theory that occurred later. It represents the thought of Niebuhr in his pre-Augustinian and pre-Marxist periods. *Does Civilization Need Reli-*

gion? attacked "sentimental optimism" but avoided a decisive break with liberalism.[45]

The disillusionment derived from postwar developments in international politics and industry was reinforced by a sense of the inevitable failure of hopes and aspirations that Niebuhr had drawn from Miguel de Unamuno and Oswald Spengler. He combined Unamuno's focus on the mortality of all with Spengler's critique of the hopes of liberal culture. He attempted to resist Spengler's conclusion that only a defiant courage in the face of the decline of Western civilization was possible. The cynicism that grew easily out of Spengler's analysis was inadequate. There still were resources for renewal. Religion contained resources for the renewal of Western civilization, but tapping these resources was more difficult than the liberals had realized.[46] He assumed with Ernst Troeltsch that Christianity was fated to be the chief source of spiritual idealism for Western culture.

The influence of Ernst Troeltsch's work *Die Soziallehren der christlichen Kirchen und Gruppen,* published in German in 1912 and in English in 1931,[47] is quite evident in Niebuhr's work of 1927. It was one of the most important works he studied during his parish years in Detroit. *Does Civilization Need Religion?* reflects Niebuhr's intellectual growth from his Yale student years. The Yale theses had been relatively innocent of social questions. They were essentially metaphysical works wrestling with the intellectual credibility of Christianity. His 1927 book summarizes in generalizations the specific issues of the industrial society in which he worked as a pastor.

In the way he handles the social issues, the influence of the Social Gospel movement is evident. It was absent in the academic writing of his theses a dozen years earlier. Added to Troeltsch's influence in analyzing the social questions were the resources of Troeltsch's sometimes friend Max Weber and the contribution of the English socialist thinker R. H. Tawney. Niebuhr's book reviews of Weber[48] and Tawney[49] in *The Christian Century* in 1925 and 1926 presented their reflections to the American audience. In the 1927 book he rewrote central insights from the reviews and broadened the scope of his reflection on their theories for his own work.

He used the new work of Alfred North Whitehead, which he had also reviewed for *The Christian Century,*[50] for the metaphysical grounding he wanted. Recent works of Albert Schweitzer were also drawn upon. He joined with Schweitzer to place major emphasis on Christian ethics for action rather than on metaphysics for intellectual credibility.

The pressures of the modern world, the social gospel, and the new writings in the sociology of religion combined in this new work in Christian social theory.

The publication of his first book helped to set Niebuhr apart from his colleagues in ministry. Boston University approached him about joining the theological school's faculty. The speaking association with Union Theological Seminary's leadership could now take on more potential as his writing gave him scholarly credentials. A praise-laden review by Francis J. McConnell, one of the most important leaders of the Social Gospel movement, made the book a significant event among the readers Niebuhr could anticipate. McConnell, the Methodist Bishop of Pittsburgh, praised the book and caught one part of Niebuhr's distinctiveness, saying, "I do not know any writer today who has a more admirable gift of generalization—or perhaps I should say of summarization."[51] The bishop was less hopeful than Niebuhr for the potential of the Christian laity to conduct social reform. He was more hopeful than Niebuhr of the capacity of the clergy to contribute to ethical reform of society. He had reservations about Niebuhr's encouragement of dualism, but he noted and welcomed Niebuhr's growing influence: "One of the promising signs of the times is that an increasing number of younger prophets in the church are thinking and speaking after the manner of Reinhold Niebuhr."[52]

Niebuhr's hopes that religion could become a source of social renewal did not depend on an optimistic evaluation of its strength. He saw religion beset by many problems and interpreted the cultural drift toward secularization as a threat to its very existence. Yet Niebuhr could not imagine religion disappearing; for him it was an essential defense of personality against the attacks of a seemingly hostile world. Religion, according to Niebuhr, defended personality in the realms of metaphysics and ethics. Properly equipped for its task, religion could provide human purposes, and it could also help make the social world more amenable to the pursuit of those purposes. Niebuhr's first book assumes a Social Gospel standpoint, examines the malaise of contemporary society, and asks what resources in religion are relevant to the reconstruction of that society. The volume is full of unresolved tensions; its author, though aware of disjuncture between the values of an increasingly secular civilization and traditional religion, had not yet reached a position that could free him from his liberalism, which presupposed a great deal of continuity between religion and politics. His doubts about the metaphysical and ethical adequacy of traditional religion were recorded in the most explicitly metaphysical writing of Niebuhr's career.

The impetus behind the chapter entitled "A Philosophy for an Ethical Religion" in *Does Civilization Need Religion?* was Niebuhr's concern to develop an ethic that would encourage action while avoiding illusion. The metaphysical reflection in the chapter was subservient to the concern for ethics. The contrast between the ideal and the real was, in its origins, an ethical problem for Niebuhr.[53] This contrast became a modern for Niebuhr's Christology, political theory, and metaphysics. Niebuhr revealed no distaste for metaphysics in this work and argued specifically that the development of an adequate metaphysics was next in importance to the development of an adequate ethic for the apologetic task of the church. Metaphysics and ethics depended on each other. The metaphysical assumption that the universe was not destructive of all the values of personality encouraged ethical action. The achievement of morality in turn prompted one to consider that the universe was not foreign to personality. Niebuhr did not carefully refine his understanding of metaphysical dualism. He did not mean to advocate total opposition between God and the universe, spirit and matter, good and evil, or spirit and nature. What he was concerned to establish was that the creative purpose met resistance in the universe and that, though the ideal was present in the real, it was also contrasted with it.[54]

Drawing upon Whitehead, Niebuhr regarded Christianity's metaphysical untidiness and tendencies toward pluralism as more inclusive of the facts of existence than monism. Niebuhr did not enter into exhaustive metaphysical analysis, but he identified himself with William James's pluralism and Whitehead's doctrine of continual creation. He regarded the latter's discussion of God as the principle of conception as a justification for religious belief: "In other words the faith of religion in both the transcendence and immanence of God is given a new metaphysical validation."[55]

Niebuhr found little affinity between the God of a robust theism and the all-knowing Absolute of monistic philosophers, which he regarded as primarily an attempt to solve the epistemological problem. God was active in the structures of the world and suffered at the hands of the world. Niebuhr regarded his dualism as metaphysically sound and close to the naive religious faith in the Bible. With William James he regarded the Absolute as destructive of practical effort to reform the world.

The Hebrew prophets drew much of their religious genius, Niebuhr believed, from a sense of the struggle between good and evil, as did Jesus. Though the capitulation of the church to Greek philosophy accentuated the countertendency to monism, the dualistic elements were preserved. Dualism helped religion in the fulfillment of its two great functions by recognizing the seriousness of the moral struggle while preserving hope for a victory over that struggle. Dualism as used by the prophets and Jesus prompted repentance of sin, but it also encouraged hope for redemption.[56]

Early Christology and Dualism

Does Civilization Need Religion? reveals the transmutation of the metaphysical dualism into Christological symbols. In later writings, Niebuhr often connected his ethics with theological symbols, but nowhere else is the metaphysical basis for these symbols so clear.

The interpreter who regards Niebuhr's Christology as central to his thought must explain the lack of a developed Christology in the early writings, Niebuhr's own claim that Christology was elaborated only in connection with an analysis of the human situation,[57] and many omissions and obvious shortcomings quickly apparent to theologians. Paul Lehmann has traced the development of Niebuhr's Christology and concluded that it is the key to understanding Niebuhr.[58] Still, Lehmann has described the early Christology as elusive and noted that Niebuhr's contemporaries did not recognize Christology as the center of his thought. This failure on the part of Niebuhr's contemporaries, Lehmann argued, was due to an "oversight" of Niebuhr's. This "oversight," which is Lehmann's principal objection to Niebuhr's Christology, is that it is not adequately trinitarian; "it is in the last analysis binitarian," resulting in the cross being "not adequately apprehended and interpreted as *operative* wisdom and power."[59] Niebuhr's writing as a whole displays little interest in the two-nature, trinitarian, or filioque controversies that have been the classical problems of Christology.

The tendency toward binitarianism that Lehmann discovered is not an "oversight"; rather, it is a deliberate tendency in Niebuhr's work. Consideration of this tendency as it first appeared will reveal that Niebuhr was more concerned with the conflict between good and evil than with elaborating Christology. Rather than being a thinker who ignored serious issues at the heart of his thought, as Lehmann portrayed him, he is a thinker who used Christological symbols to express the dualism he considered essential to a vigorous ethic. Reference to *Does Civilization Need Religion?* indicates that Niebuhr regarded the doctrines of the Trinity, incarnation, and atonement as expressions of the fundamental dualism that an adequate morality required:

> In the early Christian church the naïve dualism of Jesus was given dramatic and dynamic force through his deification, so that he became, in a sense, the God of the ideal, the symbol of the redemptive force in life which is in conflict with evil. Since no clear distinction was made between the spirit of the living Christ and the indwelling Holy Ghost, the doctrine of the trinity was, in effect, a symbol of an essential dualism.[60]

The doctrine of the atonement also symbolizes this essential dualism:

> No mechanical or magical explanations of the significance of the crucifixion have ever permanently obscured the helpful spiritual symbolism of the cross in which the conflict between good and evil is portrayed and the possibility as well as the difficulty of the triumph of the good over evil is dramatized.[61]

Treating Christological assertions as symbols of a metaphysical and ethical dualism was not new to Niebuhr in 1927. Earlier, the discovery that the cross symbolized the essential dualism of human life had revitalized the symbol of the cross for him. This 1925 statement, which connects the rediscovery of the atonement with dualism, is not fundamentally different from later statements about the cross.

> It was only a few years ago that I did not know what to make of the cross; at least I made no more of it than to recognize it as a historic fact which proved the necessity of paying a high price for our ideals. Now I see it as a symbol of ultimate reality. . . . It is because the cross of Christ symbolizes something in the very heart of reality, something in universal experience, that it has its central place in history. Life is tragic and the most perfect type of moral beauty inevitably has at least a touch of the tragic in it. Why? That is not so easy to explain. But love pays such a high price for its objectives and sets its objectives so high that they can never be attained. There is therefore always a foolish and a futile aspect to love's quest which give it the note of tragedy.[62]

Niebuhr's Christology developed beyond its fragmentary presentation in *Leaves from the Notebook of a Tamed Cynic* and *Does Civilization Need Religion?* It received its most complete elaboration in the 1939 Gifford Lectures. The dualistic background of his Christology was less obvious in this later writing, but the emphasis on the Christ as a powerless ideal destroyed by the powers of the real world survived.

Niebuhr misunderstood Lehmann's criticism that he had not done justice to the mighty acts of God.[63] He thought the criticism was directed at his use of myth, when in fact the criticism was directed at a failure to understand the cross "as operative wisdom and power." Niebuhr could not so understand the cross, because he first apprehended its significance as the very powerlessness of the ideal in the real world. This tension of the ideal and the real is constitutive of the shape of his political thought throughout his career.

Political Communities
and Their Corruption

Niebuhr's analysis of group egoism developed as his Wilsonian liberalism dissolved under the pressures of post-Versailles interpretations of World War I. His theoretical handling of the corruption of political communities was shaped, as were most of his other insights to some extent, by his interpretation of the Great War. Between 1915 and 1928 he evolved from one "trying to be an optimist without falling into sentimentality" to "a realist trying to save myself from cynicism."[64] Throughout the period, his thought returned to the analysis of the ethical potentiality in group action. The answers he derived in this period did not remain satisfactory to him, but they do point to the structure of his later thought.

The war demonstrated the conflict between the aspirations of the modern state and the aspirations of the individual.[65] Focusing on the nations of Europe destroying Western civilization, he regarded both the mass grave and the common uniform as symbolic of the destruction of individualism by nationalism. The mass grave was particularly tragic because the ends for which men were being sacrificed were generally not important to them. The primary causes of the war were regarded as economic. Possible economic gains for the nation were not worthy of the sacrifice of individuals. The moral conscience of modern man transcended the nations, but the power of the nation forced individuals into common uniforms regardless of their individual aspirations. In a spirit individualistic-universalistic protest against the claims of the nation, he declared that the individual is a world citizen.[66]

Though Niebuhr recognized that nations were self-serving and narrowly pursuing economic self-interest, his underlying idealism was apparent. He hoped that, if nations were going to sacrifice men, they would find causes that justified the sacrifice.

The failure of Wilson's attempt to harness liberal idealism and na-

46

tionalism drove Niebuhr to emphasize the egoism of the nation-state and to doubt that its policies could transcend self-interest. In his growing disillusionment with liberalism, he occasionally evoked realism, although its shape remained far from clear. For example, in 1925 he rejected as liberal a tenet of political philosophy that he later would affirm as one of the cornerstones of political realism.

> The effect of liberalism to preserve peace between warring classes and nations by pitting self-interest against self-interest was bound to fail. It only served to aggravate the fears and hatreds which the groups and nations had for one another. The Great War came to reduce the whole philosophy of unrestrained self-interest and undisciplined power to an absurdity.[67]

By 1926 he wrote that Western civilization was completely secularized and its dominant motives were beyond the reach of ethical control.[68] In 1927 he felt that if the egoism of groups could not be morally qualified, one would be driven to cynicism.[69]

Niebuhr regarded as almost impossible the task of persuading a nation to surrender its national interests for the sake of the larger society. He could not accept prudence as an adequate guide to statecraft, for World War I demonstrated how self-defeating were the counsels of political prudence. Given the situation of international anarchy, the formation of prewar alliances of the Triple Entente and the Triple Alliance were prudent actions. However, the dynamics of the alliances themselves were partially responsible for casting Europe into war. He argued for the interaction of rational and religious consideration to provide a basis for the qualification of blind national interest. He saw clearly the political nature of the problems of international politics, but his lingering idealism prevented him from proposing imaginative political solutions. The conclusions of *Does Civilization Need Religion?* were not a permanent stopping place for Niebuhr; an article written in 1928[70] indicates that, within a year, he had retreated from some of its positions.

Niebuhr took an anti–world government position which he was to develop and refine throughout his career.[71] Governments presupposed societies, and the most glaring fact of the international scene was the lack of an international society with social substance. He feared that international courts would inevitably be biased toward the status-quo nations that benefited from law and order.[72]

Niebuhr regarded international politics as plagued by the counsels of sentimentalists and cynics. Idealists who did not have a due respect for the difficulty of judging politics morally were of little help to the renewal of society; cynics who were lost in despair could not make recommendations for improvements. He pointed to the problem, but at this point in his career he lacked the resources for solving it. His failure to utilize the balance-of-power concept, which he had rejected as liberalism, and his continuing hope of transforming international politics denied him the intellectual resources he sought. He had learned the wisdom of the serpent, but that very wisdom prevented him from fully exploiting creative possibilities within traditional power politics or the innovations of international organization. He utilized the innocence of the dove—that is, a hope for a transcendence of national interest—but this innocence prevented him from seeing the possibilities of creatively expanding the concept of national interest. The polarity between the ideal and the real was contained within his thought by 1927, but the tension between the two required further development before the mature political philosophy of Reinhold Niebuhr would appear.

The Christian Ethos

Ernst Troeltsch's work on the history of the Christian ethos had decisive impact upon Niebuhr. It is hard to separate Niebuhr's work in *Does Civilization Need Religion?* from Troeltsch's *The Social Teaching of the Christian Churches*. Troeltsch saw four permanent contributions of the Christian ethos that essentially reduce to two important contributions. Christianity reinforced and inspired a high value on human personality by its theology and its ethic; also, the emphasis on the ethic of love drove toward social responsibility. These two foci, the value of personality and the ethic of love, are the driving concerns of Niebuhr's book. Beyond that, the clash between civilization and religion, the central issue of Troeltsch's book, is the theme of Reinhold Niebuhr's book and also, later, of H. Richard Niebuhr's *Christ and Culture*. The resultant history of religious ideals compromising with social reality is also similar to Troeltsch's perspective. The center of Niebuhr's book is the history of the Christian ethos in its environment. This center would continue to be a major section of many of Niebuhr's other books as part of his vocation became the historian of ethical ideas. This study of the history of ethical ideas drove Niebuhr to express what he had learned in the parish: the inevitability of social organization's resistance to reform. *Does Civilization Need Religion?* carries within it the seeds of the analysis of groups seen in 1932 in *Moral Man and Immoral*

Society. Believing that human beings need to interpret human nature in the trust that the universe supports the values of personality, he traced the history of religious ethics in the West. One third of the book is given to this historical development, and these pages reflect the heavy debt to Troeltsch and Weber. The next longest section deals with the difficulty of relating ethical ideals to the complexity of intergroup problems. His solution to the compromises of the history and the complexity of the present is the recommendation of an ascetic Protestant response. That is for those Protestants who want to renew society to discipline themselves by separating from the temptations of financial reward and nationalism. By transcending the human motivations of greed and group pride, reformers could present their ideals in a pure enough form to attract support for social reform. A withdrawal from the benefits of the structure of society is necessary to reform it. Niebuhr, in the spirit of Max Weber, reveals his strategy to be a worldly asceticism, and following Ernst Troeltsch his hopes rest in the same type of world-reforming ethic that Troeltsch had associated with Calvinist social ethics. Finally, he grounded his hopes for social reform on the possibility of the ethical renewal of religion and social reformers finding religious hopes in which to found their struggle.[73]

In New York City, Union Theological Seminary and the intellectual climate there would intersect with his disillusioned liberalism and draw him, for a time, into socialist answers for questions liberalism seemed unable to answer.

NOTES

1. Allan Nevins, *Ford: Expansion and Challenge 1915-1933* (New York: Charles Scribner's Sons, 1957), p. 3. The above paragraph and most of the remainder of chapter 2 is a reorganization of materials from chapters 1 and 2 of my book *Reinhold Niebuhr: Prophet to Politicians* (Nashville: Abingdon Press, 1975).

2. Ibid., p. 7.

3. Reinhold Niebuhr, *Leaves from the Notebook of a Tamed Cynic* (1929), p. 138.

4. June Bingham, *Courage to Change: An Introduction to the Life and Thought of Reinhold Niebuhr* (New York: Charles Scribner's Sons, 1961), pp. 101–102.

5. Niebuhr, *Leaves,* p. 34; quotations from 1990 reprint (Louisville, Ky.: Westminster/John Knox Press).

6. Ibid., p. 35.

7. Ibid., p. 36.

8. Niebuhr, "The Nation's Crime Against the Individual," *Atlantic Monthly* 18 (Nov. 1916), 609–614.

9. Reinhold Niebuhr, "Failure of German-Americanism," *Atlantic Monthly* 18 (July 1916), 13–18.

10. In 1916 Reinhold Niebuhr shared the Social Gospel movement's enthusiasm for Prohibition. "The prohibition movement has come to express the most enlightened conscience of the American people. It has the practically unanimous support of the churches and is being championed with increasing vigor by the press. It is natural that opposition to a movement that has the support of the intelligent public opinion of our country should cause resentment. . . . In this attitude, as well as in his attitude upon other issues, the indifference and hostility of the German-American to our ideals is a betrayal of the ideals of his own people." Ibid., p. 17.

11. Niebuhr, *Leaves,* p. 19.

12. William G. Chrystal, "Reinhold Niebuhr and the First World War," *Journal of Presbyterian History* 55 (1977), 285–298.

13. Ibid., p. 288.

14. Ibid., p. 290.

15. Ibid., p. 292.

16. Ibid., p. 295.

17. Reinhold Niebuhr has reflected upon his years 1915–1928 in Detroit in the short "Intellectual Autobiography" in Charles W. Kegley, ed., *Reinhold Niebuhr: His Religious, Social, and Political Thought* (New York: Pilgrim Press, 1984), pp. 4–7. A more important source for his thoughts about the Detroit years is "The Reminiscences of Reinhold Niebuhr" (Oral History Research Office of Columbia University, 1957).

18. Reinhold Niebuhr, "How Philanthropic Is Henry Ford?" *The Christian Century,* 43 (Dec. 9, 1926), 1517.

19. Samuel S. Marquis, *Henry Ford: An Interpretation* (Boston: Little, Brown & Co., 1923).

20. Niebuhr, "How Philanthropic Is Henry Ford?," p. 1516.

21. Ibid., p. 1517.

22. Reinhold Niebuhr, "Lessons of the Detroit Experience," *The Christian Century* 82 (Apr. 21, 1965), 488.

23. Report of the Mayor's Committee on Race Relations (Detroit, 1926), p. 4.

24. Reinhold Niebuhr, *The Children of Light and the Children of Darkness* (1944), p. 141.

25. The committee did not use the terms "black," "African American," or "racism," which have meanings today that would have been unknown to the committee in 1926.

26. Report of the Mayor's Committee, p. 15.

27. Ibid., p. 13.

28. Ibid., p. 14.

29. Letter to Klein of Elmhurst College (Mar. 10, 19?? New York), copy in the author's possession.

30. William G. Chrystal, ed., *Young Reinhold Niebuhr: His Early Writings— 1911–1931* (1977), p. 216.

31. Ibid., p. 215.

32. Church Bulletin of Bethel Evangelical Church, Jan. 2, 1927.

33. *The Keryx* (June 1913), quoted in Chrystal, *Young Reinhold Niebuhr*, p. 47.

34. Chrystal, *Young Reinhold Niebuhr*, p. 74.

35. Ibid., pp. 112–115.

36. Ibid., p. 108.

37. Ibid., p. 161. The frustrations with financing a women's college led him, as secretary of the General Board of Education of the Synod, to record the Board's intention to move Elmhurst toward coeducation. "Statement of General Board of Education in Regard to Education for Women," n.d., copy in author's possession.

38. Ibid., p. 163.

39. Ibid., p. 83. The phrase would appear later as a book title that reflects Niebuhr's approach to ministry: *Discerning the Signs of the Times* (1946).

40. Ibid., pp. 119–123.

41. Ibid., p. 148.

42. "25th Anniversary of Bethel Evangelical Church" (Detroit: Bethel Evangelical Church, n.d.).

43. Donald B. Meyer, *The Protestant Search for Political Realism, 1919–1941* (Berkeley, Calif.: University of California Press, 1961), p. 9.

44. See the concluding note in his 1928 diary: "Modern industry, particularly American industry, is not Christian. The economic forces which move it are hardly qualified at a single point by real ethical consideration." Niebuhr, *Leaves*, p. 152.

45. The following year Niebuhr's deep disillusionment with liberalism is stated in "The Confession of a Tired Radical," *The Christian Century* 45 (Aug. 30, 1928), 1046–1047.

46. Religion is left undefined in *Does Civilization Need Religion?* (1927), and its meaning changes slightly in various contexts. In 1927, Niebuhr usually means by the term the institution, life patterns, and ideas identified with Western Christianity.

47. Ernst Troeltsch, *The Social Teaching of the Christian Churches*, translated by Olive Wyon, introduced by H. Richard Niebuhr (New York: Harper Torchbooks, 1960).

48. Reinhold Niebuhr, "Capitalism—A Protestant Offspring," *The Christian Century* 42 (May 7, 1925), 600–601.

49. Reinhold Niebuhr, "How Civilization Defeated Christianity," *The Christian Century* 43 (July 15, 1926), 895–896.

50. Reinhold Niebuhr, "Science and the Modern World," *The Christian Century* 43 (Apr. 8, 1926), 448–449.

51. Francis J. McConnell, "A Challenge to Complacency," *The Christian Century* 45 (Feb. 16, 1928), 208.

52. Ibid., p. 210.

53. Metaphysical dualism is attributable to ethical dualism, according to Niebuhr. "The real difference between naturalistic monism and dualistic supernaturalism is derived from ethical feeling. If it is recognized or believed that the moral imagination conceives ideals for life which history in any immediate or even in any conceivable form is unable to realize[,] a dualistic world-view

will emerge. Thus classical religion with its various types of dualism grows out of the conflict of spirit and impulse in human life." Reinhold Niebuhr, *Reflections on the End of an Era* (1934), p. 198.

54. Niebuhr, *Does Civilization Need Religion?* p. 200.

55. Ibid., p. 212.

56. Ibid., p. 198.

57. Kegley, ed., *Reinhold Niebuhr*, p. 515.

58. "Christology is the leitmotiv of Reinhold Niebuhr's theology. . . . Plainly, if unobtrusively, Niebuhr's account of Jesus Christ is the presupposition of his anthropology. . . . Christology is *pivotal*, not *peripheral*, in Niebuhr's theology." Ibid., pp. 329–331.

59. Ibid., p. 353.

60. Niebuhr, *Does Civilization Need Religion?*, p. 198.

61. Ibid., pp. 199–200.

62. Niebuhr, *Leaves*, pp. 106–107.

63. Kegley, ed., *Reinhold Niebuhr*, p. 515.

64. Reinhold Niebuhr, "What the War Did to My Mind," *The Christian Century* 45 (Sept. 27, 1928), 1161.

65. Niebuhr, "The Nation's Crime Against the Individual," pp. 609–614.

66. Ibid., p. 612.

67. Reinhold Niebuhr, "Can Christianity Survive?" *Atlantic Monthly* 135 (Jan. 1925), 87.

68. Reinhold Niebuhr, "Our Secularized Civilization," *The Christian Century* 43 (Apr. 22, 1926), 508.

69. Reinhold Niebuhr, "Missions and World Peace," *The World Tomorrow* 10 (Apr. 1927), 171.

70. Niebuhr, "Confession of a Tired Radical."

71. Niebuhr, *Does Civilization Need Religion?*, p. 153.

72. Ibid., p. 158.

73. Ibid., p. 242.

3

Called
to Teach Social Ethics
1928–1960

A DEEPENING FRIENDSHIP proved crucial to the vocation of the pastor. The friend was Sherwood Eddy, a missionary, philanthropist, YMCA executive, evangelist, and organizer of Christian social reform who had come to know Niebuhr on his American seminar to Europe in 1923. (Niebuhr's friendship with Bishop William Scarlett also developed on this seminar. Scarlett would become Niebuhr's dearest friend and his confidant in correspondence in Niebuhr's old age.) Eddy recruited Niebuhr for his college campaigns and YMCA work. Niebuhr's involvement on the college-speaking circuit became so demanding that Sherwood Eddy arranged to pay for an assistant minister at Bethel Church. Eddy's worldwide contacts and academic contacts opened some of the wider opportunity Niebuhr craved. But Eddy's plans for Niebuhr to assume the editorship of *The World Tomorrow*, a socialist-pacifist journal, were not at first accepted.

After Niebuhr's book was published, Eddy approached the new president of Union Theological Seminary, Henry Sloane Coffin, about an appointment for Niebuhr. Coffin persuaded the board and the faculty, and the interview at the seminary went well enough that Niebuhr was called. Coffin, himself a liberal evangelical with pastoral experience, was moving the balance between academic study and pastoral preparation toward the latter. Niebuhr exhibited this balance and brought pastoral experience to the position.

Niebuhr has recorded this debt to Eddy:

> After that [European seminar] he enlisted me as a helper in his tour of
> the colleges and insisted on paying the salary of an assistant minister for
> my parish to free me for college work. Subsequently he was instrumen-
> tal in bringing me to the faculty of Union Seminary.[1]

Eddy himself frequently referred to Niebuhr as one of the brightest
young men of his day. On one occasion, when summing up his relationship to socialist Christianity, Eddy wrote:

> I helped to found the Fellowship for a Christian Social Order and was a
> member of the early group out of which came the Fellowship of Socialist
> Christians. I voted for Norman Thomas, and I had the privilege of paying
> Reinhold Niebuhr's salary during his first years at Union.[2]

This payment referred to a direct contribution to Union Theological
Seminary for half the salary and Eddy's subsidizing of *The World Tomorrow*, which provided the other half of Niebuhr's salary for his editorship.

Niebuhr joined Harry F. Ward in the field of Christian ethics. His
first title was Associate Professor of Christian Ethics and the Philosophy of Religion. In philosophy of religion he taught his own course,
"Religion and Ethics," throughout the year. He also joined Eugene W.
Lyman in teaching "Philosophy of Christian Religion." He joined Professor Ward in co-teaching four courses during the year 1928–29 that
had been taught by Professor Ward the previous year. The courses
were titled "Development of Ethical Ideals," "Social Teaching of the
Bible," "Modern Social Movements," and "The Social Order." John C.
Bennett was teaching as an instructor in the areas of systematic theol-
ogy and philosophy of religion during Niebuhr's first two years at
Union. After serving at Auburn Theological Seminary and the Pacific
School of Religion, Bennett would return to Union and eventually with
Niebuhr form the field of Christian ethics.

Niebuhr's remarks that he was not a theologian need to be seen in
the context of his actual teaching. His courses were offered for almost
forty years in the two areas in which he began: philosophy of religion
and Christian ethics. He did not teach systematic theology. He tended
to think in terms of Christian philosophy of religion. The remark that
he was not a theologian was not to deny that some of his work had
systematic theology dimensions. It was a vocational distinction that
was much clearer to all who knew within which areas he taught than

it was to the general public or even to some academic theologians who missed his point.

By his second academic year at Union, 1929–30, Niebuhr was evolving on his own. He now taught two courses in philosophy of religion by himself and one course in Christian ethics alone. He still shared four courses with Ward, including a new course, "Ethical Viewpoints in Modern Literature."

In 1930, he was promoted to the William E. Dodge, Jr., chair as Professor of Applied Christianity. The promotion, urged by President Coffin, was in part due to a beckoning from Yale Divinity School for Reinhold to join the faculty of his alma mater. The ethics curriculum changed to include the two-semester course "Historical Introduction to Ethics." He shared the course with Professor Ward at first, but this course would, through its various shapes, be the central course of Niebuhr's teaching career. He also added a seminar on "Ethics of the State." This seminar under various names would become a regular offering of the department of ethics. Ward continued to emphasize economic ethics while Niebuhr emphasized political ethics. His brother H. Richard Niebuhr, then Dean of Eden Theological Seminary, joined him for the summer school of 1931. Later, when Richard was Associate Professor of Christian Ethics at Yale Divinity School, he returned for the summer schools of 1932 and 1933 and for several subsequent summer schools.

As late as 1932–33, Niebuhr and Ward were still teaching together, but the catalog for 1933–34 shows that this class collaboration had ended.[3] From 1934 on, their names were sometimes listed together for a two-semester course, but each would take one semester. By 1935, Niebuhr's two-semester course in the development of ethical ideals had become a requirement for all Bachelor of Divinity degrees, and other ethics courses that he or Ward would teach were electives.[4]

The relationship with Ward began very warmly. Ward, an English Methodist educated in the United States, had become a leader of the radical wing of the Social Gospel movement. Ward's ministry in the stockyard area of Chicago conjoined with his Methodist conversionism to shape a radical critique of American society. Like Niebuhr, Ward had great energy and gave himself unstintingly to outside speaking and organizational work for social reform movements. Before coming to Union he had chaired the Methodist Federation for Social Service, writing its "Social Creed," which evolved into the social teaching of

the Methodist Church and the Federal Council of Churches. He continued to chair the Federation while at Union and added to it the role of
chairperson of the American Civil Liberties Union and the American
League Against War and Fascism. The association with Ward and
Union radicalized Niebuhr, but he never fully shared Ward's views.
Ward brought a Methodist conversionism into his expectation of society through the influence of the Social Gospel movement that was
foreign to Reinhold Niebuhr's Reformation theology expectations.
Ward's social optimism, particularly about the Soviet Union's social
direction, was not shared by Niebuhr. Ward's exposure through travel
to the Soviet Union led him to praise it in terms that Niebuhr's travel
experience in the Soviet Union found false.[5]

Both Niebuhr and Ward were investigated by the House of Representatives Committee on Un-American Activities, and both fought publicly against the committee. Ward's chairmanship of the American
League Against War and Fascism led to his being required to testify
before the committee, and Niebuhr's membership in the league was
frequently referred to in ongoing FBI inquiries into his record. Both
men were socialists and supported many of the same causes. Niebuhr
gradually became a sharp critic of Marxism. Ward remained a radical
critic of the U.S. economy long after Niebuhr could talk about pragmatically achieving a justice that was tolerable for middle-class Americans. Observing them together in 1963, I found their relations
amicable, and the greatest ethical difference between them was their
alternative readings of the Soviet Union.

Paul Tillich joined Niebuhr in the field of philosophy of religion in
1933. The other major change in courses during the 1930s was that, by
1939, Niebuhr was teaching the materials for the Gifford Lectures in
his philosophy of religion courses. Harry Ward taught his last class at
Union in 1941. In 1943, John C. Bennett, who also taught theology,
joined Niebuhr in the ethics field.

History of Christian Ethics

From 1928 through 1959, Niebuhr taught the history of Christian ethics under various titles. In its most developed form it was offered every
year as a two-semester course. It was his basic course in ethics.

The choice of history as a medium for the study of ethics was significant. It recognized the dominance of historical method in twentieth-
century theological studies. It reflected Niebuhr's own education at

Yale with Sneath. It reflected the importance of the major work Niebuhr studied as a pastor, Ernst Troeltsch's *The Social Teaching of the Christian Churches*. It marked continuity with the course on the evolution of morals inherited from Harry Ward. If history were the bearer of ethics, the historical relativity of moral positions and the engagement of ethics with historical problems were already presupposed. Finally, it demonstrated Niebuhr's own love for the history of ideas. In late-life personal recollections, he might say the field of history could have been an alternative vocation, but he found his work as a historian in the field of ethics. The material of the course appears throughout his books. From the 1927 *Does Civilization Need Religion?* to the 1965 *Man's Nature and His Communities*, he used the same sources reflected on in the course.

The second most remarkable feature of this basic course in Christian ethics was that the first semester was a study of non-Christian ethics. It was a survey of the general history of morals. The lectures ranged from sources of social conduct in primitive society through the relationships of religion to morals in the societies of Egypt, Babylon, Assyria, China, India, Persia, Israel, Greece, Rome, and Japan. The term papers required for the first semester focused on questions of the development of morality and comparative morality. Given the freedom to teach the courses he chose to teach, this long-term commitment to the teaching of the ethics of non-Christian religions indicates the breadth of Niebuhr's own mind and also the material he thought students preparing for ministry needed to know. Here in the origins of the contemporary discipline of Christian ethics, the view was broad and comparative. If the discipline has narrowed its focus as it matured, it has been to the loss of seminarians and the church.[6]

The syllabus for the course in 1942 shows 115 books selected by Niebuhr for reading, with each culture having a choice of from six to twenty books. He read widely and broadly and contributed generously to book reviews. Advanced students had the experience of thinking his offhand remarks on books were given too quickly, only to find as their own reading deepened that he had written scholarly reviews of the works being discussed.

The early lectures of the course would define ethics as the science of morals or Christian ethics as the theology of morals and reflect in general terms about the study of ethics. The study of morals would reveal historically relative standards of morality, but Niebuhr would invite the students to join him in the search for patterns of morality.

He would by his intensity and questioning method persuade the students, who were not conscious of Niebuhr's teaching the course for the twentieth time, that here was a new and vital quest.

The first week, the students would be taken into the dynamics of Niebuhr's presentation of the spirit versus nature categories. Many previous explanations of ethics would be dismissed because they had not taken the needs of nature—security, sexuality, materiality—seriously enough. But of course naturalistic theories reducing life and ethics to naturalistic impulses were not sufficiently attuned to the power of the spirit or ideal factors to shape history. Winding through generalizations about theories of ethics, the students would be led to see the possible veracity or even superiority of a Christian ethic that handled well the nature-spirit contrast that Niebuhr had set up.

Then the course would turn to primitive societies and their ethics. Typically, the study of primitive societies would occupy two and a half weeks. The discussion of Egyptian morality took about three sessions, with Niebuhr drawing out insights about the relationship of religion to imperial politics. Babylon and Persia received equal attention, with Niebuhr revealing the contributions of both toward the later emergence of Christianity. From Babylon, the Code of Hammurabi, ideas of messianic kinship, and the restoration of justice and divine drive toward social improvement were emphasized. The Persian sense of the meaningfulness of history, reflecting the provisional dualism under monistic religion, was highlighted.

On turning to the subject of Hebrew ethics in November, Niebuhr would be at his best. A former student wrote:

> Reinhold Niebuhr was a tremendous teacher. He was incapable of dullness in the classroom. Arriving a few minutes before class time, he stood at the lecturer's table like an eagle poised to jump. His lecture notes furnished a well-organized development of thought, but they were only his taking-off place. From them he roved afield, seizing upon anything relevant to his theme. Everything, however ancient or minute, came alive and contemporary.[7]

Hebrew ethics were more than a people's ethic, they contained the emergence of the first universal prophetic religion. Here Niebuhr was home. The presentation of Hebrew ethics revolved around Amos. The covenants were discussed as the fruit of prophetic religion. Apocalyptic literature was an outgrowth of the failure of prophetic justice. The prophetic teachings were the high point, and among these Amos was foremost. The moral traditions were divided by Niebuhr into pre-prophetic, prophetic, and post-prophetic.

The Old Testament department at the seminary had specialized courses on most of the material surveyed in a few days. Niebuhr recognized them as the experts and deferred to their expertise. But he had been close to Amos since his own seminary days, and the themes of the universality of God, God's transcendence above any nation, the demand by God for justice in human relations, and God as Creator were developed. In his reference in class on November 6, 1942, to the criticism of Amos by the court priest Amaziah in Amos 7:10 is foreshadowed a theme he would take up against his old enemy J. Edgar Hoover during Richard Nixon's presidency.[8]

The roots of injustice were nations and people claiming too much for themselves. Second, in the religious-ethical dimensions, the basic problem was pride or haughtiness. God was understood in Amos to redress the balance of justice. Justice was the key to prophetic religion, and in Amos justice was predominant, not love. The prophets also protested against complacency and false securities. In the name of justice, magic was rejected and ritual criticized.

Niebuhr regarded Amos as seeing God's glory in judgment. The nations continually destroyed each other as God's rough instrument of justice. The processes of history were slow, time was given for repentance, but the evil was so great that the prophets saw judgment becoming more terrible. Hope was given in the prophets for the time after destruction. Other streams of Hebrew thought developed themes of redemption—for Israel, for all, or for the repentant.

The lectures after those on prophetic ethics examined concepts of family and sexual life, property rights, and crime and punishment. These same relationships were referred to throughout the spectrum of religions under examination in the course as each religion was reviewed.

From the prophetic origins two streams of Judaism emerged in Niebuhr's overview, prophetic messianism and legalism. Niebuhr's preference for prophetic messianism was obvious. In one development it is fulfilled in Christianity, but there much of its rigor is lost in its fulfillment. Another stream, though dominated by legalism, survives in Judaism and emerges in twentieth-century America as prophetic Jews contribute to secular liberalism. In 1942, he saw three streams of fulfillment: (1) in Christ, (2) in the promised universal fulfillment of history in terms of peace on earth, and (3) in the rebirth of Zion in terms of national fulfillment.

Typically Niebuhr used three weeks, normally six lectures, to cover Greek ethical thought. This period was brief, but it was equal to the time given to Old Testament ethics.[9] After a general introduction to ancient Greece, the lectures proceeded to ethical themes in Greek drama. For some students his orations on the dramatic materials were the high point of the course. Charles C. West, a student in the class in 1942, wrote of the impact of Niebuhr's interpretation of Orestes.

> One knew that he was a man of action as well as a man of thought, and he challenged us to be both as well. I think I learned more from his interpretation of the dilemma of Orestes in Greek drama than I did from his insights as to how we should relate to the Russians in World War II.[10]

The themes of Niebuhr the political philosopher are found in these lectures on Greece. The religious problems are basic to human history. Universal truth is sought through deep understanding of particular conflicts. Ultimate order conflicts with human ordering. Pride is the danger of the creative. Lives and values have insoluble conflicts. The search for a guiltless solution leads to further and more terrible guilt. Niebuhr saw the answer of Greek tragedy to be that guilt arises to some degree without human responsibility, for the gods compelled the actors. Students listening to the lectures and reading among original and secondary sources found a teacher building upon what they had already learned in college. Niebuhr drew out the ethics, however. Both Greek and Hebrew sources were to flow into the Christianity of the professor, and neither one was despised. The dangers of Greek rationalistic thought being used as an ideological cover for the cruelties of Greek life were pointed out. As the lectures on Greece concluded with the ethics of Stoicism, one could see the Hellenistic universalism being laid out that would provide the context for the Christian sect's evolution out of Judaism.

The three lectures on Rome before the Christmas vacation covered a general dateline presentation of Roman history, a class structure analysis of Roman society, Stoic ethics, a brief Roman religious history, and a discussion of various theories of the decline of Rome from Toynbee to Gibbon. Niebuhr's own preferred interpretations corresponded to those of Charles Norris Cochrane,[11] whose thought appeared in Niebuhr's lectures. His comments about the quality of the Constantinian conversion were cynical. (They were even more scathing later in *The Structure of Nations and Empires*.[12]) Stoicism did not escape the role of ideological cover for Roman injustice and imperialism, but it was presented sympathetically. Stoicism as a universal ethic was a forerunner of Christianity as it became a universal religion. Stoic ethics in Niebuhr's perspective were Rome's public ethics even if the Romans worshiped in mystery cults. Christianity as it emerged into the public realm could learn from Stoicism, adapt, transform, and neglect aspects of it.

The weakest part of the course followed the Christmas vacation. The more ambitious of his students would complete their term papers during the Christmas two-week holiday. However, two weeks of lectures remained in January before breaking again for the reading period and the examination period. During the two weeks of January, Niebuhr would summarize his knowledge of the ethics of India, China, and Japan. The generalizations could help the students in their further reading. But there was not enough time to make an adequate presentation of the ethics of these cultures.

Niebuhr's predecessor in the course, Harry Ward, had lectured in India, China, and Japan, but Niebuhr never traveled to Asia and so the course, as was true of most world religion courses in those days, benefited from very little firsthand experience. Niebuhr's friend and sponsor Sherwood Eddy of course knew these cultures through YMCA work, and he had served as missionary to India. Students of Niebuhr, perhaps most notably Charles West, would become missionaries to China. Niebuhr furnished them with only a little of Confucian ethics. Japan's religion and ethics, even during the war years, were treated very briefly. Some years, but not every year, the ethics of Islam would be introduced.

From the perspective of the 1990s, the relatively scant coverage of oriental religions makes the survey of a general history of morals inadequate. However, the relative neglect of comparative ethics in theological education in the 1990s and the emphasis on global issues in theological education as the new emphasis of the Association of Theological Schools make Niebuhr's course from the twenties, thirties, and forties seem outstandingly ahead of its time. Even more unique is that, without requiring the course for the curriculum, he would attract enough students to fill the largest lecture hall.

New Testament Ethics

Two weeks after concluding his lectures on the general history of morals with a discussion of Gandhi, Niebuhr would begin his Christian Ethics course with a general lecture and outline. Though this course was a specifically "Christian" ethics course, the approach was summarized in the directions for the term paper: "In every case the theological basis, the socio-historical circumstances, and the resulting ethical theories and practices should be analyzed."[13]

The course raced rapidly over almost two thousand years of Christian wrestling with personal and social ethical problems. Niebuhr's typewritten single-spaced notes for the course consist of 122 pages. They are mostly in sentence fragment form with occasional handwritten additions.[14] The course, before his stroke, was given with a rapid-fire delivery style. Typically the lecture ended ten minutes before the close of the class period, and questions and answers followed. The questions could deal with the subject of the lecture, but often they involved public issues current in the news.

In Niebuhr's teaching, Jesus Christ was presented more as a messianic figure than as a teacher of ethics. The norms Jesus reflected were drawn from the Old Testament, particularly from the covenant relationship of the Creator God with Israel. Jesus used the legal traditions of his people, but he also drew upon the reality of the living God, who dealt with Israel in history in both legal and prophetic terms. Finding in the history of Israel the triumph of neither Israel nor the righteous, Niebuhr saw messianic expectations intensifying until Jesus fulfilled and changed them.

General issues that appear in Niebuhr's second or third lectures in the course were: (1) the relationship of the ultimate norm of love to the need for proximate historical norms; (2) the relationship of responsibility for human society and the radical principles of love as self-sacrifice and forgiveness; (3) the relationship of ideal expressions of justice to the rough justice of human organizations; (4) the tension between understanding love as grace and love as law; and (5), in a restatement of (1) and (2), the tension between an impulse toward perfection and the need for social responsibility. After briefly reviewing answers characteristic of seven or eight different historical Christian strategies, his lectures turned to an explication of the ethics of Jesus Christ.

Niebuhr's writings in the 1930s on the ethics of Jesus emphasized the radicalness, the purity, and the universalism of Jesus' teaching on love.[15] This ethic was not immediately applicable to social questions. The ideals of Jesus' ethic were rooted in the nature of God and therefore partially transcendent of an ethic that humans could fulfill. The dualism of the transcendent ideal and the social reality model was apparent. In the course lectures of 1942 and thereafter, the presentation is more sophisticated. Here the fuller recognition of the eschatological context of the Gospels containing Jesus' ethic is made central. In fact, the first point to make in the ordered exposition of Jesus' ethic is its eschatological character. For Niebuhr, both eschatology and the absolute love of Jesus expressed the same transcendence of life. The eschatological framework of the Gospels did not make Jesus' ethic irrelevant, as Albert Schweitzer's *Quest for the Historical Jesus* suggested. Niebuhr reflected on Schweitzer and his writings on Jesus' ethic often.

One of Niebuhr's enthusiastic students traveled to Switzerland and spent a year reading Schweitzer's works. On returning to New York, the student encountered his professor on 122nd Street.

> "You know, Dr. Niebuhr, you and Albert Schweitzer are my two intellectual and moral heroes." He seemed to stagger backward a step in genuine disorientation (mild shock). "Oh, Mr. Clark," he said, "you must not say that. You must not compare me to a man like Albert Schweitzer."[16]

In working out the role of eschatology, Niebuhr followed James Moffatt, *Love in the New Testament*,[17] in showing that many of the more radical teachings of Jesus were not set in any apparent eschatological context. He wrestled with the interpretation of the Kingdom of God which began in Jesus' ministry and was still to come in fulfillment. His lecture would utilize works by Martin Dibelius, Benjamin W. Bacon, T. W. Manson, M. C. D'Arcy, and C. H. Dodd, whom he came to call master. He would conclude by arguing that the Kingdom of God of Jesus' teaching came in Jesus as *telos*, or meaning, not as *finis*, or fulfillment in power. History itself continued as an interim, between revelation of history's meaning and the full disclosure of its meaning.[18]

The ethics of Jesus are, of course, relevant to his time, but for Niebuhr they also revealed the quality of God's love and intention for human life in all times. Following and quoting C. H. Dodd, he would argue that Jesus' teaching stirs up a human process, arousing the imagination. The precepts, sometimes quite specific, are not legislation but a qualitative input, inserting love into the moral reasoning of humanity. For Dodd, and for Niebuhr using Dodd, "The law of Christ is essentially concerned with the quality of the act and the direction in which it is moving."[19]

The love Jesus taught, Niebuhr regarded as expressing Ernst Troeltsch's phrase, "the love universalism of Jesus Christ." It was the universal law of human nature which fulfilled the humanity that was inclined to follow Jesus' commandments. The love of Jesus did not lend itself to the requirements of legislation as directly as it did to the human will. The love of course included mutual human love and was even represented by the impartialities of nature, but in its deepest expressions it was found in the willingness to sacrifice for the other and the will to forgive the other.

Niebuhr did not regard Jesus as teaching specifics for institutional change. Jesus was neither a social ethicist nor a practical political actor. Jesus' religious consciousness was focused on persons, on the community of persons he was forming into a church, and on the Kingdom of God. The implications of his teaching on love for political institutions or structures of justice or power were not spelled out. Niebuhr rejected the Social Gospel approach, which had regarded Jesus as a social reformer, and taught instead of a Jesus with a radical love ethic relatively disconnected from the political worries of his day. Niebuhr's topics for discussing Jesus' ethics were:

I. Religious dimensions and eschatological dimensions of the ethic
   1. The absolute claim of God
   2. The invitation of God
   3. Absolute trust in God
   4. The requirements of religious trust
      a. Unconcern for possessions
      b. Unconcern for social position
      c. Unconcern for the family
      d. Unconcern for life itself
      e. Unconcern for any reward
      f. The promises of rewards
II. The love commandment and the agape ethic
   1. The basic character of agape
      a. Paradox of law and law transcended
      b. Two commandments

    c. Non-calculating concern for others
2. Its dimensions and requirements
    a. The dimensions of universalism and in determining the responsibilities for the other
    b. The rigor of the commandment excluding any self-regard
3. The relationship of agape to specific laws
    a. It is the law which specific laws obscured
    b. It sets aside the lower laws
    c. It is a more rigorous law
    d. It leaves positive law and institutions unchanged
    e. It fulfills the law
    f. It seldom generates specific laws
4. The problems of agape rigorism
    a. Hebrew sense of flawed human nature
    b. Rejection of Pharisee and Publican claims of righteousness
    c. Possible with God if impossible socially
    d. Difficulties with passage of "Narrow Is the Way"
    e. No explicit statement on impracticability of ethic

Before turning to the ethics of Paul, Niebuhr would refer to the alternative theories of Rudolf Kittel's *Wörterbuch*, Hans Windisch's *The Sermon on the Mount*, and C. H. Dodd's *Gospel and the Law* but then summarize in his own terms the absolute demands relevant to an interim history. It was the confusion of liberal Christianity to confuse ultimate demands with specific practical guides for contemporary society. In addition to spending considerable time on the ethics of Jesus, Niebuhr lectured on the ethics of Paul and the Johannine literature.

Niebuhr really preferred the parables of Jesus to the theological ethics of Paul. Paul formulated his ethic from the other side of the cross than Jesus, and his message was about the kerygma or announcement of Jesus as the Christ. Paul's rigorous rejection of the law is more thorough than Jesus' relativizing of it. In Paul the theology of sin and atonement produce an ethic based on forgiveness and power. The Reformation later would emphasize Christ as forgiveness, and the sectarian movements would regard Christ as power. Some of the norms of Paul were similar to Jesus' ethic. Niebuhr found these especially in pure love, universalism, refutation of ascetic righteousness, and forgiveness. He found a difference in Paul's understanding of love being more love within the Christian community as the body of Christ. The prophetic universalism of Jesus' love was, in Niebuhr's perspective, combined with Stoic ethics and the koinonia or Christian-community emphasis in Paul. Elements of conservatism mixed into Paul's antinomian spirit as he held off the more extreme possibilities of his ethic of freedom. For Paul the emancipation from law and self-preoccupation still left one a sinner. In an off-the-cuff remark, Niebuhr said, "Paul was too theological to be an ultimate prophet. In fact it is very difficult for a theologian to be prophetic."[20]

Niebuhr isolated several distinctive elements in Paul's ethics. One such emphasis was the centering of the love ethic on the Christian community. Within the community, love as mutuality or *philia* was stressed. The ethic was historical and prudential as well as eschatological. At several points in Paul's writings, elements of law emerged. The Gentiles had the law. Minimal standards of morality were taught, as in Galatians 5:18–26. Ascetic law was applied to family life given the expected Parousia. When it is taken as the basis of law, Paul's practical advice reinforces some social hierarchy and political conservatism as well as at some points revealing male ideology.

The third and final part of the New Testament literature Niebuhr spoke about in ethics class was the Johannine literature, the Gospel and the letters. He dealt with the synthesis of Greek and Hebrew in the Christology of the Word in the Prologue to the Gospel. He stressed the particular concept of eternal life as present now. The source of sin in the flesh and the world was derived from the Hellenistic worldview. Love in the Gospel he saw as more grace than law and as related to sacrifice. The symbols of light and darkness had roots in Zoroastrianism and Hellenism. Platonic influences in the letters he thought had later effects on both Augustine and the Greek church. He relativized the second-birth narrative of Nicodemus in John 3 by seeing in it the background of the mystery cults.

The love ethic is sharply distinguished from both law and the knowledge doctrines of the mystery cults. Love for John is the new law of Christ, and it is presented in a radical and pure form. The love turns the faithful away from the world to eternal life, sinlessness, and hope of resurrection. Salvation is both transcendence over the world and a promised final victory. After finishing the Johannine lectures, Niebuhr moved on to survey the church's history of working out these ethics in the necessary compromises with historical forces.

Early Church Ethics

About the fourth week of the course, Niebuhr would move into a discussion of the ethics of the early church. These lectures ordinarily took a week and a half. He stressed the theme of Christian love having an impulse toward perfectionism in ethics and a contrary impulse toward social responsibility. Gradually the church moved toward accepting instruments of social harmony for a sinful world. Except for its ascetic expressions, it came to terms with private property, social inequality, government, and war. The ethical rigor of the early church, which had some communism of distribution in Jerusalem, a rough equality in the church, opposition to government idolatry, and pacifism, was due to the demands of both universal love and eschatological expectations. One lecture expressed this change from an eschatological sect to an established church. He saw five stages: (1) the rigor of the first two centuries; (2) the Pauline support of conservatism from Romans 13; (3) the third-century church's growing acceptance of society; (4) Constantine's joining church and empire; and then, (5) the perfectionistic reaction of the fourth century toward monastic idealism. The lectures were his interpretation of quotations from early church fathers that he had selected to correspond to his thematic interpretation.[21] The students at Union Theological Seminary would already have read in their church history courses many of the texts that Niebuhr selected. The lectures on ethics had only to draw out and interpret the moral teachings from those texts with which the student had some acquaintance.

Following a lecture on the Constantinian age and the increasing ascetic protest against church compromises with the world, Niebuhr turned to his favorite subject, Augustine. His lectures on Augustine gradually evolved from two in the early 1930s version of the course to four in later years. He had begun his study of Augustine in Detroit and deepened it while at Union through study, conversation with friends, and the contributions of his wife, Ursula.[22]

On hearing Niebuhr's lecture on Augustine, the students knew he was at home. Augustine provided Niebuhr with more than did other thinkers. Some of what Augustine provided, Niebuhr had learned first from Paul, Luther, and his Lutheran-Calvinist church. Distinctive elements in Augustine in which Niebuhr participated were the conjoining of philosophy and biblical faith, the centrality of love in ethics, the need for a socially responsible ethic, a tendency to write and speak in a dialectic fashion, the setting of ethics in historical terms, a search for a world history, and a Christian realism.

Niebuhr saw Augustine as the first Christian realist.[23] He emphasized Augustine's theologies of creation, human nature, sin, evil, the Trinity, and grace in the first lecture. The themes associated with Niebuhr, of sin as primarily pride but also sensuality, appear here. The idea that in human history evil and good are bound together is found in Augustine. Niebuhr stressed the ethics of Augustine as faith, hope, and love. He wrestled with Augustine's idea that we would find human fulfillment by refusing to love ourselves but by loving God. It was not self-sacrifice that Augustine (and Niebuhr following him) wanted to stress, but rather being freed by a sense of grace to take the focus off the self and by connecting with God and with the neighbor to find love and love of self in religious community. Finally, for Augustine the love of God was more real than love of neighbor. Of course, the neighbor if truly loved was loved for God and brought to love God.

Niebuhr presented Augustine's social ethics as realistic. Finally, though, he found Augustine too cynical about society and overly idealistic about the church. Still, an ethic of responsibility and of goals of rough or tolerable justice could be drawn from Augustine. Society was founded in force, and any peace would be imperfect. The ascetic-monastic theme was also in Augustine. Niebuhr saw Augustine's claims for the church and its closeness to the kingdom of heaven as laying the groundwork for the later claims of papal imperialism. Augustine's theory presented not a church in the empire but an empire within the church. Niebuhr's course notes show more criticism of the foundations of Roman Catholic church claims than they do of the over-realism of Augustine's social theory. In Niebuhr's later writings[24] he would criticize the social theory as too pessimistic for modern humanity's political-theoretical needs. He would also reject the dualism between those in the city of God and those in the city of earth as too extreme. But in Augustine and the great dramas of the theological meaning of history, Niebuhr felt comfortable.

Medieval Ethics

In the context of explaining the ethics of the medieval church from the fifth through the early fourteenth century, Niebuhr revealed his own preferred method in ethics. The lecture on history as a source of approximate norms is not found in any collection of his lecture notes. Human nature is that of a historical creature which can change, but the human being draws upon history as the source of law. The forces of history in their own way produce the laws that the lawgiver expresses. Niebuhr would not accept a conservative interpretation that whatever law history produced was appropriate. Nor could he conclude with John Dewey that natural law was growth or development itself. There are too many contradictions in the story of human development to accept it as the source of law. Nature is not the source of law; rather, natural law norms are derived from "the intuitions of reason." They reflect imperfectly the "universalities of moral judgment" and the "social structures of human existence." So they come from the reasoning process but not from reason itself, as they reflect the historical context. Furthermore, they do not present the depths of human moral judgment until they are regulated by love. This seems to be Niebuhr's own method: philosophical reason reflecting the social context under the inspiration and critique of love. So the history of Christian ethics really is the content of the discipline of Christian ethics. The course is basic to ethics because ethics is historical.[25]

Before he got to sorting out his own conclusions regarding principles of natural law, Niebuhr had surveyed various aspects of the medieval experience. Monasticism and asceticism had been examined, and theories of papal political power analyzed. Various aspects of medieval sexual and gender ethics were covered, from marriage as a sacrament to romantic courtly love. The problems of sexual repression and the debasement of women in both the Christian and the Aristotelian theories were considered. The combinations of Teutonic ferocity and the piety of Christian love were examined. The historic groundings of the practice of war and feudal economy were related to the articulation of Christian norms. Before considering the decline of medieval civilization, Thomas Aquinas's version of natural law was examined, and then Niebuhr's own reflections on principles of moral teaching were discussed. Here as elsewhere he was following Troeltsch's direction, but he drew upon a much wider range of sources and wove his own tapestry of the fabric of the historical articulation of Christian principles. Though a Roman Catholic historian of ethics would find the lectures brief and too full of underdeveloped or unargued generalizations, such a historian would see respect for the humanly developed ethical teachings of the church. They were not filled with anti-Catholic polemic, but they were full of fascination with the story of the expression of medieval ethics. The ethics had their own dignity; they were neither simply a stage of development of an alternative ethic nor were they, for him, expressions of economic or other hidden forces.

The medieval synthesis decayed under political pressures. The rise of France pressured the papacy. Dante in *On Monarchy* advocated a Christian universalism not centered on the papacy. Machiavelli's cynicism also undercut Christian public ethics. The political-economic order of feudalism was undermined by the rise of commerce and the emergence of an urban middle class. Philosophy also changed, and the realism of Thomas Aquinas's rationalism was undercut by Duns Scotus and by Occam's nominalism. Faith and reason held together by Thomas were pushed apart, and confidence in meaning was dissipated. Out of the decay of the medieval order, the three movements of Renaissance, Reformation, and sectarianism arose, with their respective ethics. The ethics of the Renaissance generally were based on optimism about human nature and confidence in the power of reason. There was also, in Niebuhr's words, a "subordinate note" of pessimism about the human condition seen in different ways in Petrarch, Machiavelli, and Hobbes. Niebuhr would quote from both Shakespeare and Donne to express the nobility and tragedy of the human condition. From the general idea of progress in the Renaissance, Niebuhr would either develop the ethics of modern liberalism or move to the Reformation, retaining the ethics of modern liberalism for the last section of the course.

Reformation Ethics

In late April, Niebuhr would come to Reformation ethics. In the Reformation expressions of Augustinian theology were located many of the deep roots of his own theological ethics. But as the course usually evolved, it was already late in April and classes ended the second week in May. The telescoping pressure of the calendar meant the time devoted to the Reformation was less than he would regard as appropriate. Some years he plunged straight into Luther's theology and ethics; other years he prefaced it with a lecture on Renaissance developments.

Niebuhr's emphasis on the Renaissance was a move to help close the gap between Renaissance and Reformation contributions to the modern mind. In a 1960 lecture he said he believed in human nature as the Reformation understood it. Modern culture celebrated Renaissance perspective, and he wanted to correct this by establishing a new synthesis between the two. The themes of reason against clerical and ecclesiastical authority, of the basic goodness of natural humanity, and the necessity of liberty for human development were all motifs of his own work. Of course they were qualified by the Reformation consciousness of the effect of sin upon reason, goodness, and liberty. The writings of William Shakespeare and John Donne had perhaps the most impact upon him of the Renaissance writers; he found their poetic or religious existentialism and emphases upon the incongruity of human existence persuasive. The illusions of the optimists of the Renaissance still spread confusion in the declining liberal society of the twentieth century. He would start in the 1930s to use the realism of the Marxists to criticize the liberal illusions until, as the decade ended, the illusions of the Marxists proved themselves even more dangerous.

Niebuhr introduced Reformation ethics with four theological emphases: (1) justification by faith alone, (2) the priesthood of all believers, (3) the place of work in Luther and Calvin's transforming asceticism, and (4) the authority of scripture.[26]

Martin Luther's ethics were expounded as living in freedom of grace in personal life. Love from God gave forgiveness, and the human would respond gratefully to the gift. Love for Luther as grace and forgiveness contradicted law. Niebuhr found great insight in Luther's teachings on the individual, but he found him unnecessarily reactionary and overly authoritarian in the public realm and (following Ernst Troeltsch) not of much help. In social ethics, Niebuhr found Calvin's more nuanced discussion of law helpful. For Calvin, law rightly understood could instruct conscience as well as convict of sin, and it could guide society. Luther's dualism and inadequate social philosophy renewed Niebuhr's critique, while Calvin's less radical distinction between the liberties of the Christian person and liberty in society was affirmed. The law for Niebuhr, though not absolute, was useful, and he followed Calvin here while avoiding Calvin's tendency toward bibliolatry. The Reformation ethic of subordinating natural law but not eliminating it corresponded to Niebuhr's own method and his reasons for teaching the course. Niebuhr explained the reasons for Luther's political and economic ethic, but he could not follow Luther in public ethics. Here Niebuhr was too much a creature of the Renaissance and the

Enlightenment. Luther's complicity with suppression of the peasants and anti-Semitism received Niebuhr's sharp criticism.

He found Luther's significance in social ethics in his insistence upon "maintaining the reality of the spiritual transcendent freedom above all history." But he would occasionally say in his lectures on Luther's social ethic that Luther was 90 percent wrong.[27] He was particularly wrong in denying the uneasy conscience that accompanied action in the world.

The Ethics of Calvin

In presenting the thought of John Calvin, Niebuhr sensitively discussed the subjects of the majesty of God, predestination, justification, sanctification, and providence. Niebuhr was especially critical of Calvin's use of special providence. He could appreciate Calvin's use of law, but he saw that it easily degenerated into legalism. Similarly, Calvin's use of the whole scripture tended toward biblicism. Niebuhr appreciated Calvin's moderate asceticism. He noted how Calvin's political ethics, like Luther's, were reluctant to justify resistance to the rulers. But even as Luther had eventually come to oppose illegal actions of the emperor, Calvin laid grounds for resistance to evil rule and even the deplacement of governing authority. Niebuhr stressed the later Calvinist resistance to evil rulers in looking at the Huguenot tract *Vindiciae Contra Tyrannos*, Samuel Rutherford's *Lex Rex*, and John Knox's confrontations with Queen Mary. Niebuhr spent more time on Calvin's political ethic than on his economic ethic. On Calvin's economics he followed the work of both Georgia Harkness and Max Weber. He saw clearly that Calvin did not create or cause capitalism. But he saw in the spirit of the later expressions of Calvinism tendencies that supported the development of capitalism. His lectures supported the more modest interpretations of the psychological and sociological reinforcing factors that Weber found Calvinism contributing to capitalism.

Niebuhr's appreciation for Calvinist development of political ethics is clear in the lectures. There also was appreciation for the moderate establishment solution of Richard Hooker in the *Laws of Ecclesiastical Polity*. Here church and governmental order based on natural law were established within the modern framework of monarchy and nationalism.

Niebuhr usually spent three lectures on the radical sectarians of the Reformation. He interpreted them as different expressions of the Christian impulse toward perfection expressed among disinherited people. The Reformation sectarians had been preceded by sectarian movements of protest within Catholicism. All had espoused the imperatives of the poor, expressed a new eschatology, and criticized the establishment of ecclesiastical and political authority. He distinguished three types of Reformation sectarians. Rejecting the compromises of the established churches, the sects sought to realize the Kingdom of God on earth through either fighting strategies or suffering practices. The early Anabaptists and the left wing of Cromwell's army represented the fighting sects. The Quakers and the Mennonites expressed, though differently, the second type. The pietists represented a third type of perfectionism through conversion and asceticism. Niebuhr's own sympathies were most clearly identified with "the left-wing Calvinistic sects of the Cromwellian revolution."[28] Here he found the seedbed for modern society and for Christian criticism and reform within it. The sects asserted the rights of the poor to defend themselves against oppression, demanded government by consent, sometimes sought land, requested participation in government, demanded rights, and expressed the Christian social hopes for the dispossessed.

His discussions of the perfectionist tendencies of the Mennonites, Quakers, and Methodists revealed interest and respect but no identification with these movements. His treatment of the Lutheran pietism that so influenced his own evangelical synod was very brief. The funding of homes and hospitals which he mentioned, of course, reflected his own father's work, but he does not make autobiographical or paternal references in these history-of-ethics lectures. His pietist origins are obscured and his own ethic has moved beyond them to the free-church Calvinist social-ethical type.

Another contribution of the sectarian movements and especially of the Baptists through the person of Roger Williams was the separation of church and state. In his lectures he discussed Williams's contribution in Rhode Island along with the movements to separate church and state in Virginia. Niebuhr knew there were no final solutions to the problems of church-state relationships, but he regarded separation as the American way.

In America the sects grew into churches and some of the churches became sects. His lectures traced the effects of the sectarian movement in the United States. He himself sought a balance between the classical Reformation churches and sectarian impulses. The sects tended to be too perfectionist and the Reformation "too defeatist on collective problems." Private property remained ambiguous, and if the Reformation was too complacent about its dangers, the sectarians sometimes were overly collectivist. Neither the Reformation nor the radical sects had their doctrines of government adequately developed, and experience corrected both. The radicals were wise in criticizing corruptive compromises of the Reformation churches, but they had little sense of how to deal with deep historical evils. The radical abandonment of customary ecclesiastical means of grace showed the corruptive tendencies of institutionalism, but their reliance on spontaneity was also naive.

Middle-class Protestantism in the United States became socially complacent and, in combinations of pietism, social Darwinism, and Calvinism, could produce contempt for the poor. The sectarian radicalness of the frontier could combine with pietism and social and evolutionary optimism to promote movements of social reform. The Social Gospel movement left an ambiguous heritage too, promoting reform on one hand and nationalism on the other. Much of the radicalness of the sectarians was transmuted into the doctrines of Marxism, given the church's irrelevance to the emerging industrial order. But the church's message was, for Niebuhr, justification by faith and not social perfectionism. Elements of class or self-interest were perpetually present, as were power conflicts. The sectarian impulse expressed love perfectionism and was a necessary protest against premature compromises with the powers of society. So sects became, as Niebuhr said, churches; perhaps to say they became denominations would be more accurate. As denominations they displayed the protests, but the elimination of certain abuses could not guarantee satisfactory resolutions to perennial problems.

From Renaissance
to Modern Liberalism

The development of the final section of the course[29] depended in part on the time remaining before seminary classes concluded, about May 10. In some versions of class notes, these closing lectures are very brief; in others there are extensive typed notes from Niebuhr's own typewriter. Generally, all of them traced the rise of secularism, the pushing to the side of the Christian interpretations, and the rise of the modern sciences. The class notes in their various forms discuss ethics of idealism, romanticism, naturalism, and nationalism. Brief comments are made summarizing ethical insights or theories from scores of philosophers. At first glance, it appears that students must have been swamped. But if they had studied the history of Christian thought with Paul Tillich or Wilhelm Pauck, or sat in on John Herman Randall, Jr.,'s History of Philosophy course across Broadway at Columbia University, they could have followed even the detailed lectures. But neither the generalized categories nor the lectures would have sufficed if not supported by a general knowledge of theology and philosophy, which at this point only needed to be complemented by specific references to ethics. Still, many students were indeed overwhelmed or confused by these closing lectures on modernity.

The comparison and contrast between the economic ethics of liberalism seen in Adam Smith and his followers and Karl Marx and the Marxists is present in many of these concluding lectures. Neither the ethic of liberalism nor of Marxism is seen as adequate. The inadequacies of romanticism, naturalism, and idealism set up in Niebuhr the need to move from Christian ethics to apologetics. This move was made in his courses on Christian anthropology and Christian theology of history which became his *Nature and Destiny of Man*. Though not a simple advocate of liberalism, for modern liberalism failed and elicited the revolts of Nietzsche, Marx, and Nazism, his preference for the values of liberalism is clear. In one of the summary lectures, he listed these liberal values: The community is organized by the consent of the governed, as in a social contract; the individual is an end in oneself; equality and liberty are both norms; under pluralism, toleralism is a virtue; the use of force in human affairs is to be reduced or, in optimistic versions of liberalism, eliminated; politics is to regulate economics and reduce inequality. Liberalism in itself contained truth, though many of its ideas were not profound enough to ground them.[30] His wartime book *The Children of Light and the Children of Darkness* was intended to ground those values more profoundly. His concluding remarks about Marxism, in the course, evolved with his own changing perspective on Marxism. In the course, Niebuhr's Christian ethics were laid out. The course did not conclude with a summary, for the whole course was his ethic. Christian ethics was critical reflection on these moral traditions. Preferences for combining Renaissance and Reformation, for seeing roots of democratic theory in Calvinist and sectarian ethics, preferences for free church organization, and liberal values combined with Christian theology, revealed his mind. The course concluded with the end of the semester calendar. There could always have been another lecture or two, for though Christian ethics had defining moments, particularly in Jesus, Augustine, and the Reformation, it was open-ended in its development.

Student Responses

The early years of Niebuhr's teaching were years of academic formality. Professors still wore their academic gowns to class. Niebuhr began to break down some of the formality by requesting students to ask questions and join in discussion for the final ten minutes of a lecture period. He had a genius for making something intelligible out of even relatively uniformed questions.

His presence and knowledge were intimidating, and many students were unable to challenge the professor's polemically developed positions. There were probably more students who had very little grasp of the totality of the vision than there were those who openly questioned his theology.

The overwhelming response to the questionnaire sent to graduates of Union Theological Seminary[31] was that his teaching was outstanding. Most of the graduates who responded had served as ministers or professors, and they testified to having used his major categories in their vocations. Those who were preachers mentioned quoting him in sermons, and professors of theology, history, and political science told of his influence on their courses. But the more frequent response was that his way of using the categories of sin, ambiguity, irony, justice, love, realism, human nature, and history became part of who they were in their work.

At least two groups were attracted to Niebuhr, those who took him straight, becoming "Niebuhrians," and those who melded his influence into other streams of thought. Albert Rabil, a professor at Old Westbury on Long Island, is of the second group. He wrote about two aspects of Niebuhr's influence.

> I think the influence Niebuhr had on me was great but indirect. He turned out not to be my mentor. Dr. Pauck ultimately fulfilled that role, as I came increasingly to see that history was my strong suit, the "way I thought." Niebuhr interested me indirectly in this connection, because he was always making historical generalizations, which I loved and only later came to question. What I liked about his "history" was the way he connected things, saw relations that make the past relevant to the present. This was the indirect influence: he gave religion and religious

thought "status" in the world outside religion. He had standing in that outside world. As I look back I know now that that was what I most appreciated. One could, as a religious thinker and actor, speak to and be relevant to a larger world outside the strictly religious. As a young person what I probably liked most about this was his "prophetic" stance; young people always like prophets, those they perceive to "tell it like it is."

My perception is that his influence at Union was extraordinarily great, and that also had something to do with the fact that Niebuhr (in this respect like Tillich) had a standing in the world outside the seminary that others in the seminary could not claim. He was thus a powerful connecting link between Union and the world and gave the place a sense of being important, of making a difference, of acting in both the religious community and in the larger community beyond the religious.[32]

Many former students of Niebuhr mentioned the influence of his worldly role on their understandings. Frederick Buechner replied to the questionnaire, for example, that if such an intellect who was a friend to powerful politicians, T. S. Eliot, and W. H. Auden "could give his life to teaching ministers, there must be something to this seminary."[33]

Students adopted his ideas and speech mannerisms. Some took to wearing berets in unconscious imitation. Others held their pipes the way he held his, or used their forefinger as a waving broadsword as he used his to make a strong point. James Butler of the class of 1942 wrote:

Dr. Niebuhr's influence extended to students sometimes adopting his mannerisms. For instance, a characteristic mannerism was: taking a pencil, placing it perpendicularly on the top of his head and running his fingers up and down it as he spoke. At least six or eight of the junior class [in 1937] were doing the very same thing shortly after the term started.[34]

Others mentioned this mannerism and its adoption by students. Behind the lectern he was an eagle, or an owl waving his wings and looking the students directly in the eye when responding to questions.

Tom F. Driver of the Union faculty, a drama critic, focused on Niebuhr as performer.

My memories of Reinhold Niebuhr are not of the classroom. Except one. I must have been in some class of his between 1950 and 1953, when I was a seminary student. I seem to remember him leaning over a podium, shaking his finger, and saying, "To a fox, it does not matter whether he runs through the woods in the first century or in the twentieth, but to a human it makes all the difference."

I mostly remember Niebuhr in the pulpit. I heard him preach the sermon on "Mouldy Saints" and a number of others. He contorted his body and snorted his words. I stayed out of the way but thought him benign.

I remember the open houses for students on certain evenings at his apartment in Knox Hall. He sat in a chair between two adjoining rooms, one to his left, the other to his right. Ursula Niebuhr sat off in a corner, making sardonic interjections from time to time. He held forth loquaciously, giving voice to a stream of opinions. All of us loved it. I thought he was a wily old serpent.

Looking back, I think he was a great performer. Not to diminish his gifts as a thinker. He could think pretty good, but he could perform even better. I will never forget his snarl. I would like to pay tribute to his voice, his slouched-over ability to make you draw cover and listen. He was not a mellifluous but rather an *intimidating* speaker. Who could interrogate him?[35]

The responses of Niebuhr's former students were mostly uncritical. They loved him, and many of them felt his warmth and friendship. He was more available to them than were most faculty members. The one critique that emerged several times (from former students of a particular academic bent) was that his historic generalizations might be unfair to his opponents. Hargie Likins, a student from the 1940s now a professor of education in the Pittsburgh Theological Seminary, wrote, "A number of us commented on his tendency to pick the weakest point in an individual's thought, then demolish it brilliantly and grin like a little kid. I especially remember him doing so with Freud."[36] His trip through Western intellectual life was a respectful tour de force, but it also resembled a demolition derby so that he could get on to his theological perspective. Often, however, these criticisms of his interpretations were of a vague nature rather than a direct argument. He invited direct argument and if bested would usually acknowledge it. My own experience of this was during the mid-1960s, when I decided to challenge his analysis of Plato's understanding of human nature; after all, my teachers of Plato at Oxford and Columbia universities were recognized authorities with more generous perspectives on Plato. Niebuhr responded with relevant short passages from Plato's *Republic* in Greek. I abandoned the challenge.

David Engel, a professor of education from the University of Pittsburgh who has been active in city and urban school politics, reflected on the impact of Niebuhr's public involvements on the seminary student. Engel wrote:

In the 1951–52 academic year at the Union Theological Seminary I had the privilege to have Reinhold Niebuhr as my senior thesis advisor. As a major in Christian social ethics I had had most of his courses. He was an intensely energetic man, a stimulating lecturer, the most exciting teacher I had known in all my schooling. . . .

Our first meeting was in his office in the Seminary tower at Broadway and 120th Street [now renamed Reinhold Niebuhr Place]. He reviewed bibliography and an approach to the topic. In the middle of the discussion his telephone rang. Niebuhr picked it up. I rose to leave to give him privacy. He motioned with a sweep of his arm for me to sit down and stay. As a consequence, I overheard his end of the telephone conversation.

He was talking to someone named Walter, and it seemed to me they were discussing some kind of strategy about hours of work, conditions in the workplace, and so forth. Niebuhr made such remarks as, "Walter, I think you need to consider . . . " and "Walter, a good tactic would be . . . " and "Walter, that could backfire."

The conversation with Walter lasted about ten minutes, and after it was over Niebuhr picked up the discussion with me exactly where he had left it. We finished and I left the office.

The next morning *The New York Times* carried a story about the demands made by the United Auto Workers union to the Big Three automakers in Detroit by its president, Walter Reuther. I realized then that that was the Walter, Niebuhr had been talking with the afternoon before.

In the winter of that academic year, not long before Niebuhr had his 1952 stroke, I was again in his office to discuss progress on my thesis. We were reviewing arguments associated with Martin Luther's doctrine of the two realms (the realm of Christ and the realm of Caesar) and its impact on political ethics which was central to my analysis. The telephone rang and Niebuhr picked it up and I made motions to leave the office, and he waved his arm for me to remain seated. This time he addressed the person on the other end of the line as "Beedle," and the subject of discussion was some aspect of U.S. foreign policy. Niebuhr expressed his opinion and "Beedle" spoke for some time as Niebuhr listened before he responded to "Beedle" with a succinct critique. I had no idea who "Beedle" was.

Later I described the telephone call to some classmates and one of them identified "Beedle" as Walter Bedell Smith, who became Undersecretary of State.

I always had known that Niebuhr was very much involved in current affairs and had wide-ranging associations. Those two incidents dramatized the vital role that this theological ethicist played in secular affairs.

Shortly after the "Beedle" incident, Niebuhr suffered a stroke and I did not see him again until the day before I graduated. One of my classmates called his apartment and asked if some of us could visit him. He said we could and about six of us went to his apartment in the Seminary complex and he came to the door himself, even though his gait was uncertain due to some paralysis on one side of his body. He inquired of each of us what our plans were and wished us well.

I don't know if he knew the profound effect he had on us. But in my case, even though most of my career has been outside the formal ministry, Niebuhr's thought and the example of his person has been the bedrock of my intellectual, social, and spiritual development. He was an inspiring teacher.[37]

Love and Marriage

Reinhold continued the ascetic work style at Union that he had developed in Detroit. His mother took care of many of the practical details, and he labored in his practice of Christian social action, or in his study, late into the night. Despite social engagements with women in Detroit and New York, there is no record of heavy romance before 1930. His bachelor existence gave him time and freedom for his all-encompassing work. He knew and appreciated that his lifestyle freed him for vocation in a way that married colleagues could envy.

He had just begun the fall term of 1930 as the newly appointed Dodge Professor of Applied Christianity when he met Ursula Keppel-Compton. She was the Mills Fellow or English Fellow for 1930–31, the first woman to receive the honor. President Henry Sloane Coffin had protested at receiving a woman as the English Fellow, but on receiving assurances from the committee in England that she was better qualified than the men he acceded. She had taken first-degree honors in theology at Oxford after beginning in history. The German fellow that year was Dietrich Bonhoeffer, and so began a friendship with Bonhoeffer that would deepen over the years. During the war in the 1940s, Ursula's sister, Barbara, married Gerhard Witt, a student and assistant of Dietrich's father, Klaus Bonhoeffer, and their lives were linked together in the history and tragedy of the 1930s and 1940s.

As she has recounted the meeting, Reinhold was called aside by a colleague to explain the politics of *The New Republic* to her, as she had been asked to a luncheon with the editors. John Baillie had already recommended she meet Niebuhr, a new man at the seminary. From the first meeting would come dating, love, marriage, and forty years of conversation about everything, but especially about theology and politics. Her year at Union proved fateful for the direction of both of their lives. Others sought her attention, but Reinhold prevailed easily, and by the first of May they were engaged. They attempted to keep this courtship by a thirty-eight-year-old professor of a twenty-three-year-old student from attracting the seminary's attention, and to some degree they were successful. She returned home to England; he visited her and her family at the end of the summer and then returned to Union for the fall term of 1931. They were married in Winchester Cathedral on December 22, 1931, returning in the new year to live in New York City. The extensive correspondence of their courtship across the Atlantic has been lovingly maintained and edited by Ursula in her book about their lives together. He promised very few adjustments toward slowing down to nurture the marriage. But one significant adjustment suggested in the letters was that he would not accept a fellowship to teach in India in 1933–34, as he hoped they would be starting their own family by then. In fact, Christopher was born on September 11, 1934, and Elisabeth on January 13, 1939. My own memory of their marriage in its last years was of brilliant conversation, deep affection, and unswerving trust and of Ursula's tender care for her beloved invalid husband.[38]

NOTES

1. Reinhold Niebuhr, "Introduction," in Sherwood Eddy, *Eighty Adventurous Years: An Autobiography* (New York: Harper & Brothers, 1955), pp. 126–127.

2. Ibid.

3. *Union Theological Seminary Catalogue* (New York: Union Theological Seminary, 1928–1971).

4. Ibid.

5. See Robert H. Craig: "An Introduction to the Life and Thought of Harry F. Ward," *Union Seminary Quarterly Review* 24, no. 4 (Summer 1969), 331–356. A later essay by David Nelson Duke stresses the Methodist social conversionist note of Ward but is unaware of Craig's nuanced discussion of Ward's relationship to communism. David Nelson Duke, "Harry F. Ward: From Conservative Evangelical to Social Radical," *Union Seminary Quarterly Review* 40, nos. 1 & 2 (Summer 1985), 85–98.

6. Syllabus and class lecture notes from 1942–43 provided by Charles West.

7. Roger Shinn, quoted in Henry Sloane Coffin, *A Half Century of Union Theological Seminary* (New York: Charles Scribner's Sons, 1954), p. 150.

8. See pages 181–182.

9. Conclusion from Charles West's notes 1942–43.

10. Letter from Charles West in possession of the author.

11. Charles Norris Cochrane, *Christianity and Classical Culture* (Oxford: Clarendon Press, 1940).

12. See Niebuhr's comment on Christians fawning over Constantine and

their accession to political influence in Reinhold Niebuhr, *The Structure of Nations and Empires* (1959), pp. 94–96.

13. Course syllabus: Christian Ethics 12 (1942–43), p. 1.

14. Reinhold Niebuhr Papers (MSS in the Library of Congress, Washington, D.C.), Container 24. The analysis contained here draws also upon my own notes of the taped lectures and Charles West's notes from 1942–43. My notes are from listening to the tapes while they were at Union Theological Seminary in New York City in 1966–67. They are now available for purchase from the Reinhold Niebuhr Audio Tape Collection, Union Theological Seminary in Virginia, 3401 Brook Road, Richmond, VA 23227.

15. "The Ethic of Jesus and the Social Problem," *Religion in Life* (Spring 1936), reprinted in D. B. Robertson, ed., *Love and Justice* (1957), pp. 29–40, and Reinhold Niebuhr, *An Interpretation of Christian Ethics* (1935).

16. Henry Clark, letter to author, February 19, 1991. For Clark's estimate of Schweitzer, see Henry Clark, *The Philosophy of Albert Schweitzer* (London: Methuen & Co., 1964).

17. James Moffatt, *Love in the New Testament* (New York: R. R. Smith, 1930).

18. First Lecture, History of Christian Ethics tapes. Notes in the author's possession from listening to the tapes in 1966 with Reinhold Niebuhr's permission.

19. C. H. Dodd, *Gospel and Law* (New York: Columbia University Press, 1951).

20. Lecture F, History of Christian Ethics tapes (Mar. 3, 1960).

21. "The Ethics of the Early Church" in Reinhold Niebuhr's typed notes for History of Christian Ethics, Niebuhr Papers, Container 24.

22. See Reinhold Niebuhr, "Augustine's Political Realism," in *Christian Realism and Political Problems* (1953).

23. Lecture I, History of Christian Ethics tapes (Mar. 15, 1960).

24. Reinhold Niebuhr, *Man's Nature and His Communities* (1965).

25. "The Ethics of Medieval Asceticism," Niebuhr Papers, Container 24.

26. "The Ethics of the Reformation," Niebuhr Papers, Container 24.

27. Lecture Mar. 26, 1943, from Charles West's notes.

28. "The Ethics of the Radical Reformation," Niebuhr Papers, Container 24.

29. The last section of the course had various titles on different editions of the syllabus. In the 1930s it often discussed the ethics of Marxism. This emphasis lessened in the 1940s. The Washington papers contain various different editions of the course in undated form in Reinhold Niebuhr's own typing. Some of these lectures are quite old, still being typed on the back of stationery from Edward W. Duffy Company in Detroit, Michigan; the more recent lectures are typed on the back of Union Theological Seminary stationery or on plain typing paper.

30. "The Political Ethics of Liberalism," Niebuhr Papers, Container 24.

31. See Appendix.

32. Letter from Albert Rabil, Jr., to the author, Feb. 17, 1991, in the author's possession.

33. Response to questionnaire in the author's possession.

34. Response to questionnaire in the author's possession.

35. Letter from Tom F. Driver to the author, Jan. 8, 1991, in the author's possession.

36. Response to questionnaire in the author's possession.

37. Letter from David E. Engel to the author, Oct. 10, 1990, in the author's possession. In a letter dated Feb. 4, 1992, to the author, Mrs. Ursula M. Niebuhr writes that the callers are misidentified. Letter in author's possession.

38. The account of their meeting and other facts are from Ursula M. Niebuhr, *Remembering Niebuhr: Letters of Reinhold and Ursula M. Niebuhr* (1991).

4

The Search for Economic Alternatives

1928–1956

NIEBUHR ARRIVED at Union Theological Seminary with his mother in September 1928. The crash of 1929 was still a year away, but the atmosphere when he arrived was socialist. It was a mild socialism, tempered by Christian pacifism, that influenced his colleagues on the journal *The World Tomorrow*. His fellow teacher at Union, Harry F. Ward, was a contributing editor, as were Norman Thomas, Rufus M. Jones, A. J. Muste, and other famous pacifist socialists. The journal described itself as a "journal looking toward a social order based on the religion of Jesus." Niebuhr's article against ROTC in October 1926 had been preceded by M. K. Gandhi's essay "Non-Violence—The Greatest Force."[1] Niebuhr said of the dominant Social Gospel:

> It was in full swing when I arrived at the Seminary in 1928. The Social Gospel was creative in redeeming American Protestantism from an arid Calvinistic or pietistic individualism. But it was defective in identifying the Christian faith with a mild socialism and a less mild pacifism all encased in an overall utopianism.
>
> I remember that at one of the first table conversations in which I participated, the remark was made: "All we have to do is put the sanction of the Gospel behind a collectivist conception of society."[2]

The Depression forced a deeper analysis, but it also lured many followers of the Social Gospel into more engagement with Marxism. So for approximately a decade, the social context of the Depression, the previous experience of industrial Detroit, and the intellectual context of New York City socialism meant that Marxism would become a major conversation partner for Niebuhr.

Transition from Social Gospel
to Socialism

Reflection upon the experience of the Depression in New York City led Niebuhr to abandon hope for significant reform through the two major political parties; he hoped that the Socialist Party, through effective organization and concentration on winning congressional seats, could rise to a position of power.[3] In late 1929, he urged that the socialists abandon dependence on the programs of either the communists or the American Federation of Labor. Dismissing laissez-faire economic theory as a boon to the privileged that hindered necessary progress, he advocated the removal of major sectors of the economy from private ownership, heavier inheritance taxes, increased income taxes, and extensive public welfare assistance as the necessary ingredients of political reform.

Niebuhr's essentially socialist political program was not thoroughly informed by Marxism in 1929. He cautioned that there were no guarantees that the new order would be more just than the old. He regarded Marxist hopes for the justice of the new order as romantic and the hopes of bringing forth moral sensitivity from violence as illusory. His strongly held pacifist convictions prevented him from subscribing to Marxist doctrines of revolution, though many of his penultimate goals for society fit socialist programs.[4] As the Depression deepened, so did his pessimism about the effect of liberal attempts to reform the system. In 1931 he wrote that the continued failure of the West to reorganize itself radically along socialist lines would probably lead to the system's violent end in revolution.[5] Niebuhr's use of Marxist ideas in 1932 to criticize the social thought of Walter Rauschenbusch indicates how far left he had moved.[6] He argued that middle class presuppositions had misled radical Christians to think that the just society could be obtained gradually in an evolutionary movement. The economic-social situation of the middle class reformers allowed them to advance their class interests through relatively peaceful, democratic means. The political theory of the middle class did not adequately account for group egotism and the inevitable conflict between the dispossessed and the possessor. Niebuhr credited Rauschenbusch with seeing the depth of the social struggle more clearly than most of his contem-

porary Christian social activists. However, Niebuhr charged Rauschenbusch with expecting that society could be reformed through moral
and educational means. The central weakness in Rauschenbusch's
thought, he said, was the absence of a concept of the class struggle.[7]
The Marxist idea of a class struggle expressed more adequately than
any other model the strength of group egotism.

Niebuhr's analysis was Marxist, but his prescription in 1932 was
still heavily influenced by the Social Gospel movement and particularly
by its pacifism. He recognized the need for social coercion, but he
hoped for nonviolent means of social change. For a brief period, he
tried to combine Marxist analysis with a Gandhian form of pacifist
resistance. The nonviolent techniques of social change could be justified on a pragmatic basis because, in the long run, they were more
effective. His choice of nonviolent techniques was so dependent on
pragmatic criteria that he denied any intrinsic difference between violence and nonviolence.[8] His reasons for wanting to evaluate techniques
of social change on pragmatic grounds are understandable. But his
denial of an intrinsic difference between violence and nonviolence represents a polemic move against religiously based pacifism rather than
careful analysis. Niebuhr's suggestion that the differences between violence and nonviolence were entirely pragmatic never satisfied many
religiously grounded pacifists. His defense of pacifism crumbled as the
Depression deepened and as the opponents of social reform revealed
little concern for the finer points of democratic politics. The acceptance
of the Marxist analysis of class struggle meant that pacifism held only a
tenuous position in Niebuhr's political theory.

The Influence
of British Socialism

The influence of the American Social Gospel movement upon Niebuhr's thought about politics is clear. A less important influence, but
still one of considerable significance, was English Christian socialism.
Middle class Protestantism tolerated the expression of Christian radicalism, but it criticized the more truly proletarian discontent of Marxism. Charles Kingsley and F. D. Maurice represented to Niebuhr the
English expression of mild socialism qualified by pacifism. This English
socialism was more akin to the thought of the "utopian" socialists,
Henri Saint-Simon and Charles Fourier, than to that of Marx. In England, both the chapel and the church had produced or nurtured a

great number of social reformers. Though many radicals received their inspiration from the church and then moved away from it, in England much social radicalism was contained within the church. Statesmen like Arthur Henderson and George Lansbury combined their radicalism with deep religious convictions in a way that was fruitful for both social reform and religion. Radical Anglicanism seemed to Niebuhr, in the 1930s, to serve a particularly fine purpose in uniting a passion for justice with a symbolization of the mystery beyond social reform.[9] Looking back on his socialist period, the elderly Niebuhr preferred to stress the broadness of the socialist movement and to emphasize his debt to the Christian socialists at the neglect of his debt to Marx and the Marxists.[10]

Even while most deeply influenced by Marxist ideas, Niebuhr argued that social radicalism and Marxism owed their existence to Christian inspiration. Though critical of George Lansbury's withdrawal from politics because of pacifist scruples against sanctions, Niebuhr regarded him as "the symbol of the fact that, in at least one Western nation, Christianity remains organically related to the radicalism to which it gives birth."[11] In an early survey of the various Christian radical groups, he noted their differences and criticized some of their doctrine, but he was frankly appreciative of their accomplishments. The English left-wing Christians were far ahead of their American counterparts, primarily because of their close relationship to the Labor Party.[12] To a degree, the English radical Christians had accomplished in fact what Niebuhr urged during his socialist period, an effective alliance between the Christian left wing and the secular left wing in a political party that could affect the American scene.

Niebuhr claimed that the English Christian socialists, particularly Sir Stafford Cripps and George Lansbury, had greater influence on his politics than any American socialist in the personal examples of combining Christianity and social radicalism. Niebuhr quoted George Lansbury as saying that Christianity, not Marxism, was the source of his socialism, and that he only read Marx long after his socialism was set. Sir Stafford Cripps testified, according to Niebuhr, that he never would have been elected except for the organizing work done on his behalf by Methodist Bible study groups.[13]

Niebuhr did not follow either Lansbury or Cripps in their tendency to equate socialism and Christianity. Niebuhr maintained a distinction between his faith and his socialism that Lansbury would have regarded as a dichotomy. Though the conflict of party interests and their Christian faith plagued both Lansbury and Cripps, they did not reflect in their writings the sense of an inevitable gap between politics and ethics that characterized *Moral Man and Immoral Society*. Niebuhr maintained a sense of the mystery and eternal reverence of religion, which Cripps obscured by his view of the church's vocation as the provision of moral force for social reform. The deepening of the Marxist strain in Niebuhr's own thought also led him to break with Lansbury on the question of pacifism.

The Attraction of Marxism

Several aspects of Marxist thought made it attractive to Niebuhr in the early 1930s. Donald B. Meyer has demonstrated the importance of the Marxist myth of the disinherited class, sense of catastrophe, and apocalypse in Niebuhr's thought. Meyer, however, underestimated the lure of political realism in Marxist thought for Niebuhr when he wrote that "the attractions in Marxism for Niebuhr did not root primarily in political realism. They were attractions of another order."[14] The central difference between *Does Civilization Need Religion?* and *Moral Man and Immoral Society* is the degree of Marxian analysis in the latter volume. *Does Civilization Need Religion?* raised doubts about the assumptions of liberalism, but *Moral Man and Immoral Society* reveals a break with it. Between 1928 and 1932, Niebuhr experienced a deeper sense of the difficulty confronting all programs of social reform, and Marxist thought helped him explain these difficulties. The privileged class resisted all efforts to improve the position of the underprivileged class. Marxism took account of the severity of the class conflict and recognized that the social-political power of the privileged class would have to be destroyed before significant gains in equality could be achieved. Niebuhr was drawn to Marxian analysis because the Marxists seemed to have a realistic program for achieving their dreams of social justice. He deplored their moral cynicism, but he praised their realism. In evaluating the political strategy of the "Marxian Proletarian," Niebuhr commented:

> If his cynicism in the choice of means is at times the basis of his undoing, his realism in implementing ethical ideals with political and economic methods is the reason for his social significance.[15]

This realistic estimate of the means necessary to overcome the power of the privileged was what distinguished the Marxist for Niebuhr from other, less effective socialists.

> There have been other dreams of justice and equality. The distinctive feature of the Marxian dream is that the destruction of power is regarded as the prerequisite of its attainment. . . . We have seen how inevitably special privilege is associated with power, and how the ownership of the means of production is the significant power in modern society. The clear recognition of that fact is the greatest ethical contribution which Marxian thought has made to the problem of social life.[16]

The first article of Reinhold Niebuhr's new journal, *Radical Religion,* made it clear that the editor was not primarily a democratic, revisionist socialist but a Marxist. He was also a Christian, and he held that a Christian's relationship to Marxism ought to be a discriminating one. The journal defined the clarification of the relationship between Marxian and Christian thought as one of its central purposes. While Christians and Marxists held different worldviews and disagreed about ultimate presuppositions, there could still be agreement on practical objectives. The editor committed the journal and its Fellowship of Socialist Christians to agreement on the expectation of the collapse of capitalism, to a common rejection of sentimental moralism, to a recognition of the need for a social struggle, to the view that ideals were conditioned by material forces, and to the proposition that a too-close alliance between religious institutions and the economic system muted the prophetic voice of the former. On the other hand, Marxist utopianism was rejected and the question of pacifism was recognized as an issue upon which socialist Christians would disagree.[17]

Late in the 1930s, while Niebuhr was developing a more thorough statement of the relationship of Christian theology to politics and becoming increasingly critical of Marxist anthropology, he outlined his essential agreement with Marxist thought. Marxism furnished an analysis of the economic structure of society that was essentially correct. It correctly perceived the conflict between the proletariat and the bourgeoisie as inevitable. He agreed that private ownership of the means of production was the basic cause of periodic economic crises. Marxism was right in its judgment that the communal ownership of property was a prerequisite of social justice. He accepted Lenin's view that capitalism was responsible for the economic imperialism that characterized the advanced nations.[18]

Niebuhr was attracted to Marxism by aspects of its mythical content as well as by its realism and its social analysis. The record of his greatest fascination with Marxist mythology is found in *Reflections on the End of an Era*, which he described as his "most Marxist work."[19] He urged that Christianity come to terms with Marxist mythology because it was more able to point to a meaning within the disintegration of Western civilization than either orthodox or liberal Christianity. He did not urge that Christianity surrender to Marxism, but he asked that the viable mythological insights of Marxism be recognized while using Christian insights to guard against Marxist utopianism. He regarded history as inexplicable in its own terms, requiring a mythological interpretation to ascertain meaning amid the chaos. The specific mythological insights he adopted from Marxism included the belief that capitalism was destroying itself through its own inner contradictions, the myth of the unique role of the disinherited class as the destroyers of the capitalist system, and a vision of a more just socialized society.

Critique of Marxism

Niebuhr's Marxism was never unqualified. He remained free from the illusions of fellow travelers and consistently criticized several central Marxist presuppositions. Reservations about Marxism he held as a liberal evolved into qualifications of Marxism as a Christian socialist, and the polemical attacks of the cold war turned into a scholarly critique of Marxism as the ideological ferment of the East-West struggle abated. Taken as a whole, Niebuhr's critique of Marxism is a thoroughgoing indictment on three levels: (1) the failure of Marxism in its embodiment in political institutions; (2) the inadequacy of Marxism as a political philosophy; and (3) the dangers of Marxism as a religion.

Niebuhr's reports on his trip to the Soviet Union in 1930 were characterized by both positive and negative evaluations of the communist experiment. He praised the enthusiasm of the society for industrialization, but he feared that the virtue of efficiency was being exalted at the expense of other human values. He understood why Russian orthodoxy as a supporter of the status quo before the revolution had to be attacked, but he did not regard the religious expressions of communism as adequate to human needs. He appreciated the virtues of communal property, but he doubted whether the suppression of private initiative would contribute to the general health of the community. While welcoming the advance of industrialism, he feared unchecked communism would bring it in a particularly ruthless manner. He applauded the rise of the industrial proletariat, but he decried attempts to force peasants into proletarian modes of living.

The evolution of Russian society increased his reservations about Marxism, and the purges and trials conducted by Stalin convinced him of the sickness at the center of Soviet society. As World War II approached, he argued that there was not sufficient reason to prefer communism over Nazism to sacrifice American lives in the defense of Russia. The Nazi-Soviet pact confirmed what Niebuhr had argued for years: Communism was being made to serve the aims of the Russian state rather than the Soviet Union bearing the hopes of the worldwide proletarian movement. The responses of the American Communist Party to the changes in Soviet foreign policy revealed the center of its loyalty to intellectuals who had hoped it was beyond provincial nationalism. Niebuhr severely criticized the American Communist Party's attempts to reconcile its position with that of the Soviet Union. The real tragedy of modern civilization, for Niebuhr, was that the only alternative to its self-destructive system of capitalism was a tyrannical socialism. Niebuhr's disenchantment with Marxist theory was furthered by the deficiencies he observed in the societies that claimed to be founded on Marxist theory.

Niebuhr recognized that the evils of Stalin's dictatorship were partially due to contingent historical factors, but he emphasized the mistakes in Marxist political theory that made such a development likely. Marxist thought obscured the necessity for coercion in society by regarding coercion as a product of class oppression. Once the exploiting middle class was eliminated, the need for social coercion would disappear. The failure to see the inevitable need for coercion was connected with eighteenth-century optimism about man. It was also connected with Marx's reduction of the various sources of political power to one source. Political power depended on ownership of the means of production. Marx concluded that once the means of production were responsible to the community, the political power would also be in the hands of the community.[20]

Marx did not envision an oligarchy arising to exploit the community for its own ends. According to Niebuhr, however, Marx's concept of the "dictatorship of the proletariat" had within it the seeds of a ruling party. The denial of all political power to other than the representatives of one class destroyed all checks against the development of an oligarchy. The rise of managerial power in the twentieth century proved in both communist and capitalist societies that the management of resources was a more important source of political power than the ownership of property. Marxist theory put the management of the country's resources into the hands of the group claiming to represent the proletariat and denied the necessity of checks upon their misuse of power. The very actions taken to secure the supremacy of the proletariat gave the oligarchy that spoke for the proletariat the elements of political prestige and the tools of social coercion.

> One pathetic consequence of this error is that the workers of a socialized concern, who are in theory the common owners of the property and are therefore prevented from holding any significant power, are rendered powerless against the managerial oligarchs who run the factory. The inevitable result is the accumulation of injustices more grievous than those which originally inspired the Marxist revolt against a free society.[21]

The political theory of Marxism granted one group an absolute monopoly of power and also exaggerated its inevitable self-righteousness by claims of scientific rationality for its social theory. The phenomenon of communist dogmatism reinforced by totalitarian power made it particularly difficult for communist statesmen to understand the world in which their policies operated.[22] Niebuhr was very skeptical about the possibility of achieving a verifiable social science that was, in important ways, similar to the physical sciences; Marxism claimed to have done so. Marx himself was partially responsible for the claims of Marxist social science to infallibility. Niebuhr thought Marx's essential error was to identify the method of empiricism with the doctrine of materialism. From materialism was supposed to flow certain self-evident deductions. "All the propositions dear to a revolutionary and apocalyptic idealism—universalism, collectivism, humanism, and socialism—are drawn, like so many rabbits, out of the hat of materialism."[23] Whether or not Marx's central error was to equate, as Niebuhr suggested, Lockean empiricism and materialism, Marx certainly confused descriptive and prescriptive language. The distinctions between the utopian socialists and scientific socialism are not as sharp as proponents of Marxist-Leninist science have imagined, and the pretense of scientific infallibility has given a note of fanaticism to the proponents of Marxism.

Niebuhr regarded the mythology of Marxism as its chief source of attraction to intellectuals. As his own study of Christian theology deepened, he became progressively a sharper critic of the religious elements of Marxism; his critique on the religious level is the most original element of his attack. John C. Bennett said, in commenting on Niebuhr's Marxism, "Today Communism has no opponent in this country who knows how to deal it a deadlier blow on the intellectual and spiritual level."[24]

Niebuhr thought communism met his minimum definition of a religion and contained many ingredients of traditional religion.

> Religion in minimum terms is devotion to a cause which goes beyond the warrant of pure rationality, and in maximum terms it is the confidence that the success of the cause and of the values associated with it is guaranteed by the character of the universe itself.[25]

Like Carl Becker, Niebuhr regarded faith in the doctrine of progress as essentially a religious dogma. The Marxist faith in the dialectic of history, leading to catastrophe and then utopia, was also of the character of religious dogma rather than philosophy or empirical observation. The Marxist combination of penultimate pessimism with a note of ultimate optimism was particularly fruitful for political action. The innate determinism of Marxism was overridden by the sense of participating in, and acting consistently with, the flow of history. The particular role of the proletarian class in the Marxist worldview incorporated elements of the Christian concept of the peculiar virtue of the dispossessed with messianic symbolism to make claims for the class beyond the competence of social science.

Communism was regarded by Niebuhr as having "at least one characteristic in common with all religion: it tends to oversimplify morals."[26] Rather than carefully balancing values, communism was characterized by absolute devotion to the principles of equality and loyalty to the proletarian class. Puritanism made the virtues of the rising middle class supreme, and "pure Christianity" made the ethic of love an absolute. In an analogous manner, communism made the requirements of the proletarian class in achieving an egalitarian society supreme. Detailed analysis of the value presuppositions of Puritanism, the ethics of Jesus, or the Marxian ethic hardly reveal a simple ethic. In fact, in the same article in a different context Niebuhr asserts, "Communism is a religion of mixed ethical values, but its energy proves that it is a religion."[27] Perhaps the most penetrating criticism H. Richard Niebuhr ever leveled at his brother's work was that his view of Christian ethics overly magnified the virtue of love. His brother's overemphasis on the perfect love ethic of Jesus owed more to the tradition of Adolf von Harnack than to a consideration of the fullness of the Christian ethic, according to H. Richard Niebuhr.[28]

The Marxist revolutionary creed encountered problems similar to those of other primitive creeds in preserving itself from the critical and relativizing tendencies of intelligence. Its response was typical of the responses of religious systems in the West. It created both a dogma and a church to define and defend the dogma. "Marx is its Bible and the writings of Lenin have achieved a dogmatic significance for it comparable to that which the thought of Thomas Aquinas had for the medieval church."[29] The Marxist confidence in the dialectic of history working out to certain anticipated ends seemed to Niebuhr sufficiently parallel to religious trust in a higher power to regard Marxism as a religion.[30] Niebuhr's own inclination to regard discourse about God as language about a transcendent purpose that gave meaning to human history justified, for him, the definition of Marxism as a religion.

The illusions of Marxism, which were essentially religious, reinforced the tyrannical tendencies of communism. The primary illusion was its utopianism. Great evils were approved on the grounds that every act was justified that would realize the classless society. The utopian illusions attracted intellectuals to communism but obscured the injustices perpetrated in its name. "The important point is that the ruthless power operates behind a screen of pretended ideal ends, a situation which is both more dangerous and more evil than pure cynical defiance of moral ends."[31] The criticism of Marxism was in essence the same as the criticism of liberalism: Both creeds were blinded by utopian illusions to the need for resolute political action for achievable moral ends. Marxist realism had exposed the illusions of liberalism, and Augustinian realism exposed Marxist illusions.

The Socialist Party

Niebuhr found resources within the Christian faith to challenge the conventional American two-party system. He combined an inclination toward radical politics with the conviction that a Christian's political commitments were provisional and tentative because every political system was judged by the Kingdom of God. American political conservatism was never a live option for Niebuhr, and the failure of liberalism to be sufficiently realistic pushed him further to the left.

The major parties were forced by the facts of politics to remain ideologically within boundaries set by their respective coalitions. Third parties, however, were able to take seriously the impending collapse of capitalism, the study of American society in terms of class analysis, and the socialization of the means of production. Niebuhr's acceptance of Marxist economic and social analysis drove him into the third-party movement, where such a view would be treated seriously. Niebuhr had taken the third-party alternative as early as 1928 in the League of Independent Political Action. In 1929 he dismissed the programs of both the Communists and the American Federation of Labor as irrelevant to the American political scene and urged a third-party movement.[32] He regarded the attempt to win congressional seats for Socialist Party candidates as the best strategy. Elements in his program included the nationalization of coal, heavy inheritance taxes, heavy graduated income taxes, and broad public welfare measures. He rejected an invitation of a committee of the Socialist Party to run as a candidate for governor of New York in 1930 as premature. He was too new to the party, to New York, and to his academic vocation.[33]

The collapse of German socialism and the rise of Nazism in 1933 encouraged Niebuhr's view that parliamentary, evolutionary socialism was inadequate to the crisis of the day. He regarded Germany as revealing in microcosm the problems and possibilities of Western civilization. Using lessons learned from Europe, more particularly Germany, to instruct the United States, he called for a rethinking of American radicalism. Next to the need for cohesion among the disinherited groups, he regarded as most important the disavowal of the revisionist hopes for parliamentary socialism. The revisionists, in Niebuhr's view, had held too absolute a loyalty to democratic procedure. The class that dominated a country economically could too easily exploit democracy for its own interests. He used his study of the German scene to instruct American radicals: "Recent events have proved quite conclusively that an uncritical attachment to, and an implicit trust in, the institutions of democracy will betray the workers in the hour of crisis."[34] However, the revisionists were wiser than the orthodox Marxists in admitting the need for greater subtlety in handling psychological and cultural forces. The communist ideology was a major obstacle to any alliance of the disinherited on the American scene; effective cooperation required its revision. Niebuhr advocated, therefore, "a turn left and a turn right" in American radicalism.

Niebuhr did not, however, ignore the unique features of the American scene. He thought that, if the vital rethinking of socialist positions could be carried out and the prodigious organizational work undertaken, a radical movement could arise on American soil that exploited the American revolutionary tradition.[35] He was not completely clear about the connections between the American revolutionary tradition and the proletarian revolution, but he realized European models of action needed modification for the American scene.

Niebuhr was among the young militants who with Norman Thomas gained control of the Socialist Party in 1936. The victory for the left of the party gave it a new burst of energy, but by 1937 the hopes for the Socialist Party itself were fading, and Niebuhr urged a socialist-labor alliance. Labor was essential to any development of a mass left-wing party, but the refusal of the Congress of Industrial Organizations to give support to any but labor candidates restricted the socialists to an educational and protest role.[36] The creation of the American Labor Party broke the power base of the socialists in New York.

Niebuhr ended his association with the Socialist Party in the 1940 election when he voted for Roosevelt. Elements of socialist theory continued to play a significant role in his thought as late as 1947 or 1948,[37] but his loyalty to the Socialist Party ended with Roosevelt's third-term campaign. "All this means that Roosevelt, despite anti-third term traditions, is the only hope of maintaining the real gains which have been made in the past years of the Depression."[38] Already the pragmatism that was ultimately to triumph was appearing as a source of criticism of socialism. "Doctrinaire radicalism which divides the progressive forces is just as bad as opportunism which loses sight of all ultimate goals."[39]

The failures of Russia, which were poignantly revealed in the 1937 Moscow trials, and the failure of German socialism in 1933 had discredited the alternative social system to a decaying capitalism. The failure of the Socialist Party in the United States to win mass support and the failure of its leaders to understand the international situation forced Niebuhr to regard it as irrelevant to the American political scene. By 1940, he regarded it as discredited: "Nothing is more obvious than that socialism must come in America through some other instrument than the Socialist Party."[40]

Donald B. Meyer's otherwise astute analysis of Niebuhr's relationship to third-party movements errs in maintaining that the creation of Americans for Democratic Action in the postwar years marks his return to the established two-party system.[41] While the founding of ADA did mark his abandonment of hopes for the Socialist Party, the discrediting of Marxist dogma had started before and continued after the founding of ADA in 1947. Niebuhr's founding role in and his continued support of the Liberal Party of New York State[42] is testimony to his refusal to settle easily into the two-party system. As late as 1967, Niebuhr confessed his embarrassment over the administration's Vietnam policy by hesitating to define himself as a Democrat in any other sense than that he had voted for Lyndon Johnson in 1964.[43]

Liberalism
Under Marxist Criticism

Under the influence of Marxist mythology, Niebuhr argued that a vision of catastrophe was more adequate than the optimistic illusions of liberalism. Christian theology and Marxist mythology both contained optimistic hopes on the other side of destruction. The Christian hope was otherworldly, while the Marxian hope was regarded as historical and, consequently, more prone to the dangers of utopianism. The catastrophic and apocalyptic tendencies of Marxism were no more the result of rational analysis than were the evolutionary hopes of the liberals and revisionist Marxists. But Niebuhr regarded the view that wrested hope from pessimism more productive of moral action than either sheer optimism or pessimism.

Niebuhr slipped into the language of the inevitability of history while opposing liberalism. In his Marxist period he could write confidently that the "logic of history" and the "drift of history" were toward the collapse of Western civilization. When not engaged in polemics against liberalism, and particularly while exposing the religious foundations of Marxism, he often rejected confident predictions on the direction of history. He viewed philosophies that attempted to predict the direction of history as based upon mythology. According to Niebuhr, history does not provide the data upon which predictions of the future can be based. The ultimate direction of history is too uncertain to be a basis for social policy.

> It is a question whether any scientific world view, or view of history, could be made the basis of social action. . . . The facts of history are multifarious and infinite in variety. They do not lend themselves easily to precise conclusions, and certainly not to the kind of conclusions which base political action upon certain hopes and confident prophecies about future history. . . . The philosophies . . . harmonize the facts from a particular point of view which is determined not so much by the nature of the facts themselves as by the way in which a generation or an

individual feels about the meaning of life and by what he regards as ultimate and important.[44]

There appears to be a contradiction in Niebuhr's rejection of confident predictions of the future and his criticism of liberalism for neglecting the destruction of Western civilization. Niebuhr himself knows when he moves from literal rendering of the facts to mythological speech, though it is not always clear in his works. He has no confidence that history can be predicted, and he would share the distaste of critics who deplore doctrines of the inevitability of history.[45]

Reflections on the End of an Era was written two years after *Moral Man and Immoral Society,* in the midst of a deepened Depression and increasing signs of war. It is more thoroughly Marxist and emphasizes the logic of history as thoroughly as does any other of Niebuhr's works. The following are typical examples of historical dogmatism:

> The future belongs to the worker. . . . We may deprecate or welcome that fact but we can hardly deny its *inevitability.*

> Nevertheless the proletarian seems *as certain* to rule a new civilization as it is that the commercial and industrial owner held the significant power in the social order which is passing.

> His [the laborer's] victory is certain because the *logic of history* demands his type of society rather than the one which the owner is trying to preserve.

> Thus modern society is forced by the conditions introduced by the machine to return to social ideals once held by early society. The more the intelligent portions of the community recognize this development as both *inevitable and desirable,* the quicker will be the period of transition in which society now lives and the more certainly will the dangers of barbarism be avoided.[46]

Niebuhr resisted the temptation to date the fall of capitalism in his polemics against the system. But he agreed with Marx that its contradictions doomed it to destruction and its inequalities justified its extinction. Whereas *Moral Man and Immoral Society* had been doubtful about the achievement of radical changes through either evolutionary or revolutionary change, *Reflections on the End of an Era* confidently predicted the collapse of capitalism as a result of the trend of history and concluded that liberals were too blind to see the direction of the tide. The tide was running so strongly in favor of Marxism that, if Christianity were to survive, there must be a compromise between Marxian and Christian mythology. The secularized religion of Marxism was better able to affirm the moral meaning of the current class struggle than

Christian orthodoxy. It was superior to liberal Christianity, which would be finally discredited when its naive trust in the evolutionary process was engulfed by social catastrophe.[47]

Niebuhr was polemicizing for social change in 1934, and many of his exaggerations were for political ends. He attempted to shatter the liberal mythology with a Marxist mythology, which he regarded as more adequate. There is a religious character to Niebuhr's prophecy in *Moral Man and Immoral Society* that the day of judgment is darkness and not light. The prophecy went beyond the facts, just as did liberalism's trust in inevitable progress, but he believed his prophecy more adequately encompassed the reality. However, for polemical purposes, Niebuhr occasionally allowed the myth of destruction to determine his reading of the facts and to neglect resources for improvement that others, less hindered by a myth of destruction (whether Marxist or Christian), could see. The most widely known example of this failure is his dismissal of the New Deal in its early phases. The New Deal was not bold enough to prevent the economic overlords from moving to the extreme right when they realized that power was slipping from their hands. He ruled out the possibility of a gradual transition from capitalism to socialism and predicted a drift toward fascism, which would sharpen the class antagonisms and initiate the class conflict.

> The imperilled oligarchy of our day, though it may do lip service to the sweet reasonableness of these counsels [Keynesian economics], drifts nevertheless toward fascism. The drift is inevitable because it is more natural to hide wasted strength by a desperate venture of power than to arrest its decay by a prudent restraint upon its use. . . .
>
> The net effect of fascism must therefore be to guarantee that the end of capitalism will be bloody rather than peaceful. By destroying the last possibility of resolving the conflicts of modern society in democratic terms, it makes a revolutionary end of these conflicts a practical certainty.[48]

The language of the "logic of history" and historical "inevitability" declined in inverse proportion to Niebuhr's critique of Marxism. The experience of the 1930s and 1940s taught him to be extremely wary of all schematizations of history, and he gradually moved in the interpretation of history from the category of tragedy to the motif of irony.

Critique of Pacifism

When he was a young pastor, the peculiar combination of Wilsonian liberalism and the American nationalism of a second-generation German-American led Niebuhr to disavow pacifism during World War I. The failure of Versailles and events following the war drove Niebuhr to affirm a pacifist position again in 1923. In the 1920s he became national chairman of the Fellowship of Reconciliation.

Niebuhr's pacifism collapsed under the Marxist-inspired critique of liberalism. He broke with the tradition of Christian social radicalism, which had accepted a mild form of socialism while disavowing a resort to violence. His acceptance of Marxist class analysis and a catastrophic interpretation of the end of capitalism made it impossible for him to deny the use of all violence to the forces of social change. He concluded that, because the privileged class would resist the necessary changes with violence when the instruments of legal coercion failed, it was necessary to concede the right of violence to the underprivileged class. The privileged class could, by its economic power, social prestige, and control of the legal instruments of coercion, keep a pacifist proletariat in subjection. Violence and the threat of violence were essential ingredients of the class struggle. However, Niebuhr criticized what he regarded as the romantic illusions of the radicals in regard to the redemptive effects of violence. He urged that violence be used sparingly and only where necessary. He promoted the development of instruments of nonviolent social change wherever the tactics of nonviolent resistance were relevant.[49]

Niebuhr's abandonment of pacifism led to his resigning from the Fellowship of Reconciliation in 1934. The membership was split over the resignation of J. B. Matthews as executive secretary and over the extent to which it should be consistently pacifist. A poll revealed that only 20 percent of the Fellowship was unwilling to renounce all forms of violent coercion in the social struggle. Niebuhr's statement regarding his reasons for resigning from the Fellowship demonstrated his attempt to remain a pacifist regarding international war and abandon pacifism on the domestic front.

> While respecting this position of the pure and the qualified pacifists I am bound to admit that I cannot share their position. For this reason I am forced to associate myself with 20 percent of the Fellowship who are pacifists only in the sense that they will refuse to participate in an international armed conflict. Perhaps it would clear the issue if we admitted that we were not pacifists at all. We probably all recognize the terrible possibilities of violence. We regard an international conflict as so suicidal that we are certain that we will not participate in it.[50]

The article explaining his break with the Fellowship proclaimed that a primary difference between them was that he regarded all issues of social ethics in nonabsolutist terms. Pragmatism was evoked as the guide to whether policy at a particular time should be nonviolent.

Niebuhr's decision to regard the use of violence as a pragmatic issue soon led him to disavow the pacifism he had retained in the arena of international politics. In 1935, when confronted with the League of Nations' dilemma regarding the Italian conquest of Ethiopia, Niebuhr abandoned pacifism for the policy that he thought promised the greatest likelihood of restoring peace and some semblance of justice. Recognizing that economic sanctions and their enforcement could lead to war, he still argued that the League should enforce effective sanctions, including oil, against Italy. He criticized the politics of George Lansbury, for whom he had great respect. Lansbury's refusal to support sanctions was, in Niebuhr's view, a confusion of the relativities of politics with the absolutes of the Christian faith. He praised Lansbury's insight that the League was serving Tory imperialism as well as Christian idealism but questioned his overly absolute pacifism, which refused sanctions because of the threat of war without providing an alternative policy. The enforcement of international order required the resort to or threat of armed force, because "no non-violent means of coercion can ever be guaranteed to be free of the peril of violence."[51] As World War II drew nearer, he continued to call for resistance to the threats and claims of the German, Italian, and Japanese nations, but he never personally advocated American entry into the war before Pearl Harbor. As late as 1940 he continued to object to Roosevelt's rearmament policies. Though he had given up his pacifist position, he continued to try to limit carefully those situations in which violence would be used and to argue against militarism.

Niebuhr's early criticism of the pacifism of liberal Christians focused on their tendency to confuse religious and pragmatic perspectives. He recognized both religious and pragmatic approaches to pacifism as valid on their own terms, but confusion resulted when the two were mixed. Religious pacifism was legitimate as an ascetic response to the demands of an absolute love ethic. The absolute love ethic was a perfectionist ethic of nonresistance, and adopting it should cause one to renounce all responsibility for social justice that depended on coercion, explicitly or implicitly. Religious pacifism was symbolically important but politically irrelevant.

Pragmatic pacifism, which Niebuhr himself had advocated until 1932, was the attempt to mitigate the contest between opposing forces by means of social imagination, intelligence, and arbitration. Pragmatic pacifism used political arguments to demonstrate that violence should be avoided. Niebuhr recognized it as a useful corrective to the violent tendencies of group egoism. He could not, however, remain consistently pacifist on pragmatic grounds. His social analysis led to the conclusion that violence or the threat of violence was an indispensable element in the dynamics of social change. "A responsible relationship to the political order, therefore, makes an unqualified disavowal of violence impossible."[52]

Niebuhr's argument against joining religious and pragmatic perspectives was a move to eliminate moral absolutes from the realm of political consideration. Politics was concerned with the weighing of relative values, and the weighing took place on the scales of history, which considered all sorts of contingent factors. The testimony of the absolutist against violence was necessary, but it was not immediately relevant to pragmatic considerations. In fact, Niebuhr's own pragmatism was set in and justified by particular religious perspectives. Having separated religious absolutes and pragmatic arguments for pacifism, Niebuhr could confine the religious perspective to a realm not immediately relevant to politics and advocate the use of violence when its discriminate use provided greater opportunities for justice than did the denial of violence. He recognized that he thereby justified particular policies which, while morally ambiguous in themselves, promoted the greatest good or the least evil. He accepted the implied principle that the end justifies the means in the sense that, in making ethical judgments about politics, it was necessary to subordinate one value to others. He rejected the principle insofar as it implied that one could make clear distinctions between ends and means.[53]

In 1940 Niebuhr attacked the merging of Christian pacifism and American isolationism and developed the arguments against pacifism in the church.[54] He considered pacifism appropriate as a nonpolitical expression of Christian perfectionism and appreciated the witness of the Mennonites, who disavowed political problems and tasks.[55] He regarded such pacifism as an important symbol of the ideal. But he was more familiar with the pacifism that ignored the Christian doctrines of sin and justification by faith and included a humanist optimism. Such pacifism was heretical, not as pacifism per se but because it failed to appreciate essential elements in Christian doctrine. Using the term *heretical* very loosely, he judged pacifism founded on optimism heretical because it was true neither to the full standards of the gospel nor to the facts of human existence.

The theological grounds for Niebuhr's pacifism were stated clearly in his 1940 exchange of views with Richard Roberts, a leading Canadian pacifist, in the pages of *Christianity and Society*. He asserted that the pacifists he most frequently encountered were unaware of the tragic character of human life. Pacifists tended to think that the struggle for power could be overcome by renouncing the use of violent means of social control. Their assumption followed from illusions about human nature that were opposed to the Reformation doctrine of justification by faith. Justification by faith accepted the contradictions in history between norms and achievements and pointed to divine mercy. Justification did not mean a perfection beyond history but the possibility of love *in* history. He argued that the incarnation promised no escape from history as conflict. The redemption of Christ provided a revelation of mercy, not power to overcome the contradictions of history. War was not a mere incident but a revelation of the tragic character of all human history. Pacifists seemed to be unaware of the conflict within history until it was starkly revealed in war, and then they attempted to opt out "by a supreme act of renunciation."[56]

Niebuhr admitted that his relativism could easily give way to moral cynicism and agreed that it was necessary to keep alive the tension between the ideal and the realizable relative good. But he also pointed out that it was a Christian's responsibility to preserve whatever order and decency he could in society. For Niebuhr the distinction between the barbarism of the Nazis and the imperialism of the British empire was sufficient for him to enjoin resistance to Nazi aggression. Roberts admitted the distinction but regarded it an insufficient justification for war. Niebuhr recognized the evil of war but judged it less evil than acquiescence to Nazi tyranny.

Niebuhr's critique did not remain unanswered. Pacifists replied in scores of articles and at least three pamphlets.[57] Each pamphleteer paid Niebuhr the compliment of regarding his attack upon their position as the most substantive in current Christian literature. Insofar as the critics admitted they were not attempting to provide an approach to international politics for a secular nation, their criticisms were not relevant to the task Niebuhr had undertaken. Criticisms based upon hopes of eliminating conflict through a more radical submission to the law of love fell prey to Niebuhr's attack and were of little interest to practitioners and theoreticians of international politics.

The radical ethic of absolute pacifism was combined in one of Niebuhr's British critics with a high degree of utopianism. G. H. C. Macgregor wrote:

> If only men were prepared to take God at His word, and to order their lives here and now by the laws of a transcendent Kingdom, then the power of God would answer the cry of faith, and the Kingdom would break in upon them anew and "take them unawares."[58]

One critic, John H. Yoder, drew the sharp distinction "between pacifism as a political policy for states and pacifism as an ethical principle for Christians."[59] He argued that Niebuhr failed to take seriously enough the difference between an ethic for an unregenerate society and one for redeemed Christians. Niebuhr's distinction between pragmatic pacifism and absolute pacifism is similar to the one Yoder demanded.

Niebuhr and Yoder disagreed sharply over the degree to which a Christian's political ethic is unique. Observation of the practice of Christians prevented him from making Yoder's bold claims for Christian action. Yoder was correct that Niebuhr had not fully developed a doctrine of the Holy Spirit or stressed its working in the world. Nor did Niebuhr believe, as did Yoder, that the Christian community is free of the group egoism attributed to all groups in *Moral Man and Immoral Society*. Critics have often pointed to the lack of certain emphases in Niebuhr's thought that are part of orthodox Christian doctrine. In a time of radical questioning of the meaning and cogency of Christian faith, substantial criticism of a thinker requires more than merely pointing to the absence of emphasis of a doctrine. In terms of Niebuhr's apologetic method, it is necessary to show that the theologian has erred in his judgment of the human predicament, and Yoder did not undertake that task. Yoder properly emphasized the difference between what is and what ought to be, but he used the distinction to substantiate a position that can derive an ethic for the Christian today directly from the authority of the teaching of Jesus. Niebuhr's prescription for what one ought to do always takes account of the relevant possibilities. In political ethics the delineation of the relevant possibilities is the responsibility of political analysis.

Yoder's emphasis upon the distinction between a Christian ethic and a social ethic for an unregenerated society would in dialogue soon force Niebuhr back to an accusation of self-righteousness against the Christian pacifist and to the additional charge that it is irresponsible to refuse to use the instruments of social coercion, clumsy as they are, for social justice and order. A certain imbalance in Niebuhr's thought in the 1930s results from excessively focusing on his hopes for radical social change and the approaching war. His response to a developing U.S. militarism and his position on the Vietnam struggle, which complete the story, are a later part of his perspective.

The Political Ethic

Though Niebuhr's political ethic in this period owes much to two theologians he heavily criticized, Luther and Rauschenbusch, there are five facets of the ethic that can be regarded as Marxian in inspiration. The acceptance of violence to achieve social change has already been mentioned. The tendency to regard the times as leading to a destruction of Western civilization owed more to Marxian analysis than to the direct inspiration of Amos. Niebuhr, however, regarded the Marxist "negation of the negation" as a secularized version of "the day of the Lord is darkness, and not light" (Amos 5:18). A catastrophic view of history shaped his judgment of which alternative policies were relevant to the political situation. From Marx, in particular, he learned the large degree to which the claims for morality reflected the self-interest of a person or a group. Marx's concept of social morality as ideology reflecting the economic position of the moralist revealed some of the reasons behind the protests against the threatened violence of strikes. Niebuhr's development of his political ethic in conjunction with the doctrine of sin was partially due to the connections he saw between Marx's doctrine of alienation and his political realism. An ethic without an awareness of man's brokenness was inescapably idealistic. Niebuhr's ethic was in harmony with Marx the socialist, who emphasized the need for public ownership and planning, but it was in opposition to Marx the utopian revolutionary, who envisioned a society without injustice and competition. For a brief period, though regarding Marx's utopia as illusory, Niebuhr was willing to sanction such utopias for the sake of furthering the struggle for social justice. The vision of the radical soon faded, and he came to regret the closing paragraph of *Moral Man and Immoral Society* in which he sanctioned the use of illusion.

Niebuhr regarded his political ethic as an attempt to unite political realism and morality. "An adequate political morality must do justice to the insights of both moralists and political realists."[60] The pursuit of equal justice within a society required that the degree of coercion in the life of collective man be minimized and that rational and moral factors govern its use. Agreeing with Augustine that the peace of the world is achieved through strife, Niebuhr sought ways to unite the skill of the political realist in the use of force and the wisdom of the moralist in adjusting competing interests through reason and conscience. His attempt to unite realism and morality is seen very clearly in *An Interpretation of Christian Ethics,* in which he devotes chapters to criticizing the political ethics of both Christian orthodoxy and Christian liberalism. In sweeping terms, the charge against the political theory and ethic of the church was that orthodoxy had too easily dismissed the law of love for politics while the modern liberal church had too easily affirmed its relevance. His statement of the problem of the Christian political ethic and his criticism of the answers of both orthodoxy and liberalism depend on his conception of the Christian ethic as the law of love. Like Harnack, he treated love as the central motif and interpretative principle of Jesus' ethic.

Niebuhr had learned from Ernst Troeltsch that a final Christian ethic is not achievable. Each age must refashion its Christian ethic in view of the ideal ethic of Jesus and the conditions and presuppositions of the age. The church's attempts to produce a social ethic had not been notably successful, and the ability of the contemporary church to do so was in question. He undertook to state the ethic of Jesus in its most uncompromising form: It was an ethic of the ideal of love. The ideal of love could not be realized in human history, yet it was relevant to that history because it revealed the relativity of all other standards and lifted other norms to new heights. The norm of love was described as a transcendent norm that could not be fulfilled. The tension between the ideal and the real was overcome only in the Christian's faith.

> Thus the Christian believes that the ideal of love is real in the will and nature of God, even though he knows of no place in history where the ideal has been realized in its pure form. And it is because it has this reality that he feels the pull of obligation. . . . Man seeks to realize in history what he conceives to be already the truest reality—that is, its final essence.[61]

The ethic of Jesus revealed the fulfillment of life to be that of self-sacrifice for another or a cause. All egoism was rejected as expressing sinfulness, and morality was understood as the limiting of egoism. Such an ethic was foreign to the needs of political life: "Whenever religious idealism brings forth its purest fruits and places the strongest check upon selfish desire, it results in policies which from the political perspective are quite impossible."[62]

Whatever prudential elements appeared in the ethic of Jesus were regarded as inevitable byproducts of an ethic that was founded on insight into human nature; such elements did not detract from the radical character of the ethic.

The theology of Second Isaiah's vicarious, meek, suffering servant dominated Niebuhr's thought about the bearer of the Christian ethic. Jesus bore testimony to an ideal that was powerless in the world. The crucifixion was the ultimate symbol of love's fate; the resurrection was a symbol of an ahistorical fulfillment of love. Niebuhr's portrayal of the ethic of Jesus revealed his background of perfectionism. Though not advocating asceticism, he still regarded it as the most logical outcome of the teachings of Jesus. His habit of wrestling with ideas in their extreme form colored his presentation of Jesus' ethic. He had abandoned the dualistic metaphysics that had characterized his liberal theology, but he continued to see the tension between the ideal and the real overcome only in faith. Even beyond the structure of his thought, his writing style continued to prefer dualistic modes of presentation or even paradoxical expression.

The failure of the church to develop a satisfactory political ethic and the impossibility of Jesus' ethic in the political arena encouraged Niebuhr to utilize the resources of Western political philosophy in shaping his political ethic. His tendency to criticize the political philosophers of the past obscured how many insights he had drawn from them, and his steadfast refusal to sanction a systematic political theory made him appear as a critic of the tradition. His condemnation of the illusions of rationalism prevented his readers from appreciating the extent of his dependence on the liberal-rationalist tradition. As he testified:

> A prophetic religion which tries to reestablish itself in a new day without appreciating what was true in the Age of Reason will be inadequate for the moral problems which face our generation. . . . Critical intelligence is a prerequisite of justice.[63]

Niebuhr regarded Christianity as having in its faith a foundation and a roof for the structure of an adequate morality; the walls, uprights, and diagonals that held it together were the product of discriminate political and moral judgments.[64] A trust in the meaningfulness of human endeavor and a faith that the purposes of the moral life will ultimately be vindicated were prerequisites for an adequate morality, in his view. He realized that an occasional moral philosopher could do without such religious presuppositions, but he regarded it as unlikely that many could act morally without them.

The relationship of love to justice remained an ever-present problem in Niebuhr's thought. In *An Interpretation of Christian Ethics,* the principles of equal justice were regarded as an approximate expression of the law of love, which appropriately belonged to a transcendent realm of perfection. Perfect equality was not fulfilled either, but the principles of equal justice were relevant to the world of striving men. Love then remained a principle of criticism of all principles of social morality, which in turn partially expressed the demands of love. Love also was a possibility for individual expression beyond the requirements of social coercion in the political order. *An Interpretation of Christian Ethics* emphasized the independence of the Christian ethic from culture. The emphasis upon the independence, which was partly an attack on theological liberalism, rendered dubious the relevance of the ethic to that culture.

The tensions between the law of love and political realism understood in Marxist terms, or between a dedication to political relevance and an independent Christian ethic, resulted in an admittedly dualistic ethic. This ethic was elaborated more forcefully in *Moral Man and Immoral Society* than in *An Interpretation of Christian Ethics.*

Morality was viewed largely in terms of the restraint of egoism. The egoism of individuals, sharply disapproved by the ethic of love, was amenable to religious discipline, whereas the egoism of groups was accepted as inevitable. "To some degree the conflict between the purest individual morality and an adequate political policy must therefore remain."[65] Niebuhr held to the standards of the "most uncompromising idealism" for regulation of the personal life, but he argued for the achievement of justice through the balance of power in the political arena. The two moralities are referred to as individual morality and social morality, or as the moralities of love and of justice. The gap between the two approaches is occasionally described as the gap between morals and politics. The acceptance of a "frank dualism" seemed more appropriate to Niebuhr than prematurely bridging the differences between the checks on individual and social egoism. The elaboration of this dualism was the central purpose of *Moral Man and Immoral Society.* The gap between individual and social morality that Niebuhr emphasized in the 1930s appeared so wide because he continued to speak of personal morality in perfectionist terms and social morality in terms of a Marxist-informed socialism. Also, he had not yet worked out the relationship between love and justice as fully as he would later do.

His polemics against importing irrelevant utopianism and perfectionism into political thought were more adequate than his attempt to divide individual and social morality. In one sense the individual does not exist outside the group, and the moral question does not arise in isolation from the group. Acceptance of a dichotomy between individual and social morality encourages an obliviousness to the evil use of violence, intimidation, and false propaganda. Moral thought will be furthered by recognizing such acts as morally wrong even though reasons of state may require their use. The division into two moralities makes it harder to restrain the use of such tactics. A dichotomy between personal and social life, which sociologically speaking is impossible to justify, denies to social life the limitations which man's rationality attempts to place on his egoism.

Economic Strategies
for Racial Justice

Niebuhr's 1932 book *Moral Man and Immoral Society* tried to join social realism with reforming change. Alternative strategies were sought. His own frustrations in Detroit, in both city and church, persuaded him that white people would not as a group give African Americans justice; they would have to win a place in the system. "The white race in America will not admit the Negro to equal rights if it is not forced to do so. Upon that point one may speak with a dogmatism which all history justifies."[66]

He found Gandhi's strategies of nonviolent coercion suggestive. Violent rebellion by an outnumbered and outarmed minority was hopeless. But the spiritual solvent of nonviolent coercion could, he thought, reduce the brutal response of the white majority. A combination of moral and economic pressures had advantages in winning the place of human dignity that the nation confessed it prized for all. Social ignorance and economic self-interest were against change to improve the situation of African Americans, but the tactics of nonviolent coercion showed promise for the American situation. He wrote prophetically in 1932: "The emancipation of the Negro race in America probably waits upon the adequate development of this kind of social and political strategy."[67] Urging boycotts against banks, stores, and public service corporations that practiced discrimination, he also suggested nonpayment of taxes in states that discriminated against African American education.

Religion could make a great contribution to the development of nonviolent resistance. Here the religious convictions of the common humanity of the oppressed could create attitudes that would reduce cruelty. Attitudes of repentance could be nurtured by religion, and community across social conflict could be seen by religiously informed imaginations.

> One waits for such a campaign with all the more reason and hope because the peculiar gifts of the Negro endow him with the capacity to conduct it successfully. He would need only to fuse the aggressiveness of the new and young Negro with the patience and forbearance of the old Negro, to rob the former of its vindictiveness and the latter of its lethargy.[68]

Social imagination inspired by religion and nonviolent resistance inspired by necessity were the combination he hoped to see emerge. Years later, these words were read and pondered by Martin Luther King, Jr., who began to have his view of humanity sobered when as a theological student he studied Niebuhr. *Moral Man and Immoral Society* became the only book mentioned in King's writings more frequently than Walter Rauschenbusch's *Christianity and the Social Crisis.*[69] But before King would study Niebuhr, and almost a quarter of a century before the nonviolent revolution led by King would achieve some of the gains Niebuhr hoped for, Niebuhr had another project.

A little-known extension of Niebuhr's influence was in the direction of the Highlander Center in East Tennessee. The original director, Myles Horton, had been influenced by Harry Ward and Niebuhr at Union Theological Seminary.[70] Horton had investigated many forms of Christian social ministry, under the encouragement of Niebuhr and others, including the folk-school system of Denmark. His school, later a center, was established in 1932. Reinhold Niebuhr provided advice, solicited funds,[71] and served as chairperson of the advisory board. In the 1950s Highlander became a focus of teaching strategy for integration. It was here that Rosa Parks, the heroine of the Montgomery bus boycott, received training and inspiration. She said:

> I found out for the first time in my adult life that this could be a unified society, that there was such a thing as people of differing races and backgrounds meeting together in workshops and living together in peace and harmony.[72]

Later the center was vilified by the state of Georgia with pictures of Martin Luther King, Jr., being proclaimed as attending a "Communist Training School" at the center's twenty-fifth anniversary party.[73]

The Delta Cooperative Farm

Niebuhr's work took him to the southern United States. In 1932 he visited and supported striking coal miners in Harlan County, Kentucky. In 1934 he helped establish the Fellowship of Southern Churchmen to support justice in racial and economic issues. The biracial Southern Tenant Farmers Union had attracted the support of Sherwood Eddy, Niebuhr's friend and sponsor. In 1936, Eddy and a student of Niebuhr's, Sam Franklin, were arrested and threatened while investigating abuses of sharecroppers in Arkansas. Their arrest toughened Eddy's determination to find land to develop a cooperative farm. The farm was to be interracial and to model a new form of agricultural economy for the region. Sam H. Franklin, writing about the farm in 1980, described it as "praxis": that is, it was a social action, or experiment designed for learning and further reflection.[74] Franklin had been moved by *Moral Man and Immoral Society* when he read it in 1933, and he credited Niebuhr with providing the social theology.

> It was a quest for social structures that best become those who know that humanity cannot finally be saved by social structure. The theological outlook which most of us found congenial was that of the "Biblical realism" of the president of our board of trustees, Reinhold Niebuhr.[75]

The farm was to be a "sustained action in the direction of greater justice,"[76] according to its first director.

The farm was a counter to the system of eight million people who were kept as sharecroppers or day agricultural laborers. The agricultural workers lived in squalor and poverty. Niebuhr described their conditions as the most tragic in the whole country. In extreme cases, they were reduced to semi-slavery without any legal protection. The criminal justice system itself was among their exploiters. Howard Kester, a close friend of Niebuhr's and of Norman Thomas, founded the Southern Tenant Farmers Union, and Niebuhr wrote the preface for his *Revolt Among the Sharecroppers*.

Sherwood Eddy's response to the eviction of tenant farmers he found living in tents, shacks, and caves in the South was to found the Delta Cooperative Farm. Reinhold Niebuhr became chairman of the board, and from 1936 into the early 1940s he labored to finance and organize this interracial community in the Mississippi Delta. On the farm, economic cooperation between the races was achieved as poor whites and poor African Americans labored together to throw off the tenant farming system. To Niebuhr, this cooperative movement seemed "the most significant experiment in social Christianity now being conducted in America."[77] Over against a system that in some ways was more dehumanizing than slavery, the cooperative movement tried to give the poor economic power that was a prerequisite to liberty. "Freedom that has no economic base is a bogus freedom."[78] He regarded the farm workers as a Christian proletariat. The established church turned from them, but lay Christians and ministers were organizing the Southern Tenant Farmers Union and joining relevant biblical passages to their cry, "Land to the Landless!" Niebuhr recruited Union Seminary students to participate in the farm's summer work camps, thereby giving them experiences in integrated, cooperative labor.

Eddy summarized the principles of the movement as efficiency through the cooperative principle, participation in a socialized economy, and the rights of collective bargaining, interracial justice, and "realistic religion as the social dynamic."[79] The farm was essentially a Christian cooperative movement.

The hostility of the racism of the Delta, the difficulty of operating a Christian cooperative in a secular capitalist economy, and rivalry with the Southern Tenant Farmers Union eventually led to the dissolution of the cooperative, with some of the tenants becoming landowners. A medical facility continued, and there is evidence that the Delta Cooperative Farm "provided inspiration for several of the experiments in community rescue which Franklin Roosevelt undertook in the later years of the New Deal."[80]

Niebuhr's apology for the Delta experiment used moral arguments against racism but argued that moral suasion has to be joined with economic power to liberate the poor from racism and exploitation. The project received aid from the Niebuhr-founded Fellowship of Socialist Christians, as did the Southern Tenant Farmers Union and the Fellowship of Southern Churchmen. The founding and labor on behalf of these organizations is vital in understanding Niebuhr's social ethics. Voluntary institutions were part of the tradition of social Christianity he had inherited from Calvinistic social ethics and an essential part of his social strategy. All of these were parachurch organizations that could take on ministry in areas in which the official church was reluctant to move or in ministries to which the establishment church was opposed.

Sam Franklin, the director of the Delta Cooperative Farm in Rochdale, Mississippi, described Niebuhr as the dominant influence on the philosophy of the farm, though not responsible for day-to-day decisions. Franklin described the project as one more of Niebuhr's projects, but recorded, "His influence is certainly one of the key facts in the history of our organization."[81] Sherwood Eddy was joined on the board by Niebuhr's friend Bishop William Scarlett and, originally, four others. The farm followed a program of totally cooperative or communal production, distributed its goods through a cooperative store, and sponsored a credit cooperative. The Rochdale Community Church was probably the first integrated church in twentieth-century Mississippi. By the end of the second year, the cooperative purchased another farm in Mississippi and was attracting volunteers who invested themselves in it. The farm received visitors from the nation interested in alternative economic structures. Norman Thomas went to visit in 1938 and supported the farm. Eleanor Roosevelt invited Sherwood Eddy to the White House to discuss the project. But it had to defend itself against charges that it was communist, and the racist attacks on the farm were a constant harassment.

The farm in Rochdale was sold during the war in 1942 and the project moved to Providence, Mississippi. Franklin served in the Pacific during the war, expecting to return to Mississippi. After the war his mission board prevailed upon him to take a faculty position at Tokyo Union Theological Seminary. Eddy and Niebuhr thought Franklin, who previous to founding the farm had served as a missionary, should return to Japan. Franklin mentions Eddy's many missionary visits to Japan and records that Niebuhr had planned to come to Japan to lecture, but that illness prevented it.[82]

The farm at Providence continued the Rochdale program and successfully expanded the medical and educational services. In 1955, actions against the farm by the White Citizens Council were supported by the sheriff's office. In the climate of the murder of Emmett Till and opposition to the Brown v. Board of Education decision of the Supreme Court, the community opposition was too great. The integration of the church services at Providence was a particular point of attack in the mock trial held by the White Citizens Council. When the rally demanded that the farm leave the county, there was little constructive response from the local churches. The one minister who dissented from the White Citizens Council decision was forced to leave his church. The community tried to hold out, but by mid-1956 they felt compelled to close the farm.

Niebuhr responded during the crisis by saying that the Councils "are nothing more than a revival of the old Ku Klux Klan" with a little less violence.[83] His article detailed the attacks on the farm and expressed his doubts that the cooperative would be able to hold out against "this organized terror." Recording that many ministers were losing their pastorates because of their courageous stand on race relations, he noted that more were unable to speak their convictions. Despite the problems of congregations dismissing ministers, the church could not surrender its task to strive to overcome racism. He praised Catholicism's greater ability to fight racism and called for more Protestant integrity in resisting community pressures. If the church did not maintain that "God has made of one blood all nations of men,"[84] it would reduce the church to a vehicle of sin. Despite ethnic loyalties, local customs, and cultural traditions, the requirements of the love ethic mandated the oneness of humanity.

> Any form of the Christian faith which does not subject the natural facts of life and the natural loyalties and cohesions to these ultimate perspectives and judgments becomes a very vexatious force in the community because it makes an ultimate sanctity into a vehicle of sin.[85]

In his defense of the farm Niebuhr noted the clinic, the consumers cooperative, and the credit cooperative. Most of the cooperative production had been phased out as economically unsuccessful. As Franklin put it, "Collective production, on the whole, was a failure but it was not a disaster."[86] He had also noted several successes: (1) as a means of education, (2) transcending racism in practical life, (3) solidarity between poor and culturally privileged, (4) a cooperative lifestyle, (5) a local witness to social justice in Mississippi, and (6) a model for U.S. government policy.[87]

Franklin, who recorded the farm's story, was originally inspired to return from the mission field in 1935 to work in domestic social action partly by the impact of Niebuhr's 1932 book *Moral Man and Immoral Society*.[88] After a year of study with Niebuhr at Union, he became the major force in establishing the farm, along with Eddy's financial support. Niebuhr's own commitment to working out the inevitable problems in such a venture, and his chairmanship of the board of directors, marks his involvement. Together, student and teacher demonstrate an aspect of Niebuhr's life as a professor of Christian social ethics. The teaching was not directly applied social ethics, but the commitments of the instructor were, and his help was available to students who immersed themselves in practical social ministry.

Fellowship
of Socialist Christians

In the early thirties, Niebuhr and other like-minded Christians had organized the Fellowship of Socialist Christians. Its life extended under various names for the same time period as the cooperative farms in Mississippi, ending in 1956. The fellowship became better known when it began publishing *Radical Religion* in 1935.[89] The fellowship evolved, with Niebuhr's leadership remaining a constant as it changed its name to the Frontier Fellowship and then to Christian Action in September 1951. The Christian Action form of the society had "850 members in 42 states and 9 countries" in 1954.[90]

The central supporters of the Fellowship of Social Christians and *Radical Religion* in its earliest days were Reinhold Niebuhr, Winnifred Wygal, Eduard Heimann, Joseph F. Fletcher, Sherwood Eddy, Paul Tillich, John C. Bennett, Harry Bone, and Rose Terlin. The work of the fellowship was that of social theology, and its political and economic commitments were in terms of socialism. The group was noncommunist but understood itself to be in debt to Karl Marx in terms of social philosophy, if not in metaphysics. The editor's philosophy included, in 1943, a program of socialization of major centers of property.

> It is quite obvious that these forms of "private" property which represent primarily social power, and the most potent social power of our day at that, cannot remain in private hands. The socialization of such property is a *sine qua non* of social justice.[91]

The earliest form of the society regarded Christian ethics as being in direct conflict with the ethos of capitalist individualism and its structures. The group recognized the class struggle and called for "the aggressive assertion of the rights of the exploited and the disinherited." They hoped that class warfare could be avoided by all classes coming to recognize the need for radical social change. This position recognized the "covert and overt violence inherent in the present order."[92]

The declaration of objectives called for the application of Christian ethics to individual lives, to unite radical groups within the churches to strengthen their socialist influence, to encourage revolutionary social change, and to help the radical social movement to be more infused with "the religious spirit."

Members were obligated to take on Christian socialist discipline for social action and witness, including joining labor unions, organizing within their churches, joining in public social conflicts nonviolently, supporting socialist political parties, and paying on a "graded tax schedule" for causes that supported the aims of the "cooperative commonwealth" and the society itself. The "graded tax schedule" was highly progressive and required as contribution all the net taxable income of a family beyond $8,000.

Much of the work of the society retreats and publications was theological. Both Tillich and Niebuhr were writing their major theological works during the time of the society's life.[93] Bennett listed five areas that he remembered as the major emphases of political-economic discussion in the society: (1) the continued evaluation of Soviet communism through the late 1930s, (2) response to the rise of fascism [both Tillich and Heimann were refugees from Nazism], (3) response to World War II, (4) the movement away from the Socialist Party to the New Deal with Niebuhr himself campaigning for Franklin D. Roosevelt in the closing days of the 1936 campaign,[94] and (5) evolution in the thought about socialism. A. T. Mollegen's summary of 1943 had described the society as supporting autonomous public agencies like TVA, cooperatives, socialization of centers of economic power while guarding against state tyranny, and organized labor.[95]

In the closing years of the fellowship, as it merged into Christian Action, the membership grew to 1,200 and there were about a dozen local chapters. Much of the new organization's energy was put into combating the McCarthy movement and spirit in the early 1950s. Effort was also made to distinguish Christian social action from Marxism. Other foes that received critiques were the various movements trying to synthesize capitalist individualism and Christianity. The group also encouraged a positive relationship between Christian faith and democratic political participation, and they seemed to prevail in clarifying that issue.[96]

The leaders of Christian Action were involved in many other similar causes, in their denominations and in the ecumenical movement. Niebuhr was unable to give it as much energy after his 1952 stroke. The burden of financing a national office detracted from the work. Denominations were evolving their own social action programs, and the National Council of Churches was promising a vital program in social analysis and action. All these factors combined with a conviction that fresh analysis of the political economy was needed rather than the continued application of a fading Christian socialist consensus. *Christianity and Society* was discontinued in the summer of 1956, after the national office of Christian Action was closed in February. For about twenty years these ventures of publication, fellowship, study, and support of social action had received Niebuhr's support. They also had drawn the Union Theological students into expressions of social thought and action and become part of their education. During Niebuhr's lifetime, the intellectual legacy was continued by *Christianity and Crisis* while the political work was directed into Americans for Democratic Action and the Liberal Party.

NOTES

1. *The World Tomorrow* 9 (Oct. 1926), 143.

2. Reinhold Niebuhr, "Professor's Column," *The Union Seminary Tower* (May 1960), p. 3.

3. This section and the seven that follow are an edited version of my *Reinhold Niebuhr: Prophet to Politicians* (Nashville: Abingdon Press, 1972), pp. 55–83.

4. Reinhold Niebuhr, "Political Action and Social Change," *The World Tomorrow* 12 (Dec. 1929), 491–493.

5. Reinhold Niebuhr, "Property and the Ethical Life," *The World Tomorrow* 14 (Jan. 1931), 19.

6. Reinhold Niebuhr, "Is Peace or Justice the Goal?," *The World Tomorrow* 4 (Sept. 21, 1932), 276.

7. Rauschenbusch's thought was not as devoid of the idea of class struggle as Niebuhr suggested. Rauschenbusch's idea of the class struggle was different from Marx's, but so was Niebuhr's. The concluding chapter of *Christianity and the Social Crisis* is filled with references. Rauschenbusch wrote, for example, "The class struggle is bound to be transformed to the field of politics in our country in some form. It would be folly if the working class failed to use the leverage which their political power gives them. This is a war of conflicting interests which is not likely to be fought out in love and tenderness. The possessing class will make concessions not in brotherly love but in fear because it has to. The working class will force its demands, not merely because they are just but because it feels it cannot do without them, and because it is strong enough to coerce." Walter Rauschenbusch, *Christianity and the Social Crisis* (New York: Macmillan Co., 1909), p. 411.

8. Niebuhr, "Is Peace or Justice the Goal?," p. 276.

9. Reinhold Niebuhr, "Radicalism and Religion," *The World Tomorrow* 14 (Oct. 1931), 324–327.

10. Statement by Reinhold Niebuhr, personal interview, Dec. 16, 1966.

11. Reinhold Niebuhr, "George Lansbury," *Radical Religion* 1 (Spring 1936), 10.

12. Reinhold Niebuhr, "Radicalism in British Christianity," *Radical Religion* 1 (Autumn 1936), 6–7.

13. Statement by Reinhold Niebuhr, personal interview, Mar. 3, 1967.

14. Donald B. Meyer, *The Protestant Search for Political Realism, 1919–1941* (Berkeley, Calif.: University of California Press, 1961), pp. 233–234.

15. Reinhold Niebuhr, *Moral Man and Immoral Society* (1932), p. 165.

16. Ibid., p. 163.

17. Reinhold Niebuhr, "Radical Religion," *Radical Religion* 1 (Autumn 1935), 3–5.

18. Reinhold Niebuhr, "Russia and Karl Marx," *The Nation* 146 (May 7, 1938), 530.

19. Statement by Reinhold Niebuhr, personal interview, Mar. 10, 1967.

20. Niebuhr, "Russia and Karl Marx," pp. 530–531.

21. Reinhold Niebuhr, *Christian Realism and Political Problems* (1953), p. 36.

22. Niebuhr's tendency to overestimate the rigidity of communist dogmas is represented by the following statement, made in 1953. "Significantly the hope inside and outside the party that communist inflexibility would be modified, for instance, by the western traditions of Czechoslovakia or the Confucian traditions of China, proved to be mistaken. Communism has been consistently totalitarian in every political and historical environment. Nothing modifies its evil display of tyranny." Ibid., p. 41.

23. Reinhold Niebuhr, "Introduction," in Karl Marx and Friedrich Engels, *On Religion* (New York: Schocken Books, 1957), p. xi.

24. Charles W. Kegley, ed., *Reinhold Niebuhr: His Religious, Social, and Political Thought* (New York: Pilgrim Press, 1984), p. 126.

25. Reinhold Niebuhr, "The Religion of Communism," *Atlantic Monthly* 147 (Apr. 1931), 462.

26. Ibid., p. 465.

27. Ibid., p. 468.

28. H. Richard Niebuhr, *Christ and Culture* (New York: Harper & Brothers, 1956), p. 15.

29. Niebuhr, "The Religion of Communism," p. 467.

30. Ibid., p. 468.

31. Niebuhr, *Christian Realism*, p. 38.

32. Niebuhr, "Political Action and Social Change," p. 491.

33. Letter from Reinhold Niebuhr to John C. Bennett (July 20, 1930). Photocopy in the Burke Library of Union Theological Seminary in the city of New York; used by courtesy of the library.

34. Reinhold Niebuhr, "Making Radicalism Effective," *The World Tomorrow* 16 (Dec. 1933), 682.

35. Ibid., p. 684.

36. See Donald Meyer's analysis of the socialists' relationship to labor and other groups in *The Protestant Search*, p. 236.

37. Kegley, ed., *Reinhold Niebuhr*, p. 72.

38. Reinhold Niebuhr, "The Coming Presidential Election," *Radical Religion* 4 (Fall 1939), 3.

39. Ibid., p. 4.

40. Reinhold Niebuhr, "The Socialist Campaign," *Christianity and Society* 5 (Summer 1940), 4.

41. "With the ADA, in the postwar years, he accepted the established two-party system, never to resume his nearly twenty years of agitation on the fringe." Meyer, *The Protestant Search*, pp. 236–237.

42. The Liberal Party of New York State is a coalition including the International Ladies Garment Workers Union, intellectuals from Morningside Heights in New York City, and others. Its origins are in the domination of the American Labor Party in 1944 by the Amalgamated Clothing Workers of America. The Amalgamated was open to political cooperation with Communists as the ILGWU and Niebuhr and his friends were not. The defectors from the American Labor Party in 1944 formed the Liberal Party, and Niebuhr was elected a vice president. The Liberal Party supports the national ticket of the Democratic Party and exercises independence in choosing candidates for state and local offices. In the 1966 election, the Conservative Party received more votes than the Liberal Party, thereby reducing the Liberal Party to the role of fourth party in the state.

43. Reinhold Niebuhr, in an address at Union Theological Seminary, January 11, 1967. The statement was, of course, intended humorously, and it received a response of laughter from the student assembly. It did, however, reflect his continued position of practically supporting the Democrats since 1940. His support, however, has been qualified by his criticism of Democratic administrations and his continued support of the Liberal Party of New York.

44. Niebuhr, "The Religion of Communism," pp. 462–463.

45. Morton White criticizes Niebuhr for his somewhat careless examination of the facts of history and his doctrine of historical inevitability. There is considerable evidence that the "doctrine of historical inevitability" is most apparent where Niebuhr has deliberately hung a mythological interpretation upon a few facts. See Morton White, *Social Thought in America* (Boston: Beacon Press, 1957), pp. 247–267, 277–279.

46. Reinhold Niebuhr, *Reflections on the End of an Era* (1934), pp. 146–147, 161, 239, italics mine.

47. Ibid., p. 135.

48. Ibid., pp. 53, 59.

49. While arguing that pacifism does not adequately account for the need to balance power with power to attain an approximation of justice, Niebuhr paid tribute to Gandhi's tactics and predicted that the African American advance in the United States would best be served by nonviolent coercive tactics; *Moral Man and Immoral Society*, pp. 251–254. His support of Martin Luther King in 1964 emphasized the distinction between absolute pacifism and nonviolent resistance. "The second concern is about Dr. King's position on nonviolent resistance to evil. Many of the journals and the public have confused his position with absolute pacifism, which they reject. I think, as a rather dedicated anti-pacifist, that Dr. King's conception of the nonviolent resistance to evil is a real contribution to our civil, moral and political life." Reinhold Niebuhr, "A

Foreword," *Martin Luther King et al. Speak on the War in Vietnam* (New York: Clergy and Laymen Concerned About Vietnam, 1967), p. 3.

50. Reinhold Niebuhr, "Why I Leave the F.O.R.," *The Christian Century* 51 (Jan. 3, 1934), 18.

51. Reinhold Niebuhr, "George Lansbury: Christian and Socialist," *Radical Religion* 1 (Autumn 1935), 9.

52. Reinhold Niebuhr, *An Interpretation of Christian Ethics* (New York: Meridian Books, 1960), p. 170.

53. Ibid., p. 174.

54. Reinhold Niebuhr, *Why the Church Is Not Pacifist* (London: Student Christian Movement Press, 1940).

55. Reinhold Niebuhr, "Christian Politics and Communist Religion," in John Lewis, Karl Polanyi, and Donald B. Kitchin, eds., *Christianity and the Social Revolution* (New York: Charles Scribner's Sons, 1936), p. 457.

56. Reinhold Niebuhr, "An Open Letter to Richard Roberts," *Christianity and Society* 5 (Summer 1940), 30.

57. A. J. Muste, *Pacifism and Perfectionism* (New York: [n.n.]; G. H. C. Macgregor, *The New Testament Basis of Pacifism and the Relevance of an Impossible Ideal* (Nyack, N.Y.: Fellowship Publications, 1960); John H. Yoder, *Reinhold Niebuhr and Christian Pacifism* (Washington, D.C.: Church Peace Mission, 1966).

58. Macgregor, *The New Testament Basis of Pacifism*, p. 144.

59. Yoder, *Reinhold Niebuhr and Christian Pacifism*, p. 7.

60. Niebuhr, *Moral Man and Immoral Society*, p. 233.

61. Niebuhr, *An Interpretation of Christian Ethics*, p. 18.

62. Niebuhr, *Moral Man and Immoral Society*, p. 270.

63. Niebuhr, *An Interpretation of Christian Ethics*, p. 147.

64. Ibid., p. 149.

65. Niebuhr, *Moral Man and Immoral Society*, p. 273.

66. Ibid., p. 253.

67. Ibid., p. 252.

68. Ibid., p. 254.

69. See Kenneth L. Smith and Ira G. Zepp, Jr., *Search for the Beloved Community: The Thinking of Martin Luther King, Jr.* (Valley Forge, Pa.: Judson Press, 1974), for the best discussion of King's thought and his relationship to Reinhold Niebuhr.

70. Marshall Surratt, "Myles Horton: Activism and Gospel," *Christianity and Crisis* 50 (Dec. 17, 1990), 399.

71. Ibid.

72. Ibid., p. 400.

73. Ibid.

74. Sam H. Franklin, *Early Years of the Delta Cooperative Farm and the Providence Cooperative Farm* (privately published and circulated, a copy in the Pittsburgh Theological Seminary Library, 1980).

75. Ibid., pp. 1–2.

76. Ibid.

77. Reinhold Niebuhr, "Meditations from Mississippi," *The Christian Century* 54 (Feb. 10, 1937), 184.

78. Ibid.

79. Sherwood Eddy, "The Delta Cooperative's First Year," *The Christian Century* 54 (Feb. 3, 1937), 139.

80. Paul Merkley, *Reinhold Niebuhr: A Political Account* (Montreal: McGill-Queens University Press, 1975), p. 256.

81. Franklin, *Early Years*, p. 21.

82. Ibid., p. 82.

83. Reinhold Niebuhr, "The Race Problem in America," *Christianity and Crisis* 15, no. 22 (Dec. 26, 1955), 169.

84. Ibid., p. 170.

85. Ibid.

86. Franklin, *Early Years*, p. 92.

87. Ibid., p. 94.

88. Ibid., p. 6.

89. John C. Bennett, "Tillich and the Fellowship of Socialist Christians," *North American Paul Tillich Society Newsletter* 16 (Oct. 1990), 3.

90. Reinhold Niebuhr, "The Significance of the Growth of Christian Action," *Christianity and Crisis* 14 (Mar. 22, 1954), 30.

91. Note on A. T. Mollegen, "The Common Convictions of the Fellowship of Socialist Christians," *Christianity and Society* 8 (Spring 1943), 28.

92. "The Fellowship of Socialist Christians," reprinted in *Radical Religion* 1 (Winter 1973), 7.

93. Bennett, "Tillich and the Fellowship," p. 3.

94. Conversation with Charles Brown (June 2, 1991), who presented evidence from Richard Fox, *Reinhold Niebuhr: A Biography* (New York: Pantheon Books, 1985), and independent confirmations of those who heard him speak.

95. The five points are summarized in Bennett, "Tillich and the Fellowship," pp. 3–5.

96. Robert T. Handy, "Christian Action in Perspective," *Christianity and Society* 21 (Summer 1956), 10–14.

5

War and Lectures
on Human Nature
1932–1941

IN NIEBUHR'S early years at Union, he had mastered the material for his courses, edited *The World Tomorrow*, begun an academic career, lectured and preached around the country, published two books, run for the New York State House of Representatives and the U.S. Congress, and courted and married. In these four years, which he described as the period in which the Social Gospel's influence at Union was declining, he also went through a major intellectual change.[1]

The second period, 1932–1945, was bracketed by Hitler's rise to power and the end of World War II. These are the years of Niebuhr's most significant publications—*Moral Man and Immoral Society, The Nature and Destiny of Man*, and *The Children of Light and the Children of Darkness*—and of his rise to the intellectual leadership of significant aspects of the Protestant community. It marked a movement in his scholarship from Social Gospel to Christian realism.

The events of Hitler's reign of terror shook Protestant theological education, impacting Union Theological Seminary and its students. The prewar debate at the seminary arrayed the pacifists against the interventionists. Niebuhr himself made the transition from pacifism to realism. A student from the class of 1933 wrote of Niebuhr's class in 1931, "He was in transition . . . when I took his course. He gave the best arguments I have ever heard from the pacifist position. His later change of view distressed me greatly."[2]

Niebuhr was of course a great debater, having excelled in the art at

Elmhurst College and Eden Theological Seminary, and he was quite adept at defending brilliantly a position he was abandoning. Or he would attack devastatingly a former position of his own, or one closely resembling it. Between this class in 1931 and the publication of *Moral Man and Immoral Society* in 1932, his pacifism weakened, and by the late 1930s he was arguing against it. Meantime, the Fellowship of Reconciliation and the Union Seminary student body were caught up in the turmoil.

Niebuhr's family was oriented to Europe, Gustav having returned to visit, his brother Walter serving as a World War I correspondent, and his own study seminars with Eddy beginning in 1923 with the support of his congregation. His New York City connections drew him closer to Europe, and his marriage to Ursula drew him more deeply into English culture and politics. He now had family connections to both English and German life, and his intellectual and political contacts spread across Europe. In 1933, he was influential in arranging a visiting post at Union for Paul Tillich, who had been dismissed by the Nazis from his teaching post. Niebuhr urged Tillich to come, promising that together they could create a "school." Ursula joined in the project, being the first to welcome the Tillichs to their Union Theological Seminary ground-floor apartment on 122nd Street. Niebuhr helped other refugees, but none was to have as significant an impact on Union's theological education as Paul Tillich. Eduard Heimann, Tillich's refugee friend from Germany, would teach part time in the ethics department while he was a professor at the New School for Social Research. Both Tillich and Heimann became members of Niebuhr's Fellowship of Socialist Christians, contributing papers and essays to its publications. Heimann, a Jew, converted to Christianity after his parents' death and was baptized by Paul Tillich in Union Seminary's James Chapel.

Niebuhr's trips to Europe became whirlwind affairs in which he might speak two or three times a day and spend meal breaks with political or ecclesiastical leaders. From these conversations, his own intimate knowledge of European affairs evolved. His command of German and English usually sufficed, but occasionally in Scandinavian or French-speaking areas he felt limited. On returning to Union, Ursula and he would host European visitors. The visitors would often be guests at one of the "at homes" the Niebuhrs sponsored for the students. Union served as one of the gateways to the North American continent for Christian leadership from abroad. In addition to all this personal information, gathered at home and abroad, Niebuhr read voraciously. A Union librarian told me, on the occasion of a 1980s lecture at Union on Niebuhr, of hearing the "whir of the rustling of pages as Reinhold devoured books in his study." Even if the librarian's smile revealed his exaggeration, the public record of the 1930s found in Niebuhr's published reviews of books about Europe shows his passion for keeping abreast of developments.

Moving Toward War

The Depression and the conditions imposed on Germany by the allied victors of World War I set the stage for dangerous political developments.[3] The shadows deepened in the late 1920s and early 1930s. Niebuhr, writing as a socialist essayist, focused on the economic causes of the political malaise. The various international attempts to outlaw war obscured the need for economic and social security of the central European populations. Reparations exacerbated the spiraling crises. Protectionist tariffs and commercial rivalries of the capitalist nations prevented rational economic cooperation. He concluded, "It is hardly necessary to argue at this late hour that the real root of international conflict lies in the sphere of economics."[4]

Since the early 1920s and the beginning of his European exposure, Niebuhr had been analyzing the dangers of German civilization.[5] Then, in 1933, what his soon-to-be colleague Paul Tillich saw as the eruption of the demonic seized the destiny of Germany. This emergence of evil into world affairs dominated Niebuhr's thought from its appearance to its defeat in 1945. The emphasis on sin, evil, and the need for realism that came increasingly to color his thought has its origins in his study. But the thought is in response to the horror of European and world politics.

Niebuhr was particularly hostile to the church's failure to attack the anti-Semitism of the Nazis. While praising the church for trying to preserve its independence, he criticized its quietism in regard to the "extravagances of Nazi terror." The Barthians had little to contribute to the whole struggle because, even though they were the element in the church most critical of the pretensions of the state, they would not fight for political alternatives. Outraged by the church's failure to oppose anti-Semitism, Niebuhr hastily charged, "Probably 75 percent of the church population is avowedly Nazi."[6] He coupled detailed descriptions of anti-Semitic atrocities with a plea for a worldwide Christian protest against the German government. He did not expect much help from the German churches, but the terror had passed the point where sensitivity to the feelings of German Christians should muffle protest. In August of 1933, he protested not only against the admitted facts of government policy but also against the execution of Jews in concentration camps.[7]

Niebuhr saw the United States as another threat to peace. The United States had evolved a form of imperialism (a term he used to mean a high degree of influence across international borders) without the usual trappings of empire. American imperialism depended on American business and engineering. He argued that engineers and businessmen disregarded the human factors of politics. He saw America as politically both the most powerful and the most ignorant of all major nations.[8] He particularly feared any policies that would give the United States military power to equal its economic power, believing the wedding of the two would blind the United States to the rightful claims of other nations. Regarding the labor movement in Europe as the most significant defense against imperialism, he pointed to the need for a labor movement in the United States that would resist the development of American imperialism.

Niebuhr's concession that America was an imperial power did not lead him to argue for a world power's active, responsible role in the period between the wars, as it would in the postwar period. After recognizing the combination of American power and political ineptness, he counseled aloofness from European struggles. He regarded the world, in 1934, as drifting toward the chaos of international war. The situation had deteriorated too far to be significantly improved by American entry into the League of Nations. Too many nations were contemplating aggression to expect an international pact against aggression to have much significance. The imposition of economic sanctions would probably lead to the war they were intended to prevent. In 1934, Niebuhr regarded strict American neutrality as justified under all foreseeable circumstances.[9]

During the Ethiopian conflict, his policy recommendation focused on Britain. He urged the maintenance of the collective security apparatus; if sanctions involved a risk of war, the risk was justified. He continued his ambiguous policy of recommending collective security for Europe and neutrality for the United States. The immediate problem was to prevent the outbreak of a new major war so as to buy time in which to work for a new economic system. The basic problems stemmed from economic rivalry, and the enforcement of sanctions against Italy by the successful imperialist powers had the appearance of a peace maintained by satiated robbers. Still, there was more than British interest at work in the League's opposition to Italy; the under-developed "conscience" of Europe was also being expressed. Yet the failure of British resolve to enforce oil sanctions against Italy discredited the League of Nations and revealed how little power, except that of Britain and France, was involved.

Niebuhr's writing on the Ethiopian question was quite typical of his later work on international politics, with one exception: He demanded action, strove to preserve the peace through power politics, criticized the self-righteousness of the League of Nations, and attacked moralistic illusions, but he did not emphasize American responsibility in the crisis. His reluctance to push for American intervention in European politics was due partly to his desire to restrain militarism in the United States and partly to a Marxist pessimism. He believed the anarchy of capitalism was destined to destroy itself in war, and he hoped the United States would remain aloof from the conflict. A sentence penned in commenting on the Ethiopian war is typical of his prewar pessimism: "It is therefore well to remember that the whole present structure of competitive capitalism is bound to lead to war."[10]

Gradually the two major policies Niebuhr had endorsed were exposed to him as hollow. In 1938, he admitted that a capitalist nation could not remain neutral in a major conflict. Capitalist economic motives would draw the United States into a European conflict again as they had done in the Great War. Neutrality and American capitalism were incompatible. He was also forced to admit that the democracies were unable to make a policy of collective security work. The experiences of Manchuria, Ethiopia, Spain, and China proved the inability of the League of Nations to prevent war through various collective security measures. In the spring of 1938, he thought the proper use of economic power by the democracies might stop the aggressor nations while running the risk of war, but he doubted that the political will for such policies existed. For the United States he continued to recommend a policy of abstention from the impending conflict,[11] going so far as to deplore the rearmament of the United States, even though a European war was imminent.[12]

In the late 1930s, Niebuhr saw more clearly than many that the irresoluteness of the democracies and the fanaticism of the fascists were leading the world to war. His own policy recommendations, however, were also irresolute and characterized by a drift toward the inevitable chaos. He urged that the embargo against Spain be lifted, and he engaged in polemics against the pro-Franco Roman Catholic hierarchy of the United States. His hopes for Spain were in the direction of freeing nongovernmental forces in the United States to aid the Loyalists. For a period he argued for a nongovernmental boycott of Japanese products, fearing that an official embargo would be regarded as a prelude to war. By the winter of 1938, he was urging an embargo against Japan. Gradually he drifted toward involving the United States against various forms of fascism. He deplored the Munich settlement, but he realized that criticism made from the comparative security of the United States was irrelevant. His writing between Munich and the invasion of Poland stressed the need for Britain to eliminate its equivocation and make clear to Hitler that it was prepared to resist further aggression. He praised Roosevelt's support of "so-called democracies" but did not urge that the United States commit itself militarily to Europe.

Once war had come to Europe, though regarding Nazism as a judgment on the confusion and decay of Western civilization, Niebuhr regarded Hitler's defeat as the sine qua non of a return to health. Much else had to be done to restore Europe, but the defeat of Germany was the prerequisite for the elimination of injustice and anarchy there.[13]

Niebuhr urged the United States to extend credits to the Allies and to serve as arsenal for the countries that were resisting Nazi aggression. He hoped, however, that the United States would itself stay out of the conflict. He believed it would, because he regarded it as unlikely that a democratic nation would go to war unless immediately imperiled. The division of opinion about the war in the United States convinced him that support of the Allies was the most that could be expected. He engaged in campaigns against the strict isolationists, but he himself did not urge military intervention.

With a rigidity uncharacteristic of his political thought, he persisted in the idea that a democratic nation could not be expected to engage in war until its interests were immediately affected. "We must accept the fact that nations, particularly democratic nations, do not enter a war until there is no other alternative, as both a political and a moral fact."[14] Neutrality for Niebuhr had the character of a law of politics that was forced on democratic nations until their interests were directly challenged. The case for continued neutrality was strengthened in his opinion by the probable loss of civil liberties that would accompany intervention. Entry into the war would result in the war majority suppressing the sizable minority that would resist the intervention. He renounced his previous criticism of Roosevelt's military preparedness measures and campaigned for increased aid to the Allies short of war.[15] His chairmanship of the Union for Democratic Action in 1941 indicated his two major opponents at that time, "isolationism in the ranks of labor and reaction in the ranks of interventionists."[16]

When war came, Niebuhr looked back at arguments over whether the United States should enter the war and concluded that history had overtaken debate. The choice was not as clearly in the hands of the American policymakers as both the isolationists and the interventionists had thought.[17] The attack on Pearl Harbor unified the Americans and removed the last obstacle that had prevented Niebuhr from recommending intervention. He accepted the war as a regretful necessity, to be prosecuted vigorously but without fanaticism. He became involved in relief work, work for the War Department, and efforts for the German underground.[18]

Christianity and Crisis
and the War

The first issue of Niebuhr's new biweekly paper Christianity and Crisis made it quite clear that the journal was dedicated to opposing Christian and secular forms of perfectionism and pacifism. The journal was committed to active participation in world politics and opposed to isolation in its many forms. It emphasized the need for judgment in politics. Failure to discriminate between the degrees of evil in British and Nazi imperialism, for example, was neither empirically nor morally justifiable. The journal announced that, though it would analyze various political and theological issues, the most pressing problem was the defeat of the Nazis. The threat of tyranny was regarded as more evil than participating in a war to stop tyranny, and Christianity and Crisis attempted to present an interpretation of the faith that would be relevant to the task at hand.[19]

The second article of the first issue carried the title, "The World After the War." While admitting the difficulty of articulating war aims, the editor encouraged the democratic leaders to do so and argued that five great problems would have to be dealt with: (1) reconstruction of Europe and the definition of Germany's role therein, (2) reorganization of the national and international economic systems, (3) disarmament of the nations, (4) solution of the security problems of the small nations, and (5) establishment of a world political order and the abridgment of national sovereignty.[20] This listing represents the journal's most far-reaching suggestions of postwar settlements. Although the editor would return again and again to the discussion of war aims and to just postwar settlements, his reach never exceeded the country's grasp as far as it did in that first issue.

The failure of the United States fully to aid Britain evoked his wrath. The following quotations reflect the moral fervor with which he urged increased U.S. involvement as he argued that the decisive reason for Christians to act to repeal the Neutrality Act of 1939 was the act's immorality.

> We demand the immediate repeal of the Neutrality Act because it is one of the most immoral laws that was ever spread upon a federal statute book. Its immorality was accentuated by the misguided idealism which was evoked in its support. The essence of immorality is the evasion or denial of moral responsibility. . . . Morality consists in the recognition of the interdependence of personal life. . . .
>
> As with men, so with nations. An irresponsible nation is an immoral nation, while a nation that is becoming dimly aware of its responsibilities, and acts accordingly, is moving toward morality. The Neutrality Act of 1939 was the culmination of a recent immoral trend in American life which needs to be recognized for what it is and dealt with accordingly.[21]

Throughout the war, Niebuhr continued to comment, at least biweekly, on the war's progress. He generally supported President Roosevelt's conduct both of the war and of diplomacy. His major differences with the political leadership of the United States were on four issues: (1) he disagreed with the program of saturation bombing; (2) he disagreed with the policy of demanding unconditional surrender of Japan and Germany; (3) he opposed, criticized, and organized against the internment of Japanese-Americans; and (4) he urged more positive steps by the government toward the postwar world it hoped to mold. Niebuhr's occasional writings during the war followed the twists and turns of military and political strategy.

As the war ended, Niebuhr emphasized the positive tasks of rebuilding. He foresaw that the assumption of responsibility by Russia, Britain, and America for the shattered world would evoke charges of imperialism. He saw no way to avoid the charges, and in fact he accepted the conclusion that the United States in assuming responsibility would not be consistently wise in the exercise of power. He hoped that the concern of the idealists for the rule of law would qualify the realists' tendency to trust completely some new balance of power. This meant that the major powers would have to assume responsibility for building a world organization, for protecting the rights of small nations, and for encouraging development of the rule of law.[22]

Niebuhr urged the country to remember that the spirit of vengeance had lost the peace of World War I at Versailles. Germany had suffered severely in the war and should not be punished further. The judgment of the victors, acting as judges in their own case, could not be just. Though recognizing that leading Nazi figures and war criminals should be punished, Niebuhr vigorously urged that the victorious Allies distinguish between the Nazis and the Germans and that punishment not be applied to Germany as a nation.

After the war he continued to labor in refugee organizations and in groups sending aid to Europe. He was a member, in the fall of 1946, of a U.S. State Department mission investigating the educational program of the U.S. military government. He continued in the postwar years to plead publicly and privately for the humane and wise treatment of defeated peoples. His collected papers in the Library of Congress contain numerous letters written to aid refugees, dozens of items of correspondence related to relieving postwar suffering, letters concerning the provision of books to German scholars, and evidence of hours of work invested in raising funds and in sponsoring CARE packages.[23]

Following the war, *Christianity and Crisis* reaffirmed that its original purpose had been to interpret Christian faith in a manner relevant to the threat of tyranny. Its editor committed it in the postwar period to political realism and the new opportunities for creative politics, pledging that its emphasis would be on repentance rather than despair. In terms of the general outlines of foreign policy, it counseled (1) strategic firmness and a creative economic policy, (2) support for the United Nations, (3) international control of atomic energy, and (4) support for the principles of trusteeship in problems of colonialism.[24]

Nature and Destiny
of Humanity

The dominant form of Christian theology at Union when Niebuhr arrived was evangelical liberalism. It was embodied by President Henry Sloane Coffin, and it was continued throughout Niebuhr's tenure at Union by the succeeding president, Henry Pitney van Dusen. This form of liberalism valued tolerance, freedom in thought, science, Christian social reform, and secular philosophies. It attempted following in the direction of Albrecht Ritschl to work out from a center of biblical insights and traditional Christian formulations to engage new forms of thinking and organizing.[25] Other forms of liberalism received Niebuhr's developing critique. Less traditional liberalisms were associated with the religious education department, led by Professor Harrison Elliott and reflecting the thought of John Dewey.

Also represented in the current of theological debate were various philosophical theologies, including forms of Christian naturalism; these were particularly strong at the University of Chicago. John C. Bennett also portrayed Harry Ward's tension with Niebuhr as deriving from Ward's early liberal Social Gospel thought as well as with his later sympathies for forms of Marxism and the Soviet Union.[26] In the 1930s, as Niebuhr became more and more concerned about the world situation, his attacks on these various forms of liberalism increased. Most of all, of course, he wanted to unite theological soberness about the human condition with a realistic analysis of the world political-economic situation.

In 1938, Niebuhr reduced his practical political life somewhat to undertake preparation of the Gifford Lectures. Lord Gifford's generous bequest had established the lectures at the universities of Edinburgh, Glasgow, St. Andrews, and Aberdeen to promote natural theology. Niebuhr's immediate predecessor at Edinburgh had been physiologist Charles Scott Sherrington from Oxford, who later published his lecture as *Man on His Nature*. Albert Schweitzer preceded Sherrington at Edinburgh. Karl Barth had been the Gifford lecturer at Aberdeen in 1936–38. The lectureships had become, since their initiation in 1888, the most prestigious in the English-speaking world. Richard Kroner, a refugee from Kiel who would come to Union in 1942, delivered his Gifford lecture on "The Primacy of Faith" at St. Andrews in 1939–40.

The listing of Niebuhr's lectures as given during the academic years of 1938–39 and 1939–40 has led to confusion.[27] They were given in the spring of 1939 and the fall of 1939. The Niebuhr family, with newly born daughter Elisabeth, took up residence in Scotland in the spring of 1939, lived in Sussex in the summer, and (except for Reinhold) returned home for the fall school year with the outbreak of World War II.

The influence of Niebuhr's intense preparation for the lectureship was felt at Union. In the fall of 1938 he offered, for the first time, a philosophy of religion course titled "The Christian View of Human

Nature and Human Destiny." He then took a sabbatical for the Giffords in the spring of 1939 and arrived back at Union late to complete the fall semester of 1939. The two-credit course given each semester became a mainstay of Niebuhr's teaching. Significantly, it was offered as a philosophy of religion course, though sometimes it was cross-listed as a systematic theology course. The course covered two semesters, corresponding in one term to the first lecture, on Human Nature, and in the other to the second, Human Destiny, and was given regularly until Niebuhr's retirement in 1960. Some years only one semester would be offered and other years both. It replaced his earlier courses in philosophy of religion, which he had taught since his arrival in 1928. Niebuhr's perception of his lectures as philosophy of religion was not reciprocated by Stanley L. Jaki, a historian of the Gifford Lectures, who dismissed his philosophy as dependent upon "Barthian neo-orthodoxy"[28] and the Barthian critique of metaphysics and epistemology. Jaki's comments on Dewey and James indicated that he had little understanding either of the epistemology of the American pragmatists or of Niebuhr's method.

Though Niebuhr's 1938–39 correspondence reveals some insecurity in delivering the prestigious lectures, this should not be overemphasized. He found time to prepare them even though the second series had to be completed in the United Kingdom. With a topic like human nature and destiny, he had to reach down into himself and draw upon everything he knew, from experience and literature and from studies at Elmhurst, Eden, and Yale to the present courses he was teaching at Union.

Niebuhr set himself the task of providing a Christian interpretation of the human situation. He had moved beyond correlating Christian with some form of modern thought. He was not working out how Marxist insights can enrich Christian thought. Rather, he was claiming a unique and powerful role for a Christian interpretation on its own terms. Christianity was not to be understood as located somewhere in the foundations of a Western civilization that has advanced beyond Christianity in its maturity. Rather, a Christian perspective was more profound than the alternatives—ancient, medieval, or modern. He reflected on biblical insights and traditional theologies, but he interpreted them afresh for his own constructive development of themes. It seems best to regard his work as an exercise in Christian philosophy. He used the Bible and church history, but he was not writing history or doing biblical studies. He might draw upon many sources, but he was really doing new work. He spoke and then wrote a Christian philosophy for the times, concentrating on his favorite issues, human nature and human history. In the process, he provided a Christian apologetic: that is, he defended the credibility of Christian thought. If his portraits of humanity and history persuaded his listeners or readers of their truth, then they were already thinking like a Christian on those subjects.

The Gifford Lectures were published in two volumes in 1941 and 1943 as *The Nature and Destiny of Man: A Christian Interpretation*. The works were a success; many believed in the Christian symbolism that Niebuhr expounded. More important for social ethics, the Christian social ethic now had its own foundations. Niebuhr entered into the public marketplace of ideas with a persuasive and credible Christian message on the themes he investigated. Alan Paton, author of *Cry, the Beloved Country*, spoke for many when he wrote in his autobiography, "I think him to be the wisest man I ever knew, with an understanding of human nature and of human society that no one has equaled in our century."[29]

Niebuhr's first lectures in 1939 were in the context of the evil of Nazism threatening European civilization. Those who saw Volume 1, *Human Nature*, as emphasizing the Christian doctrine of sin were correctly reading Niebuhr's intentions; those who, in the 1960s or 1970s, concluded that the picture of sin was overdrawn had forgotten the context. A helpful corrective to a decontextualized reading of *The Nature and Destiny of Man* is the reading of *Christianity and Power Politics*, published in 1940, for it presents Niebuhr's political polemics of the period. He believed in the relevance of ideas. He believed that the illusions about human nature of well-intentioned people, including his own socialist and pacifist friends, had aided Hitler's triumphs. He believed the failures of both orthodox Christianity and liberal Christianity to present Christian ideas powerfully had allowed the emergence of the cruel parareligious movements of communism and Nazism. Cynicism combined with romanticism in Nazism was too powerful for a Christianity full of liberal illusions and committed to a past order. *The Nature and Destiny of Man* is not political polemic, but it is the foundation of the Christian political polemic of *Christianity and Power Politics*. When he writes in conclusion to chapter 1, "The fateful consequence in contemporary political life of Hobbe's cynicism and Nietzsche's nihilism are everywhere apparent,"[30] he is not writing about confusion in undergraduate academic life. He is saying that Europe does not have the intellectual resources to combat the cynicism and nihilism of its contemporary politics. Search as he will through the history of ideas, he comes back to a Christian view of human nature that supports progressive, reformist, social policy to defend European civilization against the rising barbarism. The volume still inspires theological students and lay readers alike, but it needs to be seen as dealing with resistance, here of the mind, elsewhere with force, to real evil. Therefore the tones about human nature are somber, but they are about Western civilization's inadequate understanding of the evil threatening it.[31]

The lectures began: "Man has always been his own most vexing problem. How shall he think of himself?"[32] To his audience of Calvinist Scots at Edinburgh, as to his theological students from the Reformed traditions at Union, this was a familiar beginning. When the lectures progressed, they would not be disappointed, for the theology of human nature presented was fundamentally in the Augustinian-Lutheran-Calvinist tradition. These were of course problems with this tradition from past ages, but he taught it as wiser than the modern alternatives. Humanity, he argued in the first chapter and then throughout the book, was best understood in relationship to God. Calvin's *Institutes* had begun by saying, "Nearly all the wisdom we possess, that is to say, true and sound wisdom, consists of two parts: the knowledge of God and of ourselves."[33] In his 1560 French edition, Calvin had put it, "In knowing God each of us knows himself."[34] From this rooting of understanding humanity in God came the perspective of humanity as a finite, created existence with a unity of body and spirit. The uniqueness of humanity was in relationship to God and humanity's transcendence of nature, history, and self. The meanings of personality and individuality were found in God's self-disclosure, culminating in Christ. The sin of humanity was also understood as "rebellion against God." The sin is located in human freedom, and it spreads from the spiritual to the social dimensions of human life. Because humanity's self-understanding in Christian perspective views humanity's squalor and grandeur in relationship to God, it is able, Niebuhr argued, to look at humanity more adequately than other anthropologies.[35]

Critique of Alternatives

Niebuhr organizes his second, third, and fourth chapters to criticize rationalism, romanticism, and naturalism and thereby to clear the field for a Christian perspective of the human situation. There is a problem: "What is human nature?" There are false answers to be refuted and then an alternative to be presented. He presents the first critique of rationalism and romanticism in the context of a formal problem that is the relationship of vitality and form.

Modern culture, seemingly on the eve of its destruction in 1939, had no adequate sense of the unity of vitality and form in God. Romanticism had broken the illusions of idealistic formalism of the bourgeois world. But its conclusions were untenable. In its fascist form, romanticism promised only destruction. In its Marxist form, the promised revolutionary reorganizations were illusions justifying destruction. The Freudian form offered only palliatives on the personal level and adjustment on the social. The liberalism under attack had to rely on illusions of harmony which the romantic criticisms destroyed. The presentations of Nietzsche, Freud, Marx, Engels, and Schopenhauer left twentieth-century civilization critiqued, but the critics were also critiqued.

The third chapter brackets the sorry outcome of contemporary philosophy with affirmations of Protestant Christianity's commitment to grounding human individuality in Christian faith. The modern world's thought, economics, and politics join to free the individual, but in its creation of modern society it enslaves the individual. Echoes of Max Weber's *The Protestant Ethic and the Spirit of Capitalism* and Paul Tillich's *The Religious Situation* are heard in Niebuhr's critique of modernity. The chapter asserts a major theme of the book, the freedom of humanity. Most of the argument is in the presentation of the philosophical tendencies to lose the self in a general mind or in nationalism. His critique of George Herbert Mead and William James are at the points that he fears they will eclipse the dignity of the self. The free finite self is essential to Christian thought, and modern society's tendency to subvert it shows the weakness of the times.

The basic problem Niebuhr finds with modern humanity's understanding of itself is the rejection of the doctrine of original sin. Its rejection of Augustinian and reformation perspectives on humanity force it to explain away human evil rather than seeing it as constitutive of human freedom. Human failure can be located by modernity in theological superstition, government organization, civilization, private property, sexual repression, ignorance, or cultural lag, but the explanations contradicted each other. None of the specific locations of evil equipped the historical actors of 1939 to meet the evil overtaking them. His lectures and writing on the innocence-seeking character of modernity relied on wide reading, study, and analysis. Much of this study had been done in unusually feverish academic pushing in 1938. Some of it grew from class preparation, but much of it was fresh. Through this survey of modern thought from Hobbes to Whitehead, he pushed his thesis: "The easy conscience of modern culture is practically unanimous, but not quite."[36] Optimism was less general, but he followed T. E. Hulme in finding modernity united in rejecting original sin. Such a rejection was a mistake. That conclusion prepared the way for the rest of the book's presentation of a Christian view of humanity with a central place for the doctrine of sin.

Prophetic Religion

As Niebuhr presents the Christian perspective on human nature, it is clear that he presents a particular form of that perspective. He is arguing for a prophetic view that focuses on evil in society and its overcoming. It is a Protestant's perspective of a critical and world-transforming character that he argues for in chapters 5 through 10 of *Human Nature*. It is the philosophy for his particular form of social ethics. The outlines are classic Protestant thought. Human nature cannot be adequately comprehended in its greatness and its squalor outside of the relationship to God. The relationship to God is understood through Christ. Therefore, anthropology in Protestant perspective leads to Christology.

The relationship of God to humanity is glimpsed both in individual apprehensions and in social-historical constructions of religious experience. The public constructions reinforce and are reinforced by the private experience of the divine. Human consciousness itself has dim recognitions of God, or that which Schleiermacher regarded as the experience of "unqualified dependence."[37] He identifies three aspects of human experience that can be made more explicit by reference to biblical symbols. There are experiences of "reverence for majesty" or "of dependence upon an ultimate source of being," of moral obligation, and of the need for forgiveness.[38] This appeal to general religious consciousness is, of course, part of the liberal theological tradition. Then he explicates three general senses of religion in the biblical language of Creator, Judge, and Redeemer. The analysis of human experience is moved in this chapter quickly into biblical symbols. The whole interpretation is to guard against humanity's thinking too highly of itself. Humanity grounded in the creative action of God, however, rebels and is punished historically. But the historical havoc itself is not just, and the final resolution of human rebellion is found in ultimate forgiveness and not in how history can overcome its tragedies.[39] Mercy and forgiveness are expressed beyond judgment, and here atonement and justification are argued for as the answers. Forgiveness is the ultimate answer for the social ethics of Christian realism, not the remaking of history.

The argument of the book, of the course, and of Niebuhr with modern authors then proceeds in chapters 6–9 from humanity as imaging God through human rebellion and its consequences. In essence, the thesis is that humanity is God's creature reflecting the image of God and that human evil is basically the refusal to acknowledge that creatureliness before God.[40] In the presentations of aspects of the doctrine of humanity, Niebuhr presents in each case an interpretation of the biblical basis of the doctrine. He then argues the superiority of Augustine's interpretation over previous views. The Reformation interpretation is presented, usually with a Calvinist preference. He draws upon Heidegger and Kierkegaard from their German editions, and they are noted as the most profound interpreters, secularly and theologically respectively.

The image of God interpreted by Augustine uses and moves beyond the faculty of reason in human effort to transcend its limits and find its home only in God.[41] The image of God is in the blessed life conscious of the Creator, including all the virtues of Adam and of Christ.

From the image of God, Niebuhr moves into the discussion of human nature as created. Here the full biblical picture of the shortness, frailty, and dependence of human life is presented. The appropriate responses are reverence and humility. In these pages the dependence of humanity on nature and history is clear, and finitude means absorption in these realities. There is no idealism here. Yet following Kierkegaard there is a high degree of self-consciousness and freedom, however it returns to its finitude. Then he traces aspects of idealism and mysticism in Christian thought, which he regards as obscuring the basic paradox of transcendence and immanence in history and nature.

Human Sin

Niebuhr's course lectures and his writings on sin were those of a Christian theologian, and it should not be surprising if non-Christians were critical of them. A Jewish historian friend of mine told me once how persuaded he was by Niebuhr's analysis of the human situation. Then as we walked by the fountains and the statue of Alma Mater in Columbia University's courtyard, he said, "I have to make a reverse leap of faith to keep from converting to Christianity."

The writings on sin in *Human Nature* are very systematic and very theist. Sin is presented in two ways:

> The Bible defines sin in both religious and moral terms. The religious dimension is man's rebellion against God, his effort to usurp the place of God. The moral and social dimension of sin is injustice.[42]

Niebuhr's faith and passion for interpreting biblical symbols, Augustinian and Reformation theology, and Christian existentialism were the most determinative factors. However, his location as a teacher of social ethics in a mainly white, Protestant, male seminary at the time of the outbreak of World War II is also important. The portrait of sin in chapters 7 and 8, among the finest pages written in Protestant theology, reawakened confidence in their own theology for a generation of Protestant leaders. The pages seemed true in the face of the confrontation with human evil.

The footnotes of pages 186–187 show the sources of the argument. Sin is basically prideful rebellion against God, as Augustine, Luther, and Calvin all taught. This pride is expressed as "pride of power, pride of knowledge, and pride of virtue," which expresses both self-righteousness and spiritual pride.[43] From these expressions of pride all human institutions are tainted. Philosophies and religions contain no exceptions from these corruptions. Pride appears even in the recognition of the sin of pride. Most of the reflections are on sin at the religious level, but the deceptions, cruelties, and ignorance connected to pride in the historical situation of 1939 are noted.

The second chapter on sin picks up issues from *Moral Man and Immoral Society* and stays with the thesis that group egoism is even more corrupting than the egoism or pride of the self. Large political groups tend toward "sinful pride and idolatrous pretension."[44] Germany is used as a particularly heinous example of national idolatry, but he treats this idolatry as a consistent tendency in international affairs. The nations pretend to be God and convince many that they are. Fascism and Nazism "have achieved a daemonic form of national self-assertion."[45] Such nationalism is incompatible with Christianity.

In the section on "The Equality of Sin and the Inequality of Guilt," he puts quite adequately the insight that all "are equally sinners in the sight of God" in tension with the recognition that all sins are not equal. The calculations between a little more justice or a little less justice must be made, even if they are made by humans who are sinners. People who are equally sinners may of course be equally guilty, and guilt may not always be obvious. But those with power and prestige are usually particularly guilty. The prophetic polemics against the rich and the powerful are continued in the New Testament from the Old Testament. While it is true that all may become guilty as they achieve power, the biblical polemic against the powerful and their religious supporters should not be obscured. Niebuhr's sentences showing the biblical condemnation of the rich and the powerful would please a contemporary liberation theologian, but then he points out that the basic biblical concern is about ultimate matters regarding the perennial human situation, not only about social radicalism. Moral pride from the weak is also dangerous if expressed politically. Still the rich, the rulers, the whites over the blacks and the Gentiles over the Jews, are all particularly guilty to a degree that the victims are not.

Niebuhr recognized that much of the Christian analysis of sin had focused on sin as expressions of sensuality. He listed these as "sexual license, gluttony, extravagance, drunkenness, and abandonment to various forms of physical desire."[46] This sensuality he regards as a consequence of the sin of self-love or pride. It follows pride which would not trust God. Hellenistic Christianity with its tendency toward dualism was inclined to treat involvement with the sexual as sinful, and Niebuhr is moving the tradition away from this tendency. Sensuality as a secondary form of sin extended self-love into dedication to a self-defeating reality, tended to find a god in another reality, and drifted into unfree or addictive existence.[47] The dozen pages he wrote on the sins of sensuality may be the least satisfying in the book. Treating all these sins primarily on the religious level ignores the complex moral level of these problems. Of course, Niebuhr was also addressing those sins on practical levels in other writing, counseling, and group activity. The description of sin so powerfully in terms of its prideful manifestations was just right for the time of the arousal of the nations. The expressions of sensuality[48] were slighted, however, and the possibility of sins out of the underdeveloped self[49] or from sloth[50] were omitted. In a different time, critics would challenge his understanding of sin on these deficiencies.

A particularly sensitive response to the questionnaire to Niebuhr's students indicated that his theology is not without its impact on the weak, the addicted, and those imprisoned in dependency patterns.

> We have twenty-four Alcoholics Anonymous and Narcotics Anonymous groups which use our church building. As the contrapuntal unison recitation of the "Serenity Prayer" echoes through the halls, I'm sustained by Dr. Niebuhr's insistence the Gospel be embodied in practical hope.[51]

The prayer was written by Niebuhr in 1943: "God give us the grace to accept with serenity the things that cannot be changed, courage to change the things that should be changed, and the wisdom to distinguish the one from the other."

Original Sin

Following Augustine and Kierkegaard, Niebuhr taught that humanity sins in its anxiety because it is so tempted in the historical situation. That is, there is a bias but not an inevitability in the human situation that causes humanity to rebel against God. In turning from God, humanity loses its possibility of fulfilling itself in the trustful obedience to the will of God. The self can only find itself in fulfillment of God's will, but in unbelief it becomes so encumbered with contingencies and misinterpretations that the self cannot help but sin. Only in the surrender of that sinful self to the loving will of God can fulfillment be found.

His concerns were to maintain human responsibility for sinning while admitting that the tendency to sin was inevitable. He would finally choose to express it paradoxically and argue that paradox was adequate to the situation. It is not clear that he needed to express it paradoxically. He treated Adam as representative of the race. The biblical picture of Adam says nothing about perfection, a Greek conception. If Adam, as the race, is understood in human terms, our misinterpretations and evasions are inevitable, yet particular acts of misinterpretation or rebellion are not inevitable. The human feelings of guilt and remorse over particular violations of human solidarity or perceived unconditional imperatives are enough to validate both responsibility and the historical inevitability of some sin that builds as it is institutionalized. Niebuhr's understanding of original sin can be freed of his paradoxical presentation of it, but it cannot be freed from his relating of responsibility and inevitability to humanity before God. Humanity sins in its freedom.

Niebuhr's name became associated with the term "original sin," but the last chapter of his first volume is entitled "Original Justice." Original justice is not a historical perfection or a state of affairs associated with Eden. It is the dim sense by which historical humanity understood there was a better humanity which it violated. Humanity should have done better and realized it. But human history indicated humanity's inability to determine the exact meaning of the requirements of its true nature. Humanity was not willing to follow the laws of its own nature, however they were defined. In its Christian expression even the higher theological virtues of faith, hope, and love were part of this original justice. The most basic principle of this original justice was the double love commandment. Other principles of hope and faith provided the theological context for love. Natural law revealed the need for humanity to fulfill the requirements of God, and the relative constructions of natural law that humans articulated sufficed for guidance. Principles of natural law subordinated to the theological insights of the Augustinian-Reformation theology revealed Niebuhr's meaning of original justice and his own method in Christian ethics. Cynicism and utopianism were dismissed. Insistence upon human responsibility and the need for a nonself-righteous resistance to evil were grounded in Protestant theology. The presence of sin even if made clear by original justice meant that grace was not primarily power to overthrow evil but mercy toward uneasy consciences called to work in the world. Between these spring lectures of 1939 and the fall lectures of 1939, the threatened war became the reality of the emerging half decade.

Even in 1941, reviewers of his volume found him overly pessimistic. Walter Marshall Horton, for example, after a long accurate summary of Volume 1, gently criticized only the pessimism.[52] Georgia Harkness regarded it as Niebuhr's best book but argued that a greater emphasis on Jesus would have provided more direct grounds for confidence in democracy and social action. Her suggestion[53] that Niebuhr's criticism of liberalism was overdrawn and indiscriminate was echoed by James Luther Adams.[54] George F. Thomas asked for a broader understanding of sin, suggesting that greed and sensuality are not best understood as derived from pride.[55] Robert L. Calhoun explained Niebuhr as a powerful preacher-theologian rather than as a discriminating scholar.[56] But immediately following Calhoun, that very careful scholar James Luther Adams wrote, "Not since the days of Benjamin B. Warfield and Charles A. Briggs has America had a theologian who possessed such a grasp of the riches of the Christian theological tradition as does Reinhold Niebuhr."[57] He also praised Niebuhr's relating of theology to the world. Calhoun, the most acute critic, had also written, "But in few lectures of equal substance does one hear so plainly the word of judgment preached with power."[58] Adams, like Harkness a liberal whose liberalism had received Niebuhr's critique, hoped that Niebuhr's next volume would address his pessimism with more hope and sense of what the goodness of God accomplishes through humanity.

Paul Tillich, exiled from Germany, did not quarrel with Niebuhr's realism about the human situation. He disagreed with several of Niebuhr's historical judgments, thinking that Niebuhr too often confused existential religious ideas with philosophical-theoretical ideas in his comparisons. In general terms, however, he celebrated the book, proclaiming it Niebuhr's best work and suggesting it was the best study on sin in American theology. He concluded, "It is a masterpiece, and it will reintroduce large sections of the present theological generation into the profounder problems of Christian theology."[59]

All major reviewers recognized the significance of the book. A study of the reviews reveals much about the reviewers and their own theologies; none of them could free themselves from their own unique viewpoints as they responded. Even so, their critiques caught the major difficulties. Niebuhr's historical work was too polemical and partisan for those who wanted a more careful, balanced scholarship. The perspective on sin was overly focused on pride to the neglect of other forms of sin. The critique of liberalism was too sweeping. Resources for the Christian transformation of sinful self and sinful society were neglected. It seems in retrospect, given the confused Christian and liberal responses to the rise of Nazism on the eve of World War II, that Niebuhr's polemics as a social ethicist are understandable. Calhoun's interpretation that he wrote in haste is probably correct, but it was not the haste of the preacher; it was the haste of a prophet seeing the reality of destructive war.

All the foregoing theologians regarded the work as of major importance, as did *The Journal of Philosophy* reviewer. None agreed totally in 1940 and 1941 with the work, but none treated it pejoratively or minimized its importance as did the nontheologian Richard Fox in 1985. Most of them also noted its significance in the development of Niebuhr's thought, which Fox missed by confusing it with the philosophical writing of Niebuhr's B.D. thesis of 1914.[60]

Niebuhr's course in human nature was prepared for the Gifford Lectures. He continued to revise it, as the course notes make clear, but the basic content was set. His theory of human nature became a norm on which generations of theological students sharpened their skills. It also has been a focus of much of the deeper critique of his work.[61] In retirement and reflection he changed some of the emphases in his final book, *Man's Nature and His Communities.* The second series of lectures at Edinburgh were after the war had actually begun and consisted of his theology of history.

Niebuhr's teaching was enjoyable and relevant. The students knew it had consequences. The model of humanity in the Christian life as sinful yet responsible for struggling for justice was relevant to seminarians' questions about war. In 1938, 1939, and 1940, many students came to the seminary opposing international war. Harry Emerson Fosdick was an influential advocate of pacifism at both Riverside Church and Union. Professor Walter Russell Bowie, who came in 1939, reinforced the pacifism, and Niebuhr argued against it. Gradually the nonpacifist interpretation began to win over the majority of students. The chapel rang with sermons advocating either Christian pacifism or Christian responsibility leading to war. Niebuhr was in the center of the conflict in 1939–40 as he had been central to student conflicts with the seminary administration over picketing and demonstrations for various social causes earlier in the 1930s. Several of Niebuhr's students volunteered for military duty, either as fighters or as chaplains. Among those who volunteered, the names of Robert McAfee Brown, John Dillenberger, and Roger L. Shinn stand out as leaders of the next theological generation. Another eight, including three seniors who had planned on having Niebuhr read their senior theses, refused to register for the draft and were arrested and imprisoned. Among this group Don Benedict, David Dellenger, and George Houser came to be well known for critical church leadership in society. As Roger Shinn reported later:

> When Don Benedict, reading Reinhold Niebuhr's *The Nature and Destiny of Man* and doing his own thinking about power and justice, changed his pacifist connections, he enlisted in the army and served in Guam.[62]

William Lovell, who refused to register on October 16, 1940, was clear that Niebuhr deplored the action. He mentioned that while the rejection of pacifism was "often caustic in tone," Niebuhr "genuinely and considerately answered pacifist questions and comments from students in his class."[63] Another of the draft resisters recorded the meaningfulness of Professors Bowie and Niebuhr in jointly conducting a Communion service after the arrest of the draft resisters. Roger Shinn's writing on this episode in the history of the seminary has also emphasized that despite these sharp moral disagreements, resulting in war service or prison terms, the students and faculty remained in community and communication.[64]

Hideo Hashimoto, who regarded Niebuhr as his most important professor, would in later life fondly remember Niebuhr's wartime efforts to persuade the administration not to intern the Japanese. Still, his memory from his student days is of his sharp disagreements with his professor on the neutrality legislation, which Niebuhr opposed.

> After class one day, I chased after Prof. Reinhold Niebuhr, Reinie to us, dashing off with his master's gown flying. I asked if I could agree with him on theology and disagree with him on social ethics. He said, "I suppose so," or something to that effect. That has been the story of my theology and ethics pretty much since my seminary days, especially on the issue of war and pacifism.[65]

The students recognized Niebuhr's importance and felt his influence. However, even on his central themes like the relevance of the nature of humanity to issues of war and peace, the students would neither then nor later unanimously follow his leadership.

NOTES

1. Reinhold Niebuhr, "A Third of a Century at Union," *The Union Seminary Tower* 7 (May 1960), 3.

2. J. Edward Gonzalez, response to questionnaire of November 15, 1990, copy in the author's possession.

3. This section is an edited version of my *Reinhold Niebuhr: Prophet to Politicians* (Nashville: Abingdon Press, 1972), pp. 85–90.

4. Reinhold Niebuhr, "Economic Perils to World Peace," *The World Tomorrow* 14 (May 1931), 154.

5. See Niebuhr, "The German Klan," *The Christian Century* 41 (Oct. 6, 1924), 1330–1331.

6. Reinhold Niebuhr, "Religion and the New Germany," *The Christian Century* 50 (June 28, 1933), 845. This section and the following section are an edited version of my *Reinhold Niebuhr: Prophet to Politicians*, pp. 85–90, 108–111.

7. Reinhold Niebuhr, "Germany Must Be Told!" *The Christian Century* 50 (Aug. 9, 1933), 1014.

8. Reinhold Niebuhr, "Perils of American Power," *Atlantic Monthly* 149 (Jan. 1932), 90.

9. Reinhold Niebuhr, "Shall We Seek World Peace or the Peace of America?" *The World Tomorrow* 17 (Mar. 1934), 132–133.

10. Reinhold Niebuhr, "Pacifism and Sanctions," *Radical Religion* 1 (Winter 1935), 29.

11. Reinhold Niebuhr, "On the International Situation," *Radical Religion* 3 (Spring 1938), 4–5.

12. "The billion dollar defense budget of the Roosevelt administration cries to heaven as the worst piece of militarism in modern history. All the reactionary forces which have been crying for a balanced budget raise not a word of protest against this supplementary budget for which no taxation provisions are made. Our nation like England is drifting into the worst possible foreign policy. We refuse to use the non-military pressure which we have to stop the fascist nations and then build up huge armaments to fight them when they have grown strong enough to throw down the gauntlet." Reinhold Niebuhr, "Brief Notes," *Radical Religion* 3 (Spring 1938), 7.

13. Reinhold Niebuhr, "The International Situation," *Radical Religion* 5 (Winter 1940), 3.

14. Reinhold Niebuhr, "American Neutrality," *Radical Religion* 5 (Summer 1940), 6.

15. The interventionist side of Niebuhr's thought is seen most clearly in his editorship of *Christianity and Crisis* in 1941, which is discussed in the next section.

16. Reinhold Niebuhr, "Union for Democratic Action," *Radical Religion* 6 (Summer 1941), 6.

17. Reinhold Niebuhr, "History (God) Has Overtaken Us," *Radical Religion* 7 (Winter 1941), 3.

18. For an interpretation of Niebuhr's connections with the German underground, see June Bingham, *Courage to Change: An Introduction to the Life and Thought of Reinhold Niebuhr* (New York: Charles Scribner's Sons, 1961), pp. 168–171.

19. Reinhold Niebuhr, "The Christian Faith and the World Crisis," *Christianity and Crisis* 1 (Feb. 10, 1941), 4–6. The section on *"Christianity and Crisis* and the War" is an edited version of my *Reinhold Niebuhr: Prophet to Politicians,* pp. 110–111.

20. Niebuhr, "The Christian Faith," p. 3.

21. Reinhold Niebuhr, "Repeal the Neutrality Act," *Christianity and Crisis* 1 (Oct. 20, 1941), 1.

22. Reinhold Niebuhr, "Plans for World Reorganization," *Christianity and Crisis* 2 (Oct. 19, 1942), 3–6.

23. Reinhold Niebuhr Papers (MSS in the Library of Congress, Washington, D.C.), Container 22.

24. Reinhold Niebuhr, "Toward a Christian Approach to International Issues," *Christianity and Crisis* 6 (Dec. 9, 1946), 1–2.

25. John C. Bennett, "Change and Continuity in the Theological Climate at Union Seminary," *Union Seminary Quarterly Review* 18 (May 1963), 357–367.

26. Ibid., p. 361.

27. Stanley L. Jaki, *Lord Gifford and His Lectures: A Centenary Retrospect* (Edinburgh: Scottish Academic Press, 1986).

28. Ibid., p. 26.

29. Alan Paton, "Journey Continued: An Autobiography," reprinted in *Kent Quarterly* 9 (Fall 1989), 30.

30. Reinhold Niebuhr, *Human Nature* (1941), p. 25.

31. See Reinhold Niebuhr, *Human Destiny* (1943), p. 249, for a short discussion of evil of the Nazi religious nationalism and persecution of Jews.

32. Niebuhr, *Human Nature*, p. 1.

33. John Calvin, *Institutes of the Christian Religion*, ed. John T. McNeill (Philadelphia: Westminster Press, 1960), p. 35.

34. Ibid., p. 36.

35. Niebuhr, *Human Nature*, pp. 12–18.

36. Ibid., p. 120.

37. Ibid., p. 128.

38. Ibid., p. 131.

39. Ibid., p. 147.

40. Ibid., p. 150.

41. Ibid., p. 156.

42. Ibid., p. 179.

43. Ibid., p. 188.

44. Ibid., p. 210.

45. Ibid., p. 219.

46. Ibid., p. 228.

47. Ibid., p. 240.

48. Judith Plaskow, *Sex, Sin, and Grace: Women's Experience and the Theologies of Reinhold Niebuhr and Paul Tillich* (Lanham, Md.: University Press of America, 1980), pp. 62–63.

49. Susan Nelson Dunfee, *Beyond Servanthood: Christianity and the Liberation of Women* (Lanham, Md.: University Press of America, 1989), p. 19.

50. John Raines, "Sin as Pride and Sin as Sloth," *Christianity and Crisis* 29 (Feb. 3, 1969), 4–8.

51. Response to questionnaire in the author's possession.

52. Walter Marshall Horton, "Niebuhr's Essay on Man," *Christendom* 6 (Summer 1941), 430.

53. Georgia Harkness, "A Symposium on Reinhold Niebuhr's *Nature and Destiny of Man*," *Christendom* 6 (Autumn 1941), 568.

54. James Luther Adams, ibid., pp. 577–578.

55. George F. Thomas, ibid., p. 572.

56. Robert L. Calhoun, ibid., pp. 573–576.

57. Adams, p. 576.

58. Calhoun, p. 576.

59. Paul Tillich, "Review of the Nature and Destiny of Man," *Christianity and Society* 6 (Spring 1941), 37.

60. Richard Fox, *Reinhold Niebuhr: A Biography* (New York: Pantheon Books, 1985), pp. 202–204. As one of Calhoun's reviews referred to in Fox is taken from the *Christendom* symposium in which Adams, Thomas, Harkness, and others participated, his ignoring of their estimates of the significance of the work is clearly deliberate. Robert Calhoun's knowledge of the history of Christian theology is beyond dispute, but his theological differences and disagree-

ment with Niebuhr on the most significant issue of the day, the approaching war, are also well known. His review also reflects his interested position, and his attack needs to be balanced by references to the praise of others, including Paul Tillich, for an adequate, scholarly evaluation of the work.

61. Larry Rasmussen, the third occupant of the Reinhold Niebuhr chair at Union, indicates his agreement with the reservations concerning Niebuhr's understanding of human nature held by the first two occupants of that chair. Rasmussen sees Shinn as agreeing with Bennett's comment that Niebuhr dealt less adequately with sloth and indifference than he did with pride. Rasmussen reports: "Shinn goes on to say that while Niebuhr had no peer in analyzing the sins of the powerful, and understanding the dynamic of their inclinations, he says less about people buried in the struggle." He quotes Shinn at length from *Man: The New Humanism* (Philadelphia: Westminster Press, 1978), p. 160, to establish his point. This point of criticism has also been made by feminist and third world theologians. Bennett, as we have seen, has made the point since before the Gifford Lectures. Niebuhr spoke about sloth, and his concern was for the downtrodden, but when he spoke or wrote of *sin*, it was usually the sin of the powerful and usually the sin characteristic of males. Larry Rasmussen's point made elsewhere by his colleague Beverly Harrison, that the limits of Niebuhr's perspective need to be appreciated is both a helpful corrective and a Niebuhrian type of critique. Larry Rasmussen, "Reinhold Niebuhr: Court Prophet," lectures at Union Theological Seminary, November 1986.

62. Roger L. Shinn, "Conscientious Objection: Remembrance," *Christianity and Crisis* 50 (Jan. 7, 1991), 415–417.

63. Response to questionnaire in the author's possession.

64. Shinn, "Conscientious Objection," p. 416.

65. Letter from Hideo Hashimoto to the author, December 7, 1990; letter in the author's possession. Also published in *Acts of the Union Theological Seminary Class of 1940* (Portland: private circulation, 1986).

6

Theology of History and Christian Realism

1939–1945

WAR IN AFRICA and Asia preceded the Gifford Lectures of the spring of 1939. Niebuhr's journal commented on both, and his organizations responded to these world crises. The spring lectures of 1939 were given in the last year that Reinhold Niebuhr would know of peace. The invasion of Poland in 1939 began the open war in Europe among fascists, communists, and democrats that, transmuted into cold war struggles over the same territory, would continue beyond his death. He first taught the theology of history in the context of the preparation of the Gifford Lectures. It became a permanent part of his course offerings, entitled "Human Destiny." The course grew, of course, beyond the first notes prepared for the Gifford Lectures, and as war ended and turned into the long cold war, refinements appeared.

The course growing out of the lectures was not a history course, as was the course on the history of Christian ethics. It was rather a course making use of church intellectual history, constructive philosophy of religion, and the history of philosophy. However, it was a course taught in a Protestant theological seminary by a social ethicist engaged in war or cold war. That is, it was existentially committed, both politically and theologically. In fact, its teacher believed there was no general philosophy of history without commitment. If history were not self-explanatory, only theologies of history were possible.

There was no reason to be more optimistic about the world situation in the fall of 1939 than there had been in the spring of 1939. In fact, in the fall, the lectures were given to the accompaniment of the sound of gunfire and falling bombs as a nearby naval base was attacked. Words written only a little later, while Niebuhr was editing the Gifford Lectures, betray his orientation. "Western civilization is very, very sick both in terms of its international structure and its domestic policy within each nation."[1] The sickness was partly of the soul. The answers of communism, fascism, liberalism, and Christianity, Catholic or Protestant, were inadequate. He sought fresh intellectual-religious foundations for resistance to evil, new orders of domestic justice and international interdependence.[2] Meanwhile, his family returned to the United States. June Bingham, reminding readers of the delightful dedication of the two volumes to Ursula and the children, shares a story about Christopher's return. " 'The King of England,' said Christopher to his grandmother on arrival, 'told all little American boys they had to go home.' "[3]

Theology of History

The theology of history lectures did not lay out the philosophical prolegomena that characterized the spring lectures. These lectures start within the theological circle, from faith. As in the works of Paul Tillich, who read the manuscript and made suggestions, there is a method of correlation: that is, the theological answers are given to the questions arising from Niebuhr's analysis of the human question. The question concerns "how the transcendent meaning of history is to be disclosed and fulfilled."[4] The reduction begins very quickly from the question of history to historical and nonhistorical religions. Within historical religions, those that relate messianic answers to the incompleteness of history are pursued.

Hebrew prophetic religion moving toward messianic answers begins, for Niebuhr, with Amos. He finds neither the prophetic messianism nor apocalypticism quite able to answer how God will preserve the righteous when the righteous are still unrighteous. Jesus as standing within both the prophetic messianic and the apocalyptic consciousness of his time is seen to give his own revised answer of a suffering messiah. In the symbols of Christ and the cross, Niebuhr sees the divine suffering accepting the sins of humanity and providing, through suffering, grace, which provides wisdom and power. The suffering love is not triumphant in history, but it reveals the divine will, enabling people to live in this history meaningfully. So the answer to history is disclosed in Christ.

History is an interim in which there is the possibility to live freely, but with new power after Christ, but sin and evil also grow in this human history. Absolute love gives power where understood, but it guarantees no particular victories. In fact, in human history, ethical decisions are made in terms of mutual love and justice, with God's love as an *ultimate* but not the immediate norm. Within this history, Christians knowing the power in Christ's answer still have to work out their lives prudentially and responsibly. One of the ironies of Niebuhr's interpretation is that despite all his care to distinguish between an ultimate of Christ's sacrificial love and that which keeps human life in order, many critics have regarded him as demanding that the weak or poor live sacrificial love. Clearly, for Niebuhr, the poor and weak must organize their own case to achieve whatever degree of justice they can win.

> The law of love is, therefore, not a norm of history, in the sense that historical experience justifies it. Historical experience justifies more complex social strategies in which the self, individual and collective, seeks both to preserve its life and to relate it harmoniously to other lives.[5]

The Christian answer to history needs to be inwardly appropriated, because in its appropriation rests its authority. The shattering of human pride provides power to live as humans with freedom from much of the power of sin and forgiveness for that which remains. Much of Niebuhr's analysis is a repetition, in terms of biblical and theological concepts, of insights he credited to the Reformation discernment that life would not be fulfilled either by grace or by natural power. He saw history as meaningful, but pointing beyond itself for fulfillment to God. He hoped that the emphasis on human existential meaning, found primarily through justification by faith, would release the person into action and produce a growing sense of social solidarity and obligation.

He pleaded for a synthesis of humanistic hopes for truth and the development of culture through the spirit of the Renaissance, while insisting on the Reformation doctrine that humanity cannot fulfill itself. In these lectures, the atonement that related God's wrath to God's mercy is the answer. History is serious; the good needs to be achieved. Human good is not God's good, but God will forgive. Humanity is obligated, but it cannot perfectly fulfill the obligations, for only God will fulfill humanity.

The major part of the book, the first six chapters, set forth answers of atonement to the problem of sin in history. The next two apply the answer of seeking fulfillment rigorously, but not believing it to be achieved in two areas: truth and society. Truth is to be pursued. Goodness in human affairs is to be sought after. But both quests, he argues, are better served if pretensions of fulfillment are avoided. The chapter on "Having and Not Having the Truth" is not a chapter on epistemology but a chapter on the need for toleration. Most of the chapter is an interpretation of the emergence of religious toleration in Western society. The connections with the rest of the work are not obvious beyond the paradox of having and not having.

The longest and strongest chapter in the book is chapter 9, "The Kingdom of God and the Struggle for Justice." It is still relevant fifty years later as a profound introduction to faith and politics. The dialectic moves from God's absolute love and its apprehension by humans to principles of justice perceived in the history of thought to institutions of human order. Love motivates the struggle for justice and relativizes it, for in Niebuhr's theology there is no perfect fulfillment of justice. The ethics are a modified or Protestant natural law ethic driven by love and the vision of the Kingdom of God, which is not realizable in human history. Almost half the chapter is material from his history of ethics course on the Christian development of ideas of the democratic state. The Calvinist activism expressed in James Madison's draft of the U.S. Constitution is credited, along with secular theorists, for fulfilling this development. Given the audience of Scots, Scottish theorists receive a little (not much) more attention in this history than usual.[6] At the end of the chapter, Niebuhr encourages hopeful nonidealists to struggle for more order in the international community. The chapter is remarkably sanguine for 1939—or for 1943, the year of its publication. The war still had to be fought, but this chapter is mostly above the war, discussing principles and their application.

In the last lecture he discusses the Christian symbols of the end and fulfillment of history. Here, as at the beginning of the lectures, he shows how a serious but not literal reading of the ancient symbols can help dissuade people from trusting in false absolutes or presumptuous claims to control history.[7] The enemy still is the pride of modern humanity, which despite all the evidence believes in salvation through evolutionary moral progress, or thousand-year tyrannies, or revolutionary governments. What is really important to him, existentially, was the confidence that neither death, nor life, nor angels, nor principalities, nor powers, nor things present, nor things to come, nor height, nor depth, nor any other creature, shall be able to separate us from the love of God, which is in Christ Jesus our Lord.

—Romans 8:38–39[8]

He considers the symbols of Christ's return, the resurrection, and the final judgment, relating each to the incompleteness of history and the possibility of hope. The Kingdom of God, discussed in relationship to political authority in the preceding lecture, is not tied closely to the three symbols.

The preparation of the lectures and their delivery was exhausting. On returning home, Niebuhr resumed his teaching schedule, which had been concentrated due to his absence, publishing *Christianity and Power Politics,* founding *Christianity and Crisis,* lecturing, and editing the lectures for publication. This led to the need for a two-week furlough caused by nervous exhaustion, and by 1940 he was able to see the pace of his work catching up with his health. He, too, was finite, as he cautioned others to recognize. He would have further opportunity to refine, revise, and improve his thoughts on these themes in the courses at Union and also in two books that developed the arguments further, *Faith and History* and *The Self and the Dramas of History.*

Responses

One symposium on Niebuhr's book in the *Union Review* brought together reviewers from Wellesley College, the University of Chicago, Columbia University, and the Pacific School of Religion. The reviewer from Wellesley, Paul Lehmann, was the son of a former president of Elmhurst College and a former student of Union Theological Seminary. Despite giving the book great praise, Lehmann requested a more explicit Christology to undergird more direct statements about "commitment to Christian faith." Edwin E. Aubrey of Chicago found the book overly pessimistic about human nature. He also wanted more emphasis on incarnation and similarly more emphasis on God's immanence in nature as a ground for the possibilities of history. John Herman Randall, Jr., from Columbia's philosophy department, across Broadway, pushed Niebuhr's arguments toward a Christian naturalism. He wanted to recognize Niebuhr as a prophet of God, but he was less sure of Niebuhr's claim to be a "minister of the gospel." Randall's attempts to more fully secularize or naturalize Niebuhr's students extended over years in his history of philosophy course, which was required of Ph.D.

students in the joint program between Columbia and Union. In his retirement years, Randall mellowed, confessed Christian faith, and even taught at Union.

The most appreciative review was by John C. Bennett.

> This volume exceeds my highest expectations. It proves what some of us already believed, that Reinhold Niebuhr is not merely a brilliant diagnostician but that he is also a great constructive theologian.[9]

Bennett found in the volume a better balance than in Niebuhr's other writings. The Reformation and Catholicism were critiqued, as well as modern liberalism. The use of reason in theology was defended, while the dangers of the pride of reason were acknowledged. The possibilities of human nature were recognized, as well as its sin. "The usual talk about Niebuhr's almost unrelieved pessimism is nonsense."[10] However, Bennett, soon to be Niebuhr's colleague, also had criticisms, of which the major one would be picked up in the 1980s by others. He argued that more emphasis upon the sins of *inertia* was needed. How is humanity to be saved from weakness and inadequacy? Bennett also thought Niebuhr's neglect of the church was unfortunate. Finally, the perfectionism of Niebuhr's absolute of sacrificial love seemed, to Bennett, to distance it too much from mutual love. Bennett suggested also that we ought to admire the humble goodness often found in human life. Wryly he suggested that we could take time off from theological warnings to admire goodness, not in ourselves but in others. Bennett's reservation about aspects of Niebuhr's thought did not interfere with their close collaboration and friendship. Niebuhr even asked Bennett to emphasize the positive contribution of the church to social reform in his courses, when Bennett was arranging his teaching at Union. Their enduring friendship and partnership contributed to the strength of social ethics at Union and to the health of the school. As he retired, Niebuhr encouraged a partnership between Roger L. Shinn and John C. Bennett to develop.[11]

The praise and criticism of Niebuhr's primary theological work revealed the tensions and ambiguities within Protestant theology and the philosophic community with which he related. The book also represented the foundations of his work in Christian social ethics and political theory.

The Defense of Democracy

Niebuhr wrote his major treatise on democratic political theory during the period in which Allied victory in Europe was being assured.[12] He gave the Raymond W. West Lectures at Stanford in January 1944, immediately after the Teheran Conference, and finished rewriting them during the August liberation of Paris. The resulting volume, *The Children of Light and the Children of Darkness*, was a corrective to the illusions of optimism that Niebuhr regarded as supportive of democracy. Democracy as a theory for organization of community was stronger than the illusions in which it was submerged, and he thought it would be stronger for being grounded on a more secure understanding of humanity than it had previously exhibited. The essay articulates one of his perennial concerns, that people who would be morally responsible in politics must also be politically wise. It also provided an ideological defense for a system that only recently had been on the military defensive.

Niebuhr regarded World War II as bringing home to Americans, the way World War I had done to Europeans, the refutation of all optimistic estimates of human moral capacities. The book expressed the concern that, to the extent democratic ideals were connected to optimism, they too might be discarded along with optimism. The optimism he regarded as having been invalidated was that of the bourgeois classes who, seeing their own group advancing culturally, socially, and economically, had mistaken their rise for the direction of humanity. There were still traces of Marxist rhetoric in the volume, but they had little importance in the argument. The traces of Marxism were apparent in his prediction that middle class civilization was disintegrating. He then argued it was necessary to save what was permanently valid in democracy even if bourgeois society was doomed. In 1944 he did not have much evidence that bourgeois civilization was doomed, even though he made such predictions; what he was certain of was that the experience of World War II refuted dreams of the early achievement of human community on a world scale.

The thesis of the book, that neither idealism nor cynicism serves the cause of democracy, was captured in a sentence that became one of the most quoted of the Niebuhr aphorisms: "Man's capacity for justice makes democracy possible; but man's inclination to injustice makes democracy necessary."[13] This theme is played throughout the volume, with the claim being that inasmuch as humanity is a "child of light," or a moral creature, it can achieve a degree of community and harmony. Politics can, to a degree, be the art of seeking the good of the community. On the other hand, to the degree that humanity is a "child of darkness," or basically self-serving, its egoism needs to be checked to protect the community from the will to power. Politics is also the struggle between people for control of the society's resources and institutions. Democracy, according to Niebuhr, provides the possibilities of fulfilling humanity's benevolent side, but it also provides ways of checking its will to power. The greatest danger is unchecked power, and democracy is peculiarly well endowed by its systems of checks and balances, elections, and separation of the divisions of government to guard against the misuse of power.

The intellectual defense of democracy needed to be undertaken in full light of the recognition of humanity's vital capacities and its tendencies to use those capacities to fulfill itself at the risk of destroying others. Neither optimism nor cynicism would suffice if democracy were to be understood as a perennially valid form of human organization. Neither liberalism nor Marxism sufficiently understood man's nature, and this lack vitiated their respective political theories. Niebuhr attempted to articulate a deeper analysis of humanity to serve as the basis for reflection on political communities. The dynamics of human nature led him to conclude that, granted all its problems, democracy still gives the fullest expression to humanity's vitalities. Other considerations led him to regard foreign policy as the Achilles' heel of democracy.

The Weakness of Democratic Foreign Policy

Niebuhr had not put much confidence in the ability of democratic states to conduct foreign policy since the exposure of the weaknesses of the Treaty of Versailles. During World War II, he saw Western civilization threatened jointly by the barbarism of Nazism and the ineptness of the democracies. He viewed the foibles of the Western democracies' foreign policies before the U.S. entry into the war as revealing structural problems in the whole foreign policy enterprise of the democratic states.

He thought the isolationism of the United States and the pre-Munich complacency of Britain were both due to the inability of democratic leaders to force their populations to sacrifice before their own national interest was directly threatened. Hitler was able to force the German people to sacrifice for the creation of an armed force; creating a comparable armed force before the direct threat of war was not a viable alternative for the democratic states.[14]

From Niebuhr's perspective, democracy was supported by liberal culture, which trusted that all differences could be accommodated. The culture had few resources for estimating the tragic dimensions of history. A determined foe could count on an inept and irresolute response by democratic opponents. Niebuhr thought Hitler had estimated the weaknesses of liberal culture accurately and, from his estimate of the weaknesses, had grown confident that he could destroy it.[15]

A further weakness of democratic foreign policy was the inability of democratic leaders to offend significant minorities in the country by acting against their wishes for the sake of the broader national interest. Niebuhr regarded the Franco victory as the first of many defeats suffered by the democracies. He thought that Roosevelt had understood the dangers present in a Franco victory but that fear of the American Catholic hierarchy, with its connections with big-city Democratic machines, had prevented him from acting. Resolute leadership could not be counted on in a democracy; moreover, even resolute leadership could not overcome the natural lethargy of the population if opposed by a force as significant as the Catholic hierarchy.[16]

The masses of a population could not be expected to understand the quickly shifting orientation of a country's foreign policy in a world of power politics. A country with a tradition of isolationism had peculiar problems in adjusting to the needs of the hour. To the extent that the leaders of a democracy depended on the foreign policy consensus of the nation, they were limited by opinions formed in a previous situation rather than in the immediate crisis. Also, democracy was always tempted to mold its foreign policy in the shapes of its demagoguery.

The prewar failures of democratic statesmen impressed Niebuhr with the weaknesses of democracies in foreign polity. The eventual victory of the democracies did little to dispel this conviction. The postwar situation provided some evidence that republican forms of government were ill equipped for the subtleties of international politics, and Niebuhr continued to argue that oligarchic forms of government were better equipped than republican forms for the formation and execution of foreign policy.

Universal Ideals Obscure
National Egoism

The politics leading to World War II confirmed in Niebuhr's thought the thesis that, while the pursuit of national self-interest was only slightly qualified by the broader values recognized by the nation, universal ideals often served as a disguise for the pursuit of national self-interest. Nations, like men, could only rarely admit the extent to which their policies were directed to furthering their own interest.

> Every national organism seeks to defend itself, and possibly to extend its power and prestige, in competition with other nations. Every nation claims that in doing this it is fighting not only for its own existence but for certain values which transcend its existence.[17]

The residual loyalty of nations to broader values refuted the cynics, who thought international politics were totally lacking a moral dimension. However, the use of moral values as ideological cover for the inevitable pursuit of national power and prestige refuted the idealists, who thought international politics were guided by moral choices.

The claim that nations were fighting for broader interests was not wholly false, or it would not have achieved the credibility it did. However, the claims of Germany, Russia, Britain, France, and the United States to represent universal values had all been contradicted by their neglect of these values when more pressing interests of national power were concerned. The anti-Bolshevik and antifascist policies of Germany and Russia were discredited by their alliance. The loyalty of Britain and France to democracy was belied by their acquiescence with the fall of Spain. The United States could not act until its security was directly attacked at Pearl Harbor.

Niebuhr's analysis of the element of deceit in the pretensions of nation-states to be pursuing universal values was similar to his view of individuals justifying their narrow, self-seeking actions by an appeal to broader values. The nations did what individuals did, but in the case of nations it was more blatant and more nearly inevitable.

World Government Cannot
Be Realized

Niebuhr regarded the defeat of Nazi Germany as the sine qua non for a new order in Europe. He hoped the elimination of Hitler could be followed by trends toward national interdependence, the abridgment of national sovereignty, the elimination of trade barriers, and the achievement of higher degrees of justice nationally.[18] As the war ground to a halt, he wrote, "We cannot have world security without much more abridgment of national sovereignty than either the great or small nations are willing to grant."[19] He agreed with the proponents of world government that security from recurring wars demanded world government in some form, but he could not therefore conclude that world government was possible. More probably the world would continue to live in relative insecurity from war. His theological convictions merged with his estimate of the international scene to conclude that man's international relations would be plagued by conflict. The very organizations that secured order on the national scene encouraged disorder on the international scene.

He argued that, imperfect as the Dumbarton Oaks and Yalta proposals for an international organization were, they should be supported rather than risk all by promoting an unrealizable world government. The political basis for creating a world government did not exist in 1945; "the traditions and habits, the collective instincts and impulses of the nations run counter to the ideal concept."[20]

Though Niebuhr served as a U.S. delegate to a United Nations Educational, Scientific, and Cultural Organization conference and praised the work of the organization in promoting cultural understanding, in his role as adviser to George Kennan's postwar Policy Planning Staff[21] he played the role of critic when world government proposals were discussed. His position was to promote all possible international cooperation and organization, but not to allow utopian visions of world government to interfere with the complicated task of securing the precarious order and justice that were available within the existing system.

Niebuhr's critique of world government plans, in addition to attacking them in detail, emphasized two major points.

> The fallacy of world government can be stated in two simple propositions. The first is that governments are not created by fiat (though sometimes they can be imposed by tyranny). The second is that governments have only limited efficacy in integrating a community.[22]

His political philosophy emphasized the organic factors that produce national community rather than the legal structures that bind a community together. Governments were the result of many factors working together for national cohesion. The factors of economics, language, race, religion, and cultural and historical consciousness were all relevant to the formation of a government. Community, for Niebuhr, was prior to law; government was a function of community and only secondarily a creator of it.[23]

While encouraging the development of a worldwide community, Niebuhr recognized that at present the forces of particularism are stronger than the attraction of any universalism on the world scene. A few alliances, growing economic interdependence, cultural exchanges, and the United Nations are heavily outweighed by diverse cultures, ideological differences, and nationalism.

The United States Should Assume Global Responsibilities

Niebuhr's attitude toward the world role that the United States ought to play changed as the country's involvement in world politics grew. Before World War II, he had advocated the development of a system of mutual security, with the United States remaining neutral. Before Pearl Harbor, he had urged that the United States help stiffen the Allied cause without advocating U.S. entry into the war. Following American entry, he argued for active U.S. involvement in the postwar settlement, insisting that the power of the United States required it to assume a role of world leadership.

His writing on the war, which filled the columns of *Christianity and Society* and *Christianity and Crisis* and appeared frequently in *The Nation*, focused primarily on the political issues of the conflict. *Christianity and Crisis* and *Christianity and Society*, the successor to *Radical Religion*, were both founded by Niebuhr. In both he often wrote on religious or theological issues and tended to use theological concepts freely in his political analysis. Niebuhr's writing for *Christianity and Society* was much less inhibited than that in *Christianity and Crisis*, which reached a broader audience. *Christianity and Society* was read largely by people quite close to Niebuhr's position, and he rapidly produced editorials for it in his most polemical style. *The Nation*, on the other hand, generally did not carry Niebuhr's writing on theological issues. His political analyses there were much freer of theological terminology than his writing in either *Christianity and Society* or *Christianity and Crisis*. He wrote and worked actively on the perennial Christian concerns of relief and refugee work. He wrote essays and reviews interpreting the character of Germany and probing the spiritual aspects of the struggle. He commented on diplomatic conferences and the twists and turns of American society. He objected repeatedly to the policies of obliteration bombing, unconditional surrender, and the internment of Japanese citizens. However, his major emphasis was to urge the United States to adopt farsighted political policies in order to secure peace at the end of the war.

Niebuhr realized that the power of the United States would tempt it to act pridefully and arrogantly. He feared that the nation could become imperialistic, but even more he feared that it would not act to reduce the international anarchy inherited from World War II. Throughout the war he urged the United States and Britain to bear responsibility for rebuilding Europe and restoring order in Asia. He knew that a failure of the Anglo-Saxon alliance to achieve a cooperative relationship with either Russia or China meant continued instability in world politics. He recognized the difficulty of maintaining a partnership with a victorious Russia, but throughout the war he thought wise diplomacy could preserve the wartime alliance after the struggle. He argued that, despite the unsatisfactoriness of a peace settlement dictated by the great victorious powers, failure for the major powers to agree would be tragic. While welcoming the late-war proposals for an international organization, he stressed that only great-power cooperation could provide a lasting settlement and avoid another world war.

Niebuhr thought prophetic religion contained resources that the United States needed in its new global role. Prophetic religion ought not to let the nation remain secure in feelings of national righteousness. The United States needed a sense of the severe judgment which was part of great responsibilities. He thought that God had chosen Britain and the United States to play a particularly fateful role in the postwar world arena.[24] He was quite willing to demythologize the assertion to mean that at particular times various nations and classes have special missions. The churches were to contend against the American tendency toward irresponsibility and complacency in national life.[25] There was also an opposite impulse in American life toward imperialism, which needed to be countered.[26] In his attempt to expose the cultural weaknesses of the United States, which encouraged isolationism on the one hand and imperialism on the other, he advocated a humble acceptance of responsibility and urged that it be undertaken in full awareness of what was at issue religiously as well as politically.

> We must not have an easy conscience about the impurities of politics or they will reach intolerable proportions. But we must also find religious means of easing the conscience, or our uneasy conscience will tempt us into irresponsibility.[27]

After the Cairo and Teheran conferences revealed very little planning for postwar Europe, Niebuhr argued for a new European unity that would prevent international chaos and war. He feared that a division of Europe into spheres of influence would guarantee future conflict. He criticized the Allied leaders for being so preoccupied with the war that they were unable to plan for the peace.[28] At the time of President Roosevelt's death, however, he credited FDR with achieving a "higher form of political maturity than this nation has previously achieved." He praised the President for his conduct of both the war and negotiations and noted that, if the proposed measures of international accord were inadequate, the fault lay primarily in the situation rather than with Roosevelt.[29] Though the cold war frustrated hopes for a postwar coalition guaranteeing mutual security, Niebuhr's arguments in favor of an internationally responsible United States were still relevant.

Relationship to Neo-orthodoxy

The view that treats Reinhold Niebuhr, along with Karl Barth and Emil Brunner, as a leader of the neo-orthodox movement is not entirely mistaken. There are certain broad affinities in the thought of the three. They all contributed to the attacks on liberal culture, politics, and theology. They all found inspiration in Reformation thought. They each emphasized, though in somewhat different ways, the gap between the sacred and the secular. The doctrines of sin and justification by faith in Christ played determinate roles in all their theologies. Also, they all regarded man's existence and history as provisionally tragic.

However, Reinhold Niebuhr's thought on politics cannot be deduced from the theology he held in common with the representatives of neo-orthodoxy; his political position and those of Brunner and Barth had very little in common. Brunner's political thought has a conservative note that is foreign to Niebuhr. Barth's political thought is impossible to define within the normal frame of reference of political philosophy, but his specific political judgments reveal a long history of disagreement with Niebuhr. Niebuhr's political judgments are consistent with his theology, but neo-orthodoxy did not determine his political judgments. Neo-orthodoxy itself seemed to be compatible with either radicalism or conservatism.

Niebuhr indicated that, insofar as he was in debt to the neo-orthodox or crisis theology of the continent, he owed more to Brunner than to Barth. The debt to Brunner is most obvious in *The Nature and Destiny of Man*. Niebuhr studied and was very impressed by Brunner's *Der Mensch im Widerspruch*.[30] The question of the volume, "What is man?" is the question of *The Nature and Destiny of Man*. Brunner's discussion of the themes of man as sinner, man in the image of God, the connection of man's freedom with his sin, and the greatness and the misery of man are handled in ways with which Niebuhr felt no need to disagree in his Gifford Lectures. Brunner's reliance upon the Reformers, while correcting their doctrine with the insights of biblical criticism and science, is also similar to Niebuhr's position, in broad outline. The tendency to examine secular answers to the problems posed by an existential analysis and to reject them in favor of theological answers, again, is similar to the method of *The Nature and Destiny of Man.* Brunner welcomed Niebuhr's more thoroughgoing engagement with secular culture and thought. The similarities between the two works are striking, but they result from the work of both authors on the Augustinian-Reformation tradition in an awareness of the prewar crisis in man's understanding of himself, not to conscious unacknowledged borrowing. One distinguishing difference between the two studies is the increased seriousness with which Niebuhr treats the political world. The discussions of politics in *Der Mensch im Widerspruch* are perfunctory. Brunner's tendency in *The Divine Imperative* to reflect a view of the state emphasizing only its negative police functions is criticized in Niebuhr's *Human Destiny.* According to Niebuhr, Brunner's theory of natural law served the forces of social reaction by favoring the use of coercion by the forces of the status quo while denying them to the forces of revolution.

Niebuhr's debt to Brunner is clearly expressed in his own words:

> I read Brunner's book sometime before giving my lectures, and profited greatly from his analysis of the doctrine of sin in his *Man in Revolt.* Subsequently I became involved in tracing the doctrine through as much of history as I could encompass. In the process I lost sight of Brunner and did not refer to his work, though, as he confesses, I had written appreciatively to him about the book. It was a grievous error not to acknowledge my debt to him, though my omission was occasioned by finding no specific agreement or disagreement with him which would require a footnote. I may say that Brunner's whole theological position is close to mine and that it is one to which I am more indebted than any other.[31]

Reinhold Niebuhr has been interpreted as a Barthian. It is a common error on the level of journalistic writing. However, scholars also have regarded Niebuhr as a Barthian, although an American Barthian. As careful a scholar as Charles C. West has attempted "to show him as the Barthian he truly is."[32] West did not hesitate to show significant differences between Barth and Niebuhr. However, his minimization of the role of Niebuhr's substitutes for natural law and natural theology and his emphasis on the role of revelation in Niebuhr's thought tended to support his case that Niebuhr was under Barthian influence. John C. Bennett, in an appreciative review of West's book, criticized his attempts to make Niebuhr appear to be closer to Barth than Niebuhr would admit.

> I believe that he [West] is quite wrong in his assumption that these [substitutes for natural law and natural theology] are peripheral to Niebuhr's thought and that Niebuhr is really more Barthian than he admits because the effective criterion for his theological thought is revelation.[33]

The fact that he has been interpreted as a Barthian, rather than any decisive influence on Niebuhr's political thought, requires a brief discussion of Niebuhr's rejection of the Barthian position.

The bulk of Niebuhr's references to Barth are critical. In many articles written since 1928, he attacked aspects of Barth's thought.[34] Though deploring features of Barth's theology, Niebuhr directed his strongest polemics against Barth's politics.

Barth's religious socialism collapsed much earlier than did Niebuhr's. Barth never found an alternative political program; though his theology became more transcendent, his occasional political judgments and his political silence carried weight. Niebuhr's 1928 article criticized Barth for his lack of "creative social activity."[35] In part, this was the criticism of a continental theologian by an American activist, but it was also an expression of concern for the lack of moral vigor in the new theology. He asserted in 1931, "If the Barthians are socialists, I think it is not unfair to them to say that they don't work very hard at it."[36] Niebuhr feared that Barth's religious perfectionism and his shock at the failure of Christian socialism had combined to produce a defeatist attitude toward social justice.

In 1934 Niebuhr deplored the tendency, seen particularly in Friedrich Gogarten, for Barth's theology to be exploited for reactionary ends.[37] He thought Barth's theology was compatible with either social liberalism or radicalism, but it did not seem to be involved in healing the wounds of Germany. He repented of some of his polemics against liberalism after observing how orthodoxy could be used by the forces of social reaction.[38]

He welcomed Barth's opposition to the Nazis, wishing that it had come sooner and noting that ten years earlier it might have had great significance in central Europe. As a theologian, Barth opposed Nazism on two grounds: (1) it was a political religion, and (2) National Socialism was not a *Rechtsstaat*—a constitutional state.[39] Niebuhr regarded Barth's Christian opposition to Nazism as an abandonment of his earlier refusal to relate politics and faith. Barth regarded it as a shift of emphasis.

Niebuhr's criticism of Barth continued after the war. He interpreted Barth as suggesting that Christians had no guidance for the pressing political decisions required by history. "Crisis" theology, however well suited for a crisis, was inadequate for the daily decisions that determine the nature and outcome of the crisis.[40] Niebuhr criticized Barth for failing to use the resources of secular political wisdom in aiding him to make important political-moral distinctions. He expressed this attack in two points: (1) Barth's focus was consistently too eschatological for him to worry about the "nicely calculated less and more" of which political decisions are composed, and (2) Barth was overly pragmatic, refusing to use moral principles and trying to look at each event anew.[41]

Niebuhr attributed Barth's silence on the Hungarian rebellion to a "Marxist creed . . . in his subconscious," "ill-disguised anti-Americanism," and a series of political misjudgments.[42] Even if Niebuhr had recognized the particular features of Barth's neutrality as legitimate, this silence on Hungary would have been intolerable. Even Communists criticized the action and broke with the party; as Niebuhr asserted, "Surely one could have expected as much of the world's most eminent Protestant theologian as of the assistant editor of the *London Daily Worker*, who publicly disavowed all his former illusions."[43]

Niebuhr's debate with Barth reveals more clearly than many of his controversies with liberal social reformers (1) his fear that theology can be a means of escaping from social responsibility, (2) his openness to empirical studies, (3) the need for principles of social morality, and (4) his willingness to judge theological systems by their ability to produce political justice and wisdom.

Relationship to Conservatism

Niebuhr's political thought moved from the left to a radical left position and then back to left of center. The question raised by this section is, How far did the swing back to the center go? Is it helpful to regard Reinhold Niebuhr's political thought at any stage as conservative? Though there are sufficient grounds for finally rejecting the term *con-*

servative as applicable to Niebuhr's thought, the investigation into the reasons why his colleagues, friends, and a major interpreter have regarded him as conservative reveals interesting features of his thought.

Eduard Heimann doubted that the suggested political move left and theological move right programmed in *Reflections on the End of an Era* would hold together. He was correct, and the developing theological consciousness of the Christian realist contributed to the suppression of Marxism within Niebuhr's thought.

Heimann emphasizes the pragmatism of Niebuhr's thought as the source of his conservatism. Heimann believes that the essays of John Bennett, Arthur Schlesinger, Jr., and Kenneth Thompson in the volume *Reinhold Niebuhr: His Religious, Social, and Political Thought*, conclude that Niebuhr's political philosophy is "a pragmatism which finds its proper application in an authentic conservatism."[44] The three interpreters do deal extensively with his pragmatism, but none of them classifies Niebuhr as a conservative. Schlesinger emphasizes the resurgent liberalism qualified by pragmatism as the final stage of his thought. Bennett explicitly denies that Reinhold Niebuhr should be regarded as a conservative.

> There is some danger in ending on this note because it may seem that Niebuhr has merely substituted a conservative creed for the radicalism of his earlier career. This is certainly not true. . . .
>
> In recent writings, Niebuhr makes clear that he cannot be classified with the "new conservatives" who also appeal to Burke.[45]

Heimann erred in naming Bennett, Schlesinger, and Thompson as authorities who recognize Niebuhr's conservatism; his argument linking pragmatism and conservatism, however, requires further investigation. Conservatism in Heimann's opinion is the logical outcome of pragmatism. Pragmatism as a political philosophy urges the preservation of what is, through accepting necessary changes. "For if we change what no longer works as far as is necessary to make it work again, then this is preservation by means of change, change for the sake of preservation."[46] Pragmatism is a viable political philosophy, in Heimann's view, when its presupposition of a sound political structure is realized, but it lacks resources for radically altering the structure. Pragmatism "loses its applicability when that which exists cannot be preserved."[47] In Heimann's view the economic scene, both domestic and international, is characterized by structural problems for which pragmatism provides no solutions. Heimann, a socialist, disagrees with

Niebuhr's break with socialism and regards his pragmatism as influential in the break. Niebuhr's pragmatism binds him to the modification of the status quo in a day when an adequate analysis reveals that radical social change is required. However, Heimann's short essay leaves the hard questions unanswered. He does not prove that the present economic system is headed for disaster. Nor can he quote Niebuhr to prove that the latter is opposed to changing the economic system domestically or internationally. Niebuhr's rejection of socialism does not in itself make him a conservative; there are many alternatives to socialism on the political spectrum. Niebuhr's participation in and leadership of Americans for Democratic Action and support for programs commonly identified in American politics as liberal make a classification of Niebuhr as one who supports the status quo with modification difficult to sustain. Niebuhr's sense of the movement of history does not allow him willingly to defend that which is destined to change. Heimann's real disagreement is with Niebuhr's refusal to read the movement of history through socialist glasses.

Will Herberg also regarded Reinhold Niebuhr as a conservative. Herberg refers to "Niebuhr's brand of conservatism," which admittedly is not the conservatism of those who describe themselves as conservatives in American politics. Exact definition of this peculiar conservatism is not provided except for reference to the fact that "it is enough apparently to establish a kinship with Burke."[48] Herberg thinks Niebuhr's awareness of the relative character of political institutions and his "emphasis on the historic continuities of social life" made Niebuhr's political thought conservative.[49] Although Herberg is correct that these elements are present in Niebuhr's thought, neither element is proven by Herberg to be foreign to the broad stream of American political liberalism. Herberg himself could be regarded as among the "new conservatives," but more substantial arguments need to be produced to place his mentor in that group. Herberg's association of Reinhold Niebuhr with Edmund Burke has continued through two more generations of Drew University scholarship.

Gordon Harland regards Niebuhr's conservatism as an important ingredient of his political philosophy. Harland reflects the emphases of both Heimann and Herberg. Niebuhr's conservatism is implied in his criticism of liberalism and related to both his "prophetic radicalism" and his pragmatism. Harland admits, while wanting to retain the term *conservative*, that Niebuhr is not associated with American conservatism or with the defense of the status quo. His relationship to "historic conservatism" is essentially, for Harland, Niebuhr's respect for its emphasis on factors of power and organic processes of social cohesion rather than abstract schemes.[50] He clearly disassociates Niebuhr from "the conservatism of scholars like Kenneth Kirk" on the basis of Niebuhr's own criticism of Kirk's political thought. Harland's work indicates how difficult it is to label Niebuhr a conservative. Harland retains the term, conceding that it is not the common use of the word but failing to provide an alternative definition.

The most developed work of the Drew University Burke–conservative Niebuhr hypothesis is that of Vigen Guroian. From his doctoral dissertation he has produced at least three lively essays on the subject. There are interesting similarities and differences between the political theories of Burke and Niebuhr. Usually Guroian does not claim that Niebuhr learned his political thought from Burke. He writes in his third essay, "Neither will it do to speak of Burke as a formative influence on Niebuhr. He was not."[51] Guroian's effort in its careful mood is to show "a confluence of important themes, concepts, and normative recommendations about the nature and practice of politics."[52] Niebuhr knew of the similarity and often quoted *Reflections on the French Revolution* to support his own judgments, but Niebuhr left no evidence of having read widely or deeply in the thought of Edmund Burke. Many of the parallels Guroian finds between Niebuhr and Burke are from Burke's works, which there is no evidence that Niebuhr ever read.

The problem of the argument being in the definitions arises again. Guroian in one instance writes, "According to Niebuhr's analysis and in this writer's judgment, Burke has a place within the broad liberal movement which eventually spawned free societies."[53] In another, he refers to Burkean "liberal conservatism." So the reader is left with an argument that the Burkean conservative Niebuhr is seen as similar to may really be a Burkean liberal. Guroian wisely recognizes the plurality of interpretations of both Burke and Niebuhr. It is too much to say "that on balance Niebuhr belongs to a school of modern politics that is considerably indebted to Edmund Burke."[54] The discussion between Niebuhr and Burke needs to be on "contrast" as well as "comparison." Burke's failure to recognize the social realities inspiring revolution, his defense of the ancien régime, his polemics against government aid to the poor, and his appreciation for historical institutions because they are in place all contrast with Niebuhr's thought. But beyond the differences, some of which are due to historical context, is the political misuse that openness to redefining the term *conservative* has in the

American context. Niebuhr had no eighteenth-century liberal whig option as did Burke. In his life, he voted for progressive, socialist, democrat, labor, and liberal candidates, and the causes he worked for embodied those politics. The term *conservative* does not fit.[55]

Niebuhr himself encouraged his classification as a conservative in three ways: (1) he recognized wisdom in political conservatism, (2) he evoked the names of Edmund Burke and Winston Churchill as political guides, and (3) he attacked liberalism. The attack on liberalism, already discussed, has been revealed as largely an attack on humanistic optimism. Edmund Burke was relatively unimportant in Niebuhr's writing; he used Burke as a weapon against abstract idealists and the errors of the French revolution. The references to Burke in Niebuhr all come from selected passages in *Reflections on the French Revolution* and emphasize what Niebuhr elsewhere describes as political realism. The references to Churchill do not commit him to Churchill's total political outlook but indicate deep respect for his uniting moral purpose and artful politics in the defense of Britain against Nazism.[56] He praised Roosevelt for similar brilliance in leading the United States in the struggle. In Niebuhr's usage and in common political usage, Churchill was regarded as a conservative and Roosevelt as a liberal, yet in foreign policy they had many of the same virtues. The qualities of realistic politics which Niebuhr occasionally praised in political conservatism were not intrinsically related to conservatism.

Niebuhr did not use the term *conservative* in a precise sense. He considered a careful definition of the term unnecessary. In his chapter "The Foreign Policy of American Conservatism and Liberalism," he wrote, "Perhaps it is as useless to define the ideal conservatism as to restore exact meaning to the word liberal."[57] In that context he did not define conservatism precisely but pointed to its characteristics, including (1) support for the status quo, (2) loyalty to aristocratic interests, (3) commonsense wisdom, (4) awareness of the factors of power and interest, (5) pragmatism, and (6) politics understood as the art of the possible. Except for the first and second characteristics, neither of which Niebuhr valued highly, these characteristics were as applicable to liberals as to conservatives, particularly liberals like Franklin D. Roosevelt. Niebuhr's frequent failure to define his terms and to use them carefully is partly responsible for the treatment of him as a conservative. When he praised conservatism in the following statement, for example, he should have used the term *realism:* "In part, this conservatism is the product of Christian rather than 'idealistic' approaches to the perennial facts of human nature."[58] His desire here was to emphasize the need for historical, empirical approach and for the consideration of factors of human egoism. The term *realism* is much more appropriate than the term *conservatism*, which denotes a predisposition to defend existing political institutions and connotes a defense of privilege, neither of which is intrinsic to Niebuhr's political philosophy.

He returned to definitions on the occasion of Russell Kirk's publication in 1954 of *The Conservative Mind*. He associated Kirk with *traditional conservatives* who, while understanding factors of social hierarchy, interest, and power in politics, defend the status quo. He thought *traditional liberals* were committed to social justice but lacked awareness of the issues of power and interest and were too optimistic about society's possibilities. He then describes his own position as a *realistic liberalism* and notes that the realism is "drawn from the Christian estimate of the perennial character of human sin."[59] His impatience is expressed with Russell Kirk's use of Burke, on the one hand, and with traditional liberals on the other. He sees Kirk using Burkean realism to accept conformity, inequality, and so on. He sees traditional liberals as confused by realistic liberalism, thinking that a liberal using realism should also be conservative. Illusions about human nature are not necessary to promote "liberty, equality, and justice." Though the definitions are not satisfying, there is no doubt that Niebuhr understood himself in 1954 as a Christian realist liberal.

The rejection of the term *conservative* as applicable to Niebuhr's political philosophy leaves unanswered the degree to which his political philosophy is in debt to pragmatism. The definition of this pragmatism and its relationship to his Christian faith, on the one hand, and his political liberalism, on the other, is taken up in chapter 8. By the end of World War II, Augustinian realism had replaced Marxism as a source of the criticism of American liberal optimism. Politically, Niebuhr was trying to integrate elements of his socialist politics into the realistic liberalism of his wartime philosophy.

NOTES

1. Reinhold Niebuhr, "Editorials," *Christianity and Society* 5 (Spring 1940), 10.
2. Ibid.
3. June Bingham, *Courage to Change: An Introduction to the Life and Thought of Reinhold Niebuhr* (New York: Charles Scribner's Sons, 1961), p. 280.

4. Reinhold Niebuhr, *Human Destiny* (1943), p. 3.

5. Ibid., p. 96.

6. The section moves from Plato through James Madison with the usual Niebuhr emphasis upon Augustine, Calvin, and Luther. Edmund Burke does not yet appear as part of this interpretation of significant political theory.

7. The central thesis of the whole lecture series was that a revised Augustinian theology of history, often called biblical view, was more dynamic than classical views and more realistic than the modern views of history. Augustine had been a subject of Niebuhr's since Detroit. Ursula also enriched his perspective on Augustine from her historical and theological studies at Oxford. His review of Charles Cochrane, *Christianity and Classical Culture: A Study of Thought and Action from Augustus to Augustine* in the *University of Toronto Quarterly* (July 1941), pp. 305–310, documents the congruence of his perception of Augustine's theology of history with his own developed views. Incidentally, he described the book as having "given me more unalloyed pleasure than anything I have read in the past decade."

8. Niebuhr, *Human Destiny*, pp. 320–321.

9. John C. Bennett, "Human Destiny—Reinhold Niebuhr: A Symposium," *Union Review* 4 (Mar. 1943), 24.

10. Ibid., p. 25.

11. Ibid., p. 26; Reinhold Niebuhr letters to John C. Bennett, copies in Burke Library, Union Theological Seminary.

12. The rest of this chapter is an edited and in part revised discussion from my *Reinhold Niebuhr: Prophet to Politicians* (Nashville: Abingdon Press, 1972), pp. 111–128.

13. Reinhold Niebuhr, *The Children of Light and the Children of Darkness* (1944), p. xiii.

14. Reinhold Niebuhr, *Christianity and Power Politics* (1940), pp. 65–66.

15. Ibid., p. 69.

16. Ibid., p. 63.

17. Ibid., p. 108.

18. Reinhold Niebuhr, "The International Situation," *Radical Religion* 5 (Winter 1940), p. 3.

19. Reinhold Niebuhr, "The Spiritual Problem of the Coming Decades," *Christianity and Society* 10 (Summer 1945), 7.

20. Reinhold Niebuhr, "Is This 'Peace in Our Time'?" *The Nation* 160 (Apr. 7, 1945), 383.

21. The staff was formally created on May 5, 1947, with George Kennan as director. It had the broadest of mandates to formulate and develop long-term foreign policy programs and to recommend their adoption to the appropriate officials of the State Department. George F. Kennan, *Memoirs 1925–1950* (Boston: Little, Brown & Co., 1967), p. 327.

22. Reinhold Niebuhr, *Christian Realism and Political Problems* (1953), p. 17.

23. Niebuhr, *Children of Light*, pp. 153–190.

24. Reinhold Niebuhr, "Anglo-Saxon Destiny and Responsibility," *Christianity and Crisis* 3 (Oct. 4, 1943), 2.

25. Ibid., p. 4.

26. Reinhold Niebuhr, "American Power and World Responsibility," *Christianity and Crisis* 3 (Apr. 5, 1943), 2–4.

27. Ibid., p. 4.

28. Reinhold Niebuhr, "We Are in Peril," *Christianity and Crisis* 3 (Oct. 18, 1943), 2–3.

29. Reinhold Niebuhr, "The Death of the President," *Christianity and Crisis* 5 (Apr. 30, 1945), 5.

30. Emil Brunner, *Der Mensch im Widerspruch* (Berlin: Furche Verlag, 1937).

31. Charles W. Kegley, ed., *Reinhold Niebuhr: His Religious, Social, and Political Thought* (New York: Pilgrim Press, 1984), p. 507. Brunner had protested that he could find "no mention" of the influence his work *Man in Revolt* had exerted upon *The Nature and Destiny of Man* (ibid., p. 32). Niebuhr assumed Brunner was correct that he had failed to mention Brunner's work. In fact there were footnote references to Brunner's *Man in Revolt* on pp. 237 and 272 of volume 1 of *The Nature and Destiny of Man*. Thus Brunner's criticism was overdrawn and reflected careless reading on his own part. Richard Fox continued the careless reading and chose to let Brunner's remark appear in a caustic and sarcastic manner. The references to Brunner were detailed in my 1972 book which Fox reviewed in *The Nation* (June 1973, pp. 823, 824) and referred to in his 1985 work. Furthermore, a more careful historian than Fox, Charles Brown, lists an additional six references to Brunner in *The Nature and Destiny of Man*. See Charles Brown, *Niebuhr and His Age* (Philadelphia: Trinity Press International, 1992).

32. Charles C. West, *Communism and the Theologian* (Philadelphia: Westminster Press, 1958), p. 14.

33. John C. Bennett, "Review of Communism and the Theologians by Charles C. West," *Union Seminary Quarterly Review* 14 (Jan. 1959), 65.

34. Collected in D. B. Robertson, ed., *Essays in Applied Christianity* (1959), pp. 141–196.

35. Ibid., p. 146.

36. Ibid., p. 148.

37. Ibid., p. 151.

38. Ibid., p. 156.

39. Ibid., p. 166.

40. Ibid., p. 172.

41. Ibid., p. 187.

42. Ibid., pp. 188–198.

43. Ibid., p. 190.

44. Eduard Heimann, "Niebuhr's Pragmatic Conservatism," *Union Seminary Quarterly Review* 11 (May 1956), 7.

45. Kegley, ed., *Reinhold Niebuhr*, pp. 130–131.

46. Heimann, "Niebuhr's Pragmatic Conservatism," p. 7.

47. Ibid., p. 8.

48. Will Herberg, "Christian Apologist to the Secular World," *Union Seminary Quarterly Review* 11 (May 1956), 15.

49. Ibid.

50. Gordon Harland, *The Thought of Reinhold Niebuhr* (New York: Oxford University Press, 1960), p. 186.

51. Vigen Guroian, "The Conservatism of Reinhold Niebuhr: The Burkean Connection," *Modern Age* 29 (Summer 1985), 226.

52. Ibid.

53. Vigen Guroian, "The Possibilities and Limits of Politics: A Comparative Study of the Thought of Reinhold Niebuhr and Edmund Burke," *Union Seminary Quarterly Review* 36 (Summer 1981), 199.

54. Guroian, "Conservatism," p. 231.

55. Vigen Guroian, "On Revolution and Ideology: Convergence in the Political Legacies of Niebuhr and Burke," *Union Seminary Quarterly Review* 39, nos. 1 and 2 (1984), 25–39. Whatever Burke's reaction to Jacobinism, Niebuhr's reaction to communism is that of a realistic liberal: the program of Americans for Democratic Action.

56. An example of Niebuhr's critique of Churchill reveals the deep differences between the two, even on the foreign policy of the Allied democracies. "Churchill's great achievements as leader of an embattled nation cannot hide the fact that the Indian policy has been a blind spot for years in his career. He has been consistently wrong about India." Reinhold Niebuhr, "Common Counsel for United Nations," *Christianity and Crisis* 2 (Oct. 5, 1942), 1.

57. Niebuhr, *Christian Realism*, p. 71.

58. Ibid., p. 72.

59. Reinhold Niebuhr, "Liberalism and Conservatism," *Christianity and Society* 20 (Winter 1954–55), 3.

7

History and Theology
in Cold War
1945–1952

WHEN NIEBUHR presented retiring President Henry Sloane Coffin with the Festschrift he had edited, the war in Europe was over and the war with Japan had been decided.[1] The world environment had changed, and Union Theological Seminary had changed also. Niebuhr had been very close to Coffin, who brought him to the seminary and persuaded him to stay despite the offers of other universities.[2] The close personal friendship would continue with Henry Pitney van Dusen, a peer of Niebuhr's in age and tenure at the seminary. Van Dusen's broad view of the world importance of ecumenical theology met Niebuhr's own expanding perspectives as the world was more united in an emerging world history through war.

Teaching Ministers

For the first six postwar years, the seminary grew, reaching 647 students in 1951.[3] During this period and until Niebuhr's retirement in 1960, the faculty doubled to a total of over 50. It was a grand period of prestige and expansion for the seminary at a time when many of its star lecturers were at the height of their powers. Union benefited from its location in New York City, which, with the new United Nations headquarters influencing diplomacy and Wall Street dominating world economics, seemed to approach the status of a world capital. All students (from the classes of 1929 to 1960) who responded to the question about Niebuhr's dedication to and influence at the seminary regarded him as very loyal and very influential. His presence was irenic, while exerting a leadership based on his attraction of students and his reputation beyond the seminary. Many students came to Union to study with him; others fell under his influence on arrival. A Professor Emeritus of Pittsburgh Theological Seminary who majored in ethics under Niebuhr wrote:

> I had never heard of Reinie while in college. The first time I heard his name was on the bus going from Iowa to New York in 1935 when a young man from Oregon, I believe, turned out to be going to Union also. When I asked him "why?" he said it was to study with Reinhold Niebuhr. Taking his courses made me want to major under him.[4]

Niebuhr regarded the postwar years of Union as a fourth period in his tenure there.[5] It was, for theological ethics, a time of coming to grips with the dilemmas of nuclear terror, confrontation with tyranny, and cold war. The seminary seemed to be in a secure time of growth, freed from internal tumultuous social conflicts and with strong presidential leadership. Niebuhr's recollection of this era, as he retired, was that the theological temptations had not been optimism but flight from conflicts into biblicism, eschatological escapism, or an undue emphasis on the uniqueness of church. For his part, he praised the Union students of this period for finding mature responses to the insecurities of their time.

Niebuhr's influence was a factor in drawing many to theological studies. But he did not himself recruit for the ministry. That was a call beyond any teacher. In fact, Niebuhr would advise inquirers not to pursue the ministry unless there was a strong compulsion from the divine and their own selves. In an address to potential students for the ministry, he suggested themes from Churchill of blood, sweat, and tears but then became biblically serious. In a time of crisis, he said, Gideon was told by the Lord, "Whoever is fearful and trembling, let him return home" (Judges 7:3, RSV). He hoped the courageous could be attracted while the others found some alternative vocation.[6]

He did not, in his lectures, sermons, and seminars, reflect very much on his own ministry. In the total body of his work, there is not much autobiographical reflection except for the diary of his ministerial years and a few other occasions when such reflection was requested. In lecturing on ministry, he warned future pastors of the dangers of pride:

> I remember when I was a young parson, two Sunday school girls were playing under the window of my study. One said, "Let's not make too

much noise, we will disturb Mr. Niebuhr," and the other little girl said, "Who is Mr. Niebuhr?" The first child answered, "Don't you know? He is the pastor in this church. He knows all about God." This shocked me, but reminded me of the pretenses to which the ministry is prone.[7]

In the same lecture he advised younger candidates for the ministry to examine themselves in their own hours of private prayer. If they would confront the world with Christ, they needed to understand their own pride and their own illusions. Those who heard him preach in chapel and lead in prayer knew that here was a person of private prayer as well as public. He was in chapel almost every morning, and he often led the services. School of Sacred Music students and candidates in education who often did not take his classes have recorded his impact on them through chapel services.[8]

Niebuhr's teaching was through several mediums, and some alumni have said that the particular course was not as important as the person of the professor. Frederick Buechner made this point: "In the last analysis, I have always believed it is not so much their subjects that the great teachers teach as it is themselves."[9] Originally he took most meals in the refectory, and after marriage he continued to lunch there often. Students would crowd around him for conversation as they did in the social hall. The seminary was a close-knit community, with the focus of life moving among chapel, refectory, library, classrooms, and, to a lesser degree, the social hall. Niebuhr's presence was evident in all of these, as well as in his office. As most faculty lived in the quadrangle complex between West 120th and 122nd streets bounded by Broadway and Claremont Avenue, they were around most of the time. He added another opportunity to meet students by inviting them to his "at homes." These were initiated when his mother lived with him and continued, with Ursula as hostess, after their marriage. The serving of refreshments, which came to include beer, prompted Ralph R. Sundquist to remember that the young men in Hastings Hall would sing, to the tune of the Rheingold Beer song; "My beer is Reinhold, the Niebuhr." Usually Niebuhr would hold forth on some subject, usually current events, and respond to questions. Sometimes there were guests of national or international importance, who would present remarks to focus the discussion. His faithful devotees would attend, but those others who were not so close would come as well. Ursula was well known in the Union community for her brilliance, wit, and wide and deep study. Yet the "at homes" were for the students, and Reinhold and she did not usually intervene. However, whenever she did, and particularly if it was to tease or differ from her husband, her remarks would be shared the next day around the seminary quadrangle.

James A. Martin, a student in 1940–44 and later Danforth Professor of Religion in Higher Education at Union, wrote:

> The informal "at homes" in his apartment were memorable. Sometimes when the likes of T. S. Eliot or W. H. Auden were present, there could be something of a tug of war between Reinie and Ursula. At other times persons on the frontline of domestic and international debate were present, and the conversation was both stimulating and engrossing.[10]

He went on to relate an occasion of Ursula's humor:

> At one of the meetings of the Fellowship of Socialist Christians . . . the discussion turned to the possible dangers of overconfidence in proclaiming the views of the group. . . . Reinie was offended, and spoke at length about his sense of mutual sin and of the dangers of *hubris* on both sides. He said that sometimes this sense so overcame him that he sank to his knees in humility—or words to that effect. The meeting broke into appropriate humor when Ursula spoke out: "Not very often, dear!"[11]

Donald G. Dawe, professor of systematic theology at Union Theological Seminary in Virginia, also chose to share a memory from the "at homes."

> One of my fondest recollections of Reinhold Niebuhr was at one of those "at home" evenings the Niebuhrs had in their apartment in Knox Hall. Students, faculty, and visiting church leaders from all over the world would appear at these informal sessions. We sat on the couches or on the floor as a fascinating free-flowing conversation took place. At that time, 1951–52, Niebuhr was still closely in touch with people in the State Department and had an intimate knowledge of world affairs. In addition his voracious appetite for reading kept his mind stocked with the latest ideas. He blended these together in fascinating responses to questions of all sorts.
>
> However, there were some themes that kept recurring. One of these was his distaste for much Anglican theology and ethical reflection. One evening in response to a question, he was indulging at considerable length in Anglican bashing. All of us sat there receiving his words as veritable oracles of truth. When all of a sudden from the next room there was a clear carrying feminine voice that said, "It's not that way at all, Reinie." It was Mrs. Niebuhr. We all turned to see the source of this contradiction of our oracle. She then gave an extensive set of counter-comments on Anglican theology just to set the record straight. I recall that the rest of the evening went on in a somewhat more subdued tone and we hastened rather quickly to the distribution of refreshments.[12]

Niebuhr's primary work was the teaching of theological students. As they spilled out of seminary to lead churches, teach college and university students in various fields, and administer church and parachurch welfare, service, and action agencies, his vocation was fulfilled. Union Theological Seminary was his basic community, and among associates he sought advice and shared his insights. Social or political crises would find Niebuhr and his colleagues talking over the phone, in offices and hallways, and on walks on Riverside Drive. The journals and organizations he founded or joined were for the church but also for the wider society. His method of pushing the public meaning of Christian ethics prevented him from making too clear a division between church and society. His theology, of course, prevented him from claiming very much uniqueness or special righteousness for the church, for in such claims the primary sin of religious pride always lurked.

Although Niebuhr often castigated the church for an otherworldly mysticism neglectful of the needs of people, or for a sentimental activism neglecting the depths of the Christian faith, the church was his primary instrument of change. His essays and books sometimes were addressed to the intellectual despisers of religion, but more often were addressed to the devout. He gained fame for social wisdom, but his daily work was preparing ministers for their tasks.

His theology of church was shaped by his Reformed-Lutheran heritage and Congregational policy of the United Church of Christ and by his ecumenical commitments. Service for the Federal Council of Churches and its successor, the National Council of Churches, was matched by efforts to shape the World Council of Churches' social thought. His ecclesiology remained congregational and conciliar, leaving Roman Catholics and Episcopalians to doubt the seriousness of his ecclesiology. He understood the high claims for the church preferred by those in the Catholic traditions, but his own preference was closer to that of low-church polity. When asked about the social location of Reinhold Niebuhr, one must recall what he did: He taught ministers. This vocation is more important than class analysis in explaining his position. One could say he was a middle class intellectual, but first he had experienced the genteel poverty of the parsonage of his parents, and his social attitudes were established in his early ministry at Bethel Church in Detroit. The students he taught at Union were not anticipating lives of affluence, and Union's policy of paying all senior full professors equally meant that his own income was never at the level of the more prestigious pastors or of the higher paid professors at wealthy universities. It varied from $4,500 to $10,000 from 1928 to 1960, plus apartment. So while correlating his social thought with perspectives shaped by class analysis may inform an analysis of his thought, the commitment to theological scholarship for the equipping of the American churches is more fundamental to understanding his contribution.

The recognition of Niebuhr's primary work as a theological educator brings into perspective both his ministry at Bethel Evangelical Church in Detroit (1915–1928) and his critique of American religion. At Bethel he learned of the inadequacies of his liberal theological education in dealing with social conflict, economic injustice, and international strife. During the rest of his life as a theological educator he labored to join Christian faith to a realistic analysis of people and society. This led him to criticize sharply the inadequacies of American spiritual life, while training seminarians to correct those deficiencies.

The Weakness of American Religion

Niebuhr deplored the lack of vitality in American religious life, particularly his own Protestantism.[13] His criticism of Roman Catholicism mellowed after the 1930s when Roman Catholicism made tragic political alliances in Europe. He welcomed the reforming spirit of the Second Vatican Council but was not surprised to see the curia delay the implementation of reforms. Shortly before his death, he noted particular signs of vitality in Dutch Roman Catholicism and urged American Catholics and Protestants to take note.[14] His treatment of Judaism emphasized its rigorous response to problems of social justice. Protestantism, however, was his inspiration and target of attack.

He confided that on Christmas Day in New York he liked to attend the Cathedral of St. John the Divine.[15] The liturgical services preserved the drama of the high holidays of the Christian year better than most preaching. His tendencies toward improving the worship of his own Protestantism were deepened by his marriage to Ursula Keppel-Compton in Winchester Cathedral.

He recorded the engaging dialogue between his Anglican wife and himself over the relative merits of Protestant preaching services and Anglican liturgical services. Ursula usually had the edge because of her background and greater interest in art and culture. Also, her interest in religion was more radically involved in acts of devotion than was his activist Protestantism. In an essay,[16] she revealed deep faith and rigorous scholarship, demanding that religion's strength be evaluated by its own intrinsic value. Reinhold would agree, but she would dismiss the pragmatic criteria quicker than he would.

Long before the recent liturgical renewal, he attacked the sentimentality and awkwardness of common patterns of worship. He enumerated some of his charges:

1. The pastoral prayer is both too long and too formless. . . .
2. Without the discipline of traditional and historic prayers there is a tendency to neglect some of the necessary and perennial themes of prayer. . . .
3. The language of the prayers of common worship is either too common, too sentimental, or too extravagant. . . .
4. The use of Biblical ideas in prayer is necessary not merely to purify the expressions but to correct the thought. . . .
5. The free worship tends to be too personal in every respect. . . .
6. The reading of the Scripture in Protestant worship leaves much to be desired. . . .
7. The participation of the congregation in the worship service is too minimal. . . .
8. Choir music in the nonliturgical churches and in some liturgical ones is still affected by the sentimentality which began to corrupt religious music in the latter part of the last century. . . . [17]

Niebuhr often criticized American Protestantism for its disunity. He labored hard in the ecumenical movement but felt that the Protestant churches seeking unity had delayed too long. In 1924 he criticized those who boasted of the churches moving together.

> The church has lost the chance of becoming the unifying element in our American society. It is not anticipating any facts. It is merely catching up very slowly to the new social facts created by economic and other forces. The American melting pot is doing its work. The churches merely represent various European cultures lost in the amalgam of American life and maintaining a separate existence only in religion.[18]

The major reason he wanted more unity among the churches was so that each tradition could borrow the elements of the fullness respective groups had preserved. The spectacle of competition among the denominations was a scandal. However, he rejected arguments for unity based on notions of a united front against Catholicism or of more power and prestige.

He also criticized American churches for failing to provide moral leadership, because spiritual vigor and social intelligence were missing in American Protestantism. People needed to be confronted with the ethic of love so that the essential selfishness and poverty of American life could be exposed. The church did not have to become a political agency, yet must be involved in the contentious issues of American common life. Reinhold Niebuhr was a true child of the Social Gospel movement. He articulated the relevance of the gospel to American social problems. In his writings on the churches' need for an adequate social ethic, his dual attitude of love for and critique of the church is most obvious. He was a Protestant clergyman with his whole heart, but he delivered scathing criticisms of the church's failure to fulfill its ethical tasks. His book *Man's Nature and His Communities* leveled its strongest criticism at the self-righteousness religious communities encouraged. Religious self-righteousness and strictly legalistic moral codes sealed off the gates of grace and vital ethical concerns. The ideal of humility was lost by the tendency to reinforce community mores. Instead of becoming a constant source of community renewal, religion had obscured the need for it.

In one of the last few published interviews, Niebuhr's interlocutor, Patrick Granfield, a Catholic, pushed him on the church issue in his thought.[19] "Some have said that in your social picture of redemption you do not adequately emphasize the role of the church," Granfield noted. Niebuhr's response was shrewd, pointing toward the ecclesiastical assumptions of the critics and toward the historical realities of the church of which its educated critics were aware.

> Many of my friends, especially Anglicans, have made that objection, and I think it may be valid. . . . But I have been influenced by the historical realities of the church as I know it—both Protestant and Catholic. . . . I have also been influenced in this respect not by sectarian Protestantism, but simply by the critical attitude of some of my secular, political-scientist friends. They viewed religious communities only as they became involved in corruption.[20]

In his lecturing to theological students he had stressed that while the gospel was most naturally and easily appropriated by the poor and the oppressed, the rich and the powerful needed it as well. A temptation of ministry was to compromise the gospel so that it became less than a word of confrontation to the powerful. The task was to find the way to confront the ruler's pride, as Nathan had done in leading King David to condemn his own sin. He warned the students in 1953 that in criticizing the sins of the American nation which portrayed itself self-righteously the minister faced the danger of being labeled a Communist. Hearing Niebuhr's warning in the early 1950s, most students had no idea that Niebuhr was speaking personally.

Under Investigation, 1942–1969

The Federal Bureau of Investigation's package of papers on Niebuhr provided under the Freedom of Information Act totals 623 pages, but much information has been withheld or is blacked out on the pages provided. The FBI conducted a loyalty investigation of Niebuhr in 1951 and 1952. He had sponsored an anti–Joseph McCarthy rally and spoken out against the House Un-American Activities Committee, but it was his employment by the Department of State that unleashed this investigation.

The released documents identify him as Consultant to the Policy Planning Staff of the Department of State in 1949 and 1950. He had been Acting U.S. Representative to the General Conference of the United Nations Educational, Scientific, and Cultural Organization in September of 1949 and an unpaid consultant to the Department of State in November 1949. The 1951–52 investigation, of course, was in the context of the general hysteria over charges from Senator McCarthy and others about Communists in the State Department.

The 1951 investigation turned up a previous investigation in 1942. On that occasion, a request for compensation for travel expenses to Archibald MacLeish's Office of Facts and Figures for a report Niebuhr did on religious freedom related to the war effort had triggered an investigation. Also, his role as a consultant to the Office of War Information and his lecturing for that office in England during the war was noted. The investigations, once launched, continued on their own momentum, with the files being provided to different government offices.

The investigation did not focus on what Niebuhr said or did for the government, but, rather, on his multifaceted social action, political writing, and organizational work. Within the reports are many unsupported charges of Communist leanings and dangerously radical teaching. Material was collected, but the file reveals very little ability on the part of the FBI to evaluate the charges or check their veracity. The FBI was still collecting information in 1961 and 1963, particularly relating to activities critical of the House Un-American Activities Committee. The final use made of the material provided by the FBI was a summary memo sent by J. Edgar Hoover in October 1969 to the Honorable [sic]

John D. Ehrlichman, Counsel to the President, on Reinhold Niebuhr, reporting that the

> investigations, while largely favorable as to Niebuhr's loyalty, disclosed that he had been identified . . . as a member, endorser, or supporter of a large number of organizations cited as Communist fronts which extended over a period of twenty years. . . . Because of his long-standing prominence in Socialist and other left-wing political circles, Dr. Niebuhr has been described as a "Christian Revolutionary."[21]

His connections with the American Labor Party, reputed to be under the control of the Communists in Manhattan, and the Liberal Party were mentioned. The FBI seems to have been able to determine when one affiliated with an organization but then unable to learn when or why one left an organization.

Hoover's memo to Ehrlichman is ludicrous. Driving both Hoover and Ehrlichman in October, however, was probably Niebuhr's August attack on the travesty of the White House chapel and its ringing pronouncements of White House virtue and American self-righteousness. Niebuhr's article provoked more of a national furor than anything else he wrote in the last two years of his life.[22] He had reached down into the depths of his understanding of critical Protestant faith and attacked what he perceived as false piety, covering cruel politics domestically and in Vietnam. The title "The King's Chapel and the King's Court" was taken from the high priest Amaziah's silencing of Amos by telling him not to preach justice, for this was the king's chapel and the king's court. Niebuhr's comparison of J. Edgar Hoover to the court priest Amaziah in the article may have been more to the point than he realized when he wrote it.

The investigators were thorough, interviewing people at all Niebuhr's past educational institutions, former neighbors, and acquaintances; acquiring pamphlets from organizations he associated with; and collecting some of his own writings. The very thoroughness of the investigations meant that many people were interviewed by the FBI, and some of them talked later, much to Niebuhr's embarrassment. An isolationist, for example, tried to discredit Niebuhr with stories that his loyalty was under investigation, while a pastor at a nearby church concluded that Niebuhr was preparing to leave Union for wartime employment in Washington, D.C.

Niebuhr's protests involved first Archibald MacLeish, who had authorized the investigations which had included Niebuhr and others, and then Attorney General Francis Biddle. The matter came to J. Edgar

Hoover's attention from the Attorney General. Niebuhr was given an opportunity to submit his own statement, but he was not allowed to see the file, at the express direction of J. Edgar Hoover, so he declined to add to it. Mention of the FBI's approach to an isolationist member of the America First Committee in *The Nation* (April 4, 1942) caught the Bureau's attention, and an excerpt of the notice went in the file. The FBI investigation reproduced the references to Niebuhr in the August 1938 to October 1939 hearings of the House Un-American Activities Committee. This report lists seventeen references to Niebuhr's activities, involving his condemnation by J. B. Matthews using Niebuhr's *Reflections on the End of an Era*. Theodore Graebner of Concordia Seminary of St. Louis also accused Niebuhr of associating with Communists. The report claimed he was associated with fourteen such groups. Later hearings of the House Un-American Activities Committee kept referring to Niebuhr.

The FBI report finally collected the names of almost two dozen organizations to which Niebuhr had belonged, contributed, or addressed, or acted as a sponsor for, which some government group considered subversive or Communist. The investigation did not stop but continued to collect information on Niebuhr into the 1950s and 1960s. Sources were as varied as informants who had happened to attend his lectures, or references to him in *The Daily Worker*, or a letter he signed to President Truman protesting, in 1951, the government's loyalty program and the FBI's participation in it.

In December of 1951, Hoover was repeatedly sending telegrams to the New York FBI office demanding they expedite the investigation of Niebuhr. Hoover mentioned that other government agencies were interested in the loyalty investigations being undertaken by the FBI. Given that Niebuhr in 1951 was no longer in the employ of the federal government, Hoover's interest in pursuing the case is irregular. Hoover himself got caught up in the red-scare hysteria. On other occasions, he exhibited an extraordinary compulsion to discipline religious dissenters from American policy. The 1952 report from New York to Hoover was much more responsible than the 1942 report. More testimony was collected about Niebuhr's loyalty and his non-front organizations, and his opposition to communism was more obvious in 1952 than it had been to FBI agents in 1942. His resignation from the American Labor Party and from the Socialist Party were present in the report, which was sixty-seven pages long and included extensive appendices. One of the agents even excerpted a few quotes from *Moral Man and Immoral*

Society of 1932. Interviews with scholars, apparently from Union Theological Seminary, also deepened the report. Some of the nastiest pages in the whole file were written by "religious" people who feared Niebuhr's influence in the church. They pleaded for Hoover to investigate this "Judas." They asked for results of the FBI investigations of Niebuhr so they could persuade publishers of Sunday school publications not to use his work. They told Hoover that the Communists were going to take over America by first converting the theological seminaries to atheism. Hoover, for his part, could only tell them that the Bureau's files were not available for such uses, but he sometimes warned them, as in a note as late as April 7, 1966, that Niebuhr was well known in "Bureau files for his left-wing activities."

The files were added to from time to time in an apparently random manner. The last entries were in regard to Niebuhr's opposition to the Vietnam War, starting with the formation of a Minister's Vietnam Committee on July 11, 1963, to protest U.S. involvement.

The founding of Clergy Concerned About Vietnam on January 30, 1967, with Niebuhr on the executive committee, was reported. He was listed as a sponsor of a Negotiations Now organization, petition, and rally in Philadelphia on July 27, 1967. On October 14, 1969, Niebuhr was associated with a *Sun Times* ad in Chicago by the Business Executive Move for Vietnam Peace.

Niebuhr's attacks on the developing cold war internal security system were also noted. One report from the *People's World* of November 16, 1963, listed Niebuhr as asking President Kennedy to repeal the Smith Act of 1940, the McCarran Internal Security Act of 1950, and the Communist Control Act of 1954.

So, Niebuhr had worked in some organizations with Communists and had struggled to keep Communists out of control. When he lost, or when a journal became, in his judgment, too uncritical of the Soviet Union, he resigned. He had been a Socialist Party theoretician, party officer, and candidate twice for public office. He had written as a Christian Marxist, and at least one Marxist publication, *Revolutionary Socialist Review*, had called him Comrade Niebuhr.

But overall, the FBI investigations were inept. They failed to study his denunciations of communism or to interview his most significant friends in government; they did their research out of an unnecessary red paranoia. His loyalty to the United States was explicitly and systematically attacked in the report for: (1) supporting the democratic forces in Spain against the fascists, (2) organizing opposition to the

Japanese invasion of China, (3) urging the diplomatic recognition of the Soviet Union, (4) organizing German refugees to work for a more democratic and unified Germany after the war, (5) opposing U.S. war preparation in the 1930s, (6) opposing the internment of Japanese citizens, (7) writing for social publications, (8) organizing relief funds for striking textile workers, (9) working as an officer of the NAACP, (10) supporting Borough President Stanley M. Isaacs's appointment of a suspected Communist to his staff, and (11) attacking, in print, the internal loyalty system and the FBI. To say that *The Protestant Digest*, of which Paul Tillich was the chairman, "faithfully propagated the Communist Party line" is ridiculous, but the file tars Niebuhr for his contribution to that little journal as well. What the report needed was a study of some of the more serious organizations, like the League for Industrial Democracy and the American Labor Party, to determine if there was some subversion and, if so, who the subverters were, but the agency lacked the intellectual resources to do this. To label those who participated in the flexible, ever-changing political organizations left of center as dangerous, radical, subversive, or disloyal would have been silly if it had not done so much damage to American politics.

FBI File No. 121-033418 did have one reference to the fact that Niebuhr taught a popular course at Union Theological Seminary entitled "Christianity and Communism."

Christian Ethics 394: Christianity and Communism

In the academic year 1949–50 Professors John C. Bennett and Charles W. Iglehart joined Niebuhr in a new course, "Christianity and Communism." As the course was for theological students who were studying Christianity in almost every other course in their program, the emphasis was on communism and a Christian response to it. The course dealt briefly with Marxist theory but was really about the movement of communism as it was embodied in institutions. Professor Searle M. Bates joined Bennett and Niebuhr in 1951, and that ensured even more that the course was about communism in history. A former missionary historian of China, Bates brought a passion for historical detail to the course. Bennett brought theological sophistication and an unusual sensitivity to emerging third world issues. Niebuhr's passion was for the practical strategies of coexistence with communism. Professor Bates's lectures on the history of communism could become tedious, but his vast knowledge of Asia anchored the course in reality. His passion for detail meant that a few of his favorite students did not dare show up on campus without having learned the content of the morning's *New York Times*. Bates would waylay the unwary student on his way for a morning cup of coffee with questions about the meaning of the latest development in Sri Lanka or Tibet. Any self-respecting student would want to know at least as much as the morning newspaper had to say. John Bennett, known for his quiet humility, could be aggressive in his teaching also. A student fresh from the Midwest quoting from *U.S. News & World Report* would be politely told in front of the class that "that journal was not considered authoritative here." A student's opinion from the James Chapel pulpit or in a student newspaper might also result in an invitation to Bennett's office to help the student see that a more moderate expression might be helpful. Bennett succeeded Niebuhr as Dean of the Faculty when Niebuhr's health led him to resign from the position in 1955.

The new course was restricted to seniors and graduate students. Despite the disparate nature of lectures given by three different professors, it became very popular. Its catalog description indicated its breadth.

> A course on the nature of Communism and on the Christian approach to Communism. There will be study of the classical Marxist theory and of the contemporary theory and practice of Communist parties. Emphasis will be placed on the problems created by Communism for the Christian church, for its world mission, and for its younger branches overseas.[23]

In a typical semester, Niebuhr would give four or five lectures. His lecture on the roots of Marxist philosophy stressed materialism, Hegelianism, apocalypticism, perfectionism, and romanticism. For him, the mistake of Marx and, following him, Engels was to confuse the long history of materialism with empiricism. Marx had written his dissertation on the Greek atomists, but Niebuhr thought he equated materialism with empiricism and that this implied communism as the way to liberate humanity.[24] The Hegelian historical dialectic was used to explain the material issues of the historical class conflicts, which, drawing upon traditions of apocalypticism, perfectionism, and romanticism, promised a new heaven and a new earth. It was in essence a secularized and materialistic view containing much in common with Christian, particularly sectarian, visions of history. Of course, the Marxist view of history differed from the Christian by being tied to a particular political program, class, and party.

A second lecture dealt with freedom and determination in revolution. In this lecture, he emphasized Engels, Trotsky, and Lenin and again the hope for a Marxist utopia. He emphasized the utopian character of Engels and Lenin's writing. The lecture also focused on Stalin's theories of Marxist-Leninist truth and the inevitability of revolution, and of Russia's emancipation leading the world revolution. A powerful section of the lecture on the realities compared with the dream was followed by remarks on Trotsky on the revolution betrayed.

He lectured on the ethics of communism. He saw communism rejecting Christian ethics as an ideology that preached submissiveness to those who needed to revolt. Contemporary Christianity had, according to communism, inculcated undue reverence for authority. He saw a stress on equality in communism resembling in some aspects a secularized Christian love ethic. But there was an advance beyond "formal bourgeois equality" in theory in advocating "From each according to ability, to each according to need." The ethical ideals of uncoerced harmony and the overcoming of class conflict were utopian, but within the tradition of Western thought. The ideals of universal humanity were developed in Marxism, but on the basis of a proletarian ideal. He thought Marxism left liberty out of its ethics except as the fruit of the overcoming of the state. He pointed out that Christian ethics were not necessarily opposed to the political ethics of communism on (1) the use of force, (2) the right of revolution, (3) the class struggle, or (4) the theory that the end may justify the means. All four subjects were of course developed differently in communist theory than in a Christian context of thought.

He also lectured on the Marxist interpretation of history and on communism in Europe. The lectures on history are similar to material in his written works. The lecture on communism in Europe drew on his extensive continual reading and also his personal experiences and meetings in Europe, which had taken place about every other year, from his first trip with Sherwood Eddy in 1923 to his stroke in 1952. Details showing the difference in personalities and historical backgrounds among the various Communist parties of Europe were more obvious in these lectures than in the more sweeping generalizations in his books.

At the time he taught the course, Niebuhr was a critic not only of Russian communism, which he had been since his visit to Russia in 1930, but also of Marxism in general, and even of democratic socialism. In 1948, when the name of the Fellowship of Socialist Christians was changed to Frontier Fellowship, Niebuhr had still identified with socialism's commitment to socialize major industries. By the time he published "The Anomaly of European Socialism" in 1952, he was more critical of socialism, and specifically for its Marxist heritage.[25]

Niebuhr taught the students that Marxism contained seven errors.[26] The most important was its trust in creating a heaven on earth, its utopianism. The radical distinction between good and evil people, which denied the universality of evil, encouraged fanaticism. Evil was derived in communist theory from a social institution rather than from human nature. Ownership was overestimated as a basis of power, neglecting managerial power. The state was underestimated; political power was unduly subordinated in theory to economic power. The economic motivation was overestimated as a source of egotism and ideology. There were other faults also. Finally, the whole Marxist logic of history was fantastic. He believed therefore that communism was not well equipped to check power in its organizations or to challenge dogmatic and moral pretensions. Believing that such failures were of the essence of communism, Niebuhr was not hopeful of its evolution out of tyranny or its capacity for empirical judgments.

Niebuhr's colleague John C. Bennett was more hopeful of positive evolution within communism. Bennett thought that Niebuhr's critique of communism in the book Niebuhr dedicated to him was overdone. The differences between these two close friends and colleagues are noticeable to the reader of the book Bennett prepared from the development of the course, *Christianity and Communism Today*.[27] Bennett remained more moderate in his criticism of communism than Niebuhr. He was less inclined than Niebuhr to stress the world conflict of the West with communism, placing more emphasis on centers of energy other than the two superpowers. He was more hopeful than Niebuhr about Marxism's revolutionary role in the third world. He was also more hopeful than Niebuhr about communism's evolution into humane government.

Student response to the course was generally enthusiastic. Richard P. Poethig reported on the first time it was given.

> My first experience of Niebuhr as teacher came in a 1949–1950 seminar on "Christianity and Communism" with a focus on China. The Communists had just taken over the mainland and Chiang Kai-shek had fled to Taiwan. John Bennett and Niebuhr drew upon the experience of missionaries who were present at Union. The seminar holds vivid memories. It was as relevant as the latest news coming off the press-wire. It was an

experience in shared knowledge. Niebuhr and Bennett respected what others had to say about the situation.[28]

Professor Beverly W. Harrison's memory of the course from 1955–56 expressed more ambivalence.

Christianity and Communism was truly awful pedagogically, with three unrelated lecturers. But Kerensky took the course, so that was interesting. To hear Kerensky's accounts of his and Lenin's conversations the night before the Bolsheviks formed a government was worth the price of admission. His and Niebuhr's conversations about these matters were fascinating and provided the best sessions of an otherwise dismal seminar.[29]

Faith and History

Niebuhr's postwar writing continued the themes of his second Gifford Lecture series of 1939. The first major publication after *The Nature and Destiny of Man* was *Faith and History* (1949), which repeated the themes published earlier. Paragraphs were not republished, but there is not much new development of thought. The 1949 volume was drawn from lectures at Yale Divinity School in 1945, at the universities of Glasgow and Aberdeen in 1947, and at the University of Uppsala in a time of compulsive work. Not only does the volume reemphasize ideas from *The Nature and Destiny of Man*, but the chapters review the thoughts of preceding chapters. Given their lecture series origin, this is understandable, but it weakens the book and leaves it hard to read rigorously if one is already familiar with Niebuhr's previous work.

The book is for a theologically educated readership, and it works more explicitly out of its Christian sources than do Niebuhr's other books on history. The investigation of the concept of God is fuller than in *The Nature and Destiny of Man* and shows his use of Alfred North Whitehead's philosophy very clearly. The chapter "Beyond Law and Relativity" is one of his best statements on his method in ethics, in the use of historical standards of justice under the critique of and from the motivation of love.

The central thesis is that modern humanity tries to find meaning in a variety of inadequate understandings of history. The overwhelming modern view of history is to find history's meaningfulness in progressive development to better forms of human life. Niebuhr argues that historical progress in human affairs has been refuted. History has partial meanings, and its ultimate meaning is best represented in Christ's vicarious bearing and forgiving of the sins of history. God's judgment runs through the destruction by humans of human projects, but as there is no progressive development, meaning is found in God's self-disclosure.

The provisional pessimism of Niebuhr for which he is so often criticized is seen here as a necessary apologetic understanding. If historical optimism or progressive human evolution contains the meaning of history, there is no need for Christ. The meaning of the Christ symbol requires a provisionally pessimistic reading of human history. Given repentance and humility, the good of humanity can be realistically sought.

Despite its repetitiveness, the book is an excellent theological statement of Niebuhr's war and postwar understanding. It shows his theological depth better than some more widely read works. His two major academic biographers have differed greatly on the significance of the book. Paul Merkley, who argues strongly that the center of Niebuhr's philosophy and politics is his personal Christian faith, regards *Faith and History* highly.[30] Richard Fox, who seems to be, like Max Weber, unmusical in regards to Christian faith, lightly dismisses the book.[31] This difference in judgment is rooted in their quite different perspectives on Niebuhr. Study of *Faith and History* reinforces the view of the centrality of personally held theology to Niebuhr's work.

A contemporary reviewer, Arthur Schlesinger, Jr., concluded:

> *Faith and History* is written with Dr. Niebuhr's usual vigor, erudition, and precision of expression. It is an indispensable contribution to the revolution of our culture with which this age is inevitably concerned and in which Dr. Niebuhr has already played so brilliant and distinguished a role.[32]

A note of difference from Niebuhr's prewar works is seen in his increasing use of irony. He draws in *Faith and History* on the perspective in Psalm 2:4: "He that sitteth in the heavens shall laugh: the Lord shall have them in derision." This move toward irony and a gradual displacement of tragedy as a central concept for history would lead to the framework of his last book before his stroke, *The Irony of American History* (1952). The professor's close work with his students, and the ability of the students he attracted, is seen in the group who helped with proofreading and indexing. Roger L. Shinn was to become his successor, John E. Smith would become head of the Yale philosophy department, and Langdon Gilkey moved to Chicago to become a leading systematic theologian.

Reflections on History

The word *history* contains a certain ambiguity.[33] It refers both to events that have occurred and to the record of those events. Niebuhr uses *history* as a series of events when he argues that, though history itself is not meaningful, it bears all the meanings which can be found. His own writing of history emphasizes the interpretation of events over the recording of the events for their own value.

Niebuhr's focus was on the meaning of the story rather than on the detail of the occurrences. He had many friends who were professional historians, and he was willing to defer to friends like Arthur Schlesinger, Jr., and Wilhelm Pauck on questions of the verification of events. He did not seek to escape from the discipline of history, but neither did he shoulder its burdens. He wrote and waited patiently for specialized historians to correct him if he had erred. He tried to stand humbly before the historians while offering them his understanding of the meaning of the events they tried to verify and relate. In his preface to *The Irony of American History* (1952), he expressed this humility: "I must add that I have no expert competence in the field of American history; and I apologize in advance to the specialists in this field for what are undoubtedly many errors in fact and judgment."[34] Reactions to his writings on U.S. history were, of course, mixed. Evidence of a positive response is noted in Henry F. May's 1968 article. He began: "In 1952 many historians of the United States were deeply impressed by Reinhold Niebuhr's *The Irony of American History*."[35]

Niebuhr's usual practice in arguing for the acceptance of an idea was to trace its history. In discussing justice he would trace the idea of justice from its Greek and Hebrew roots, through the early years of Western civilization, to its emergence in medieval Europe, into the complexities and various alternatives of the concept in Reformation, Renaissance, and Enlightenment thought; and for a conclusion he would analyze its contemporary meaning. Or if he were attacking a policy of the government, for example Vietnam, he would trace with biting irony the mistakes of the various administrations that had led to the quagmire. So if it is true that his reflections on history lacked the precision of a careful historian, his social criticism and philosophy included more historical detail than philosophers usually consider.

The deftness with which he generalized about historical epochs drove both his students and his family to historical research. The Niebuhrs' family life was often the center of far-ranging debates over interpreting history and what history was as opposed to sheer interpretation. Ursula's Oxford education, combined with the discipline of teaching ever-questioning Barnard undergraduates, often gave her the advantage in debates over historical points. Particularly on British history she often corrected her husband. *The Irony of American History* is dedicated to their son, Christopher, whose approach to historical materials stands in contrast to his father's. Christopher's mind retains massive amounts of detail, and his rapid-fire delivery can overwhelm his listeners. In later years, Christopher often corrected his father, to the father's alternate pride and chagrin.

A visitor to Reinhold Niebuhr's retirement home on Yale Hill in Stockbridge, Massachusetts, shortly before his death was inevitably awed by the power and depth of the elderly Niebuhr's mind. He also felt in Christopher the vitality that reminded many of Reinhold in his youth. In their talk he saw the son's mastery of the slightest detail and sensed the father's impatience to get on to the overarching interpretation of the data. Ursula tended to be more modest in her generalizations than Reinhold, as she emphasized more the counterpoints that forced qualification of the broader generalization. She laced her conversations with a critical wit that forced one to participate in the encounter every bit as completely as one did when engaged with her husband. Conversation at the Niebuhr home inevitably involved the problem of the historical, from the history of Stockbridge, at which they all were experts, through problems of biblical history, in which Ursula had an edge, to issues of American history, in which Christopher mastered the details and Reinhold was allowed to interpret. The pace of the dialogue was breathtaking, and visitors left the beautiful stone-and-wood house awed and better informed than on their arrival.

The Irony of History

Niebuhr's adoption of irony as the major motif of his interpretation of history is significant. It reveals the decreased importance of three previous motifs, and it also indicates a trend toward a less dogmatic and more empirical approach to history. The second chapter indicated how the liberal motif of progress had been unable to deal with the tragic character of history. The third chapter discussed the failure of the

Marxist dialectic of history to dominate Niebuhr's thought. The motif of tragedy was of continued importance to Niebuhr into the 1940s. Even the volume of essays entitled *Beyond Tragedy* (1937) regarded a provisionally tragic interpretation of the human situation as essential to the Christian apologetic.[36] His first full treatment of irony as a motif for interpreting history appeared in *The Irony of American History* in 1952.

Robert E. Fitch's essay on Niebuhr's philosophy of history failed to examine carefully the evolution of Niebuhr's thought about history and tended to blur the distinctions between pathos, irony, and tragedy. While he admitted that Niebuhr's development of the theme of irony is as recent as 1952, Fitch argued that it had been important to his thought since 1934.[37] Fitch's essay tended to stress the continuity of Niebuhr's philosophy of history and to blur some distinctions between his philosophy of history in his Marxist and Christian realist-liberal periods. There is, of course, a continuity; it is the same man thinking about the problem of history. An argument that stressed the continuity of the philosophy of history while acknowledging the significant differences between Marxism and Christian realism could only, with difficulty, stress the centrality of the philosophy of history in Niebuhr's thought. Fitch's case hangs on his supposed discovery of the use of irony in *Reflections on the End of an Era*. Unfortunately for Fitch's purpose, Niebuhr used *pathos*, not *irony*, to interpret the aspect of history that he described.

> One of the pathetic aspects of human history is that the instruments of judgment which it uses to destroy particular vices must belong to the same category of the vice to be able to destroy it. Thus some evil, which is to be destroyed, is always transferred to the instrument of its destruction and thereby perpetuated.[38]

The term *pathos*, as defined by Niebuhr,[39] fits the feature described more adequately than does irony.[40]

Fitch's other evidence for the development of the theme of irony in Niebuhr's thought deals with tragedy and humor, not with irony as a category for the interpretation of history.[41] Fitch's failure to marshal proof for Niebuhr's early use of irony as a motif for the interpretation of history allows the interpretation that (1) Niebuhr's distinctions between pathos, tragedy, and irony were important to his thought and (2) the shift from tragedy to irony correlated with other shifts in his thought. The gradual replacement of tragedy by irony in his philosophy of history indicates a new openness to human accomplishment and a less dogmatic approach to history in the post–World War II era.

Irony was differentiated from pathos, for Niebuhr, by the actor's increased degree of responsibility. It was differentiated from tragedy by the fact that the involved weakness was an unconscious fault rather than a conscious resolution.[42] Irony was more than comedy, though it contained a comic element. Irony revealed a hidden relationship in the incongruity that was the essence of comedy. The most succinct definition of irony is found in Niebuhr's volume *The Irony of American History*: "Irony consists of apparently fortuitous incongruities in life which are discovered, upon closer examination, to be not merely fortuitous."[43] Ironic situations are characterized by a tendency to dissolve when the actors become aware of the irony. For the awareness means the discovery of "the hidden vanity or pretension by which comedy is turned into irony."[44]

It was the possibility that the United States might turn away from the hidden vanities and pretensions of American life that prompted Niebuhr to write on the ironies of American history. He no longer was as bitter in his castigations of America's liberal culture, for he saw that it had realized a higher degree of justice than its critics thought possible. Yet he still thought the United States was hindered by "pretensions of virtue, wisdom, and power." *The Irony of American History* is more the work of a moralist than a historian or philosopher of history. It is the work of a moralist who wanted to free his country from illusions that hindered its wise conduct of foreign policy.

Even in Niebuhr's special use of irony, it is not a particularly theological concept. Niebuhr relates it to his theology, however, and claims that it is the normative way for Christians to view history.

> Yet the Christian faith tends to make the ironic view of human evil in history the normative one. Its conception of redemption from evil carries it beyond the limits of irony, but its interpretation of the nature of evil in human history is consistently ironic. This consistency is achieved on the basis of the belief that the whole drama of human history is under scrutiny of a divine judge who laughs at human pretensions without being hostile to human aspirations. . . .
>
> The Biblical interpretation of the human situation is ironic, rather than tragic or pathetic, because of its unique formulation of the problem of human freedom.[45]

The Christian view of history is not tragic because human actions are not necessarily evil. The development of the concept of irony inclined Niebuhr away from the more pessimistic notes of his Marxist and Christian-realist writings. Developing the ironic interpretation of history, he wrote:

> Nevertheless, a purely tragic view of life is not finally viable. It is, at any rate, not the Christian view. According to that view destructiveness is not an inevitable consequence of human creativity. It is not invariably necessary to do evil in order that we may do good.[46]

The Ironies of American History

Niebuhr's commitment to American ideals and to the country drove him to the role of social critic for whom a favorite form of critique was irony.

He was drawn to the figure of Don Quixote perhaps through Unamuno, whose writings on death and the decline of Western civilization had influenced him earlier.[47] Don Quixote had refuted the ideals of chivalry by espousing them. The reader whose mind was stimulated by Miguel de Cervantes could see the refutation of the ideals even though Don Quixote himself was oblivious to the absurdity of his portrayal of values of knight errantry.[48] As Cervantes had laughed at chivalry through Don Quixote, Niebuhr set out to laugh at the foibles of a bourgeois American culture. The laughter he desired to provoke would be accompanied by understanding of the hidden incongruities of American life. He hoped that an understanding of the ironies of American history would help to dissolve those ironies and to reduce the pride and pretensions of the country. Condemnation of the weakness of the United States accomplished little; the use of irony, he hoped, would avoid the hostility of injured pride and result in an "abatement of the pretensions which caused the irony."[49]

After *The Irony of American History*, in 1952, Niebuhr continued to reveal to the country the ironies of which it was only dimly aware in a book of essays published in 1958 under the title *Pious and Secular America*;[50] in 1963 he wrote with Alan Heimert of Harvard *A Nation So Conceived*,[51] which had a similar purpose. *The Democratic Experience*,[52] which he wrote with Paul E. Sigmund in 1969, had a related thrust in Part I, though it reflected on the broader democratic experience of Europe also and was less explicit about the use of "irony." In all these books Niebuhr argued that history was not tragic. Human beings did not have choices only between evil alternatives, for they could with sufficient understanding of their own predicament act creatively. The books revealed a similarity of purpose and sometimes of examples as he ranged over the data of American history to attack American illusions.

Niebuhr piled ironies upon ironies, using the term so frequently that it seemed to lose the rather careful meaning he had given it. The fact that the dreams of agrarian isolationist innocence of the young America had been reduced to irrelevance by the growth of the United States was regarded as ironic.[53] The fact that American idealists attempted to escape the realities of international politics by articulating schemes for world order was labeled irony.[54] The awareness that the nation had been better able to assure its security in the days of its youth than in the day of nuclear power was seen as irony.[55]

The height of irony to Niebuhr was that the foe, Marxism, in the hands of the Soviet Union, had transmuted weaknesses in liberal culture into a dangerous creed that threatened to destroy democracy.[56] The ideas of humanity's control of its destiny, equality, and the innocence of man, which had fueled liberal illusions, were combined into a religious-political mythology in Marxism that, protesting against the ills of bourgeois culture, threatened humanity. Bourgeois culture and communist culture shared illusions, and their conquest of the power of nature through science threatened the world. Against the misunderstandings of the cold war and the discredited mythologies involved in the struggle, Niebuhr responded again in the spirit of scripture: "He that sitteth in the heavens shall laugh."[57]

In the four books mentioned above, Niebuhr attacks the complacency, sentimentality, utopianism, and parochialism he thinks the American rise to power has encouraged in Americans who held on to overly simple views of their heritage. He uses irony in a rather general way as a label for an incongruity between American myth and reality. Marcus Cunliffe, professor of American history at the University of Manchester, in the preface to the British edition of *A Nation So Conceived*, points to the central purpose of all four volumes by writing, "The second value of the book is in providing a sample of a special category of current American historiography—that which is devoted to the destruction of clichés."[58]

An irony of Niebuhr's writing on the ironies of American history was that he gave so little attention to racial strife in the four books. In the introduction to the last published volume, this omission was noted: "In the United States, we are conscious, as we were not a few years ago, how difficult it is for democratic politics to deal with the problem of race, especially when it is reinforced by economic handicaps."[59] The book itself dealt with the problem of race in the United States only superficially. The other three books on American history had only one chapter of eight pages and a few scattered references to the race problem in the United States. Niebuhr's editorials and magazine articles did focus on aspects of the race problem, as did the post-retirement seminar on social ethics, but the race problem as such was not the center of his concerns about American history in these books. If there is irony in the manifestation of militant African Americans charging liberal whites with failure to take seriously their liberal creeds, the Constitution of the United States and the Declaration of Independence, it is even more ironic to find Niebuhr, to whom many African American theologians look as an ally, guilty by omission of neglecting African Americans in American history. Niebuhr has not tried to exclude himself from those Americans who are subject to illusions about the American past. However, a major article, "The Negro Minority and Its Fate in a Self-righteous Nation,"[60] written during the summer of 1968 in his old age and ill health in the style of his reflection on the ironies of American history, filled the gap that his books on history had left.

Niebuhr knew that human beings were tempted by sloth as well as pride. He recorded this standard insight of Christian thinking about sin in 1952.

> Nations as individuals may be assailed by contradictory temptation. They may be tempted to flee the responsibilities of their power or refuse to develop their potentialities. . . . There is therefore no nice line to be drawn between a normal expression of human creativity and either the *sloth* which refuses to assume the responsibilities of human freedom or the *pride* which overestimates man's individual or collective power. But it is possible to discern extreme forms of each evil very clearly; and to recognize various shades of evil between the extremes and the norm.[61]

Reinhold was not tempted by sloth. He worked compulsively. He loved his vocation and it drove him relentlessly. Ever since 1939, he had had recurring bouts of exhaustion and depression, but after finishing *The Irony of American History* in January of 1952, he hit his own limit. The tape recording of a University of Chicago lecture that month reveals a tired man. His voice is still powerful, but there is not the rapid-fire delivery of earlier lectures. The contrast between "Transvaluation of Values" at Chicago and the Amsterdam World Council of Churches address in 1948 is striking in voice and delivery.[62] After a

197

bout with flu over Christmas 1951, January was difficult. On February 15, after a spasm, he was taken to St. Luke's Hospital.[63] Spasms recurred, leaving him by the end of the summer with reduced energy, a crippled left arm, slurring speech, and an increased tendency toward depression.[64]

The circuit preaching was ended: he was sidelined. From constant overwork he was limited to a few hours each day. His life, which had been in his work, was drastically curtailed at age sixty. Paul Merkley reports his work time, after a series of strokes, was reduced to three hours per day.[65] June Bingham[66] reported that after having exploratory brain surgery, a procedure called pneumoencephalogram in which he remained conscious, he immediately jotted down some notes for *The Self and the Dramas of History*. He would work on that book during his convalescence. Ursula later would refer to the strokes as cerebral incidents; apparently insufficient blood entered the brain. He recovered to continue his teaching, but literary work was cut back, and travel and outside speaking were basically ended. Ursula's life changed. Reinhold was now home, and she took on the nursing care of her husband. Other professional help was arranged, but her own academic vocation was put on hold. Reinhold would often speak and write of her sacrificing her vocation to his care.

NOTES

1. Reinhold Niebuhr, ed., *This Ministry: The Contribution of Henry Sloane Coffin* (New York: Charles Scribner's Sons, 1945).
2. Robert T. Handy, *A History of Union Theological Seminary in New York* (New York: Columbia University Press, 1987), p. 208.
3. Ibid., p. 214.
4. Response to questionnaire from J. Gordon Chamberlin in the author's possession.
5. Reinhold Niebuhr, "A Third of a Century at Union," *The Union Seminary Tower* 7 (May 1960), p. 3.
6. Speech delivered in 1953 and published in Ursula M. Niebuhr, ed., *Justice and Mercy* (1974), p. 128.
7. Ibid., p. 129.
8. Responses to questionnaire in the author's possession.
9. Frederick Buechner, *Now and Then* (San Francisco: Harper & Row, 1983), p. 12.
10. Response to questionnaire in the author's possession.
11. Ibid.
12. Response to questionnaire in the author's possession.

13. This section is a contemporary editing of pages 219–240 of my *Reinhold Niebuhr: Prophet to Politicians* (Nashville: Abingdon Press, 1972).

14. Reinhold Niebuhr, "Toward New Intra-Christian Endeavors," *The Christian Century* 86 (Dec. 31, 1969), 1622–1667.

15. D. B. Robertson, ed., *Essays in Applied Christianity* (1959), p. 29.

16. Ursula M. Niebuhr, "The Testing of Our Calling," in Martin Caldwell, ed., *Lift Up Your Hearts* (New York: Morehouse-Gorham Co., 1956), pp. 35–53.

17. Robertson, ed., *Essays in Applied Christianity*, pp. 57–63.

18. Reinhold Niebuhr, *Leaves from the Notebook of a Tamed Cynic* (1929), p. 90.

19. D. B. Robertson has written the best essay on Niebuhr's perspective on the church. See "Introduction," in Robertson, ed., *Essays in Applied Christianity*. In addition to the book of essays Robertson published on the subject, chapter 14 of Niebuhr's *Faith and History* (1949) is particularly useful.

20. Patrick Granfield, *Theologians at Work* (New York: Macmillan Co., 1967), p. 66.

21. File No. 121-33418 on Reinhold Niebuhr provided by Federal Bureau of Investigation under Freedom of Information Act in the author's possession.

22. Reinhold Niebuhr, "The King's Chapel and the King's Court," *Christianity and Crisis* 29 (Aug. 4, 1969).

23. *Union Theological Seminary Catalogue* (1953), p. 82.

24. Lecture on "The Roots of Marxist Philosophy" in class notes; "Christianity and Communism," Reinhold Niebuhr Papers (MSS in the Library of Congress, Washington, D.C.), Container 24; also "Marx and Engels on Religion" (1964) in Ronald Stone, ed., *Faith and Politics* (1968), pp. 47–54.

25. Reinhold Niebuhr, "The Anomaly of European Socialism," *The Yale Review* 42 (Dec. 1952). Reprinted in *Christian Realism and Political Problems* (1953), pp. 43–52.

26. Lecture on "The Errors of Marxism" in class notes; "Christianity and Communism," Niebuhr Papers, Container 24. Also "Why Is Communism So Evil?" in Reinhold Niebuhr, *Christian Realism and Political Problems* (1953), pp. 33–42.

27. John C. Bennett, *Christianity and Communism Today* (New York: Association Press, 1940).

28. Response to questionnaire in the author's possession.

29. Response to questionnaire in the author's possession.

30. Paul Merkley, *Reinhold Niebuhr: A Political Account* (Montreal: McGill-Queens University Press, 1975), pp. 202, 214–215, 220–221.

31. Richard Fox, *Reinhold Niebuhr: A Biography* (New York: Pantheon Books, 1985), pp. 237–238.

32. Arthur Schlesinger, Jr., "Book Review of Faith and History," *Christianity and Society* 14 (Summer 1949), 26–27.

33. The further discussion of history in chapter 7 is an edited version of my *Reinhold Niebuhr: Prophet to Politicians*, pp. 137–145.

34. Reinhold Niebuhr, *The Irony of American History* (1952), pp. viii–ix.

35. Henry F. May, "A Meditation on an Unfashionable Book," *Christianity and Crisis* 28 (May 27, 1968), 120. May is Margaret Byrne Professor of History at the University of California, Berkeley.

36. "Christianity's view of history is tragic insofar as it recognizes evil as an inevitable concomitant of even the highest spiritual enterprises." Reinhold Niebuhr, *Beyond Tragedy* (1937), pp. x–xi.

37. Charles W. Kegley, ed., *Reinhold Niebuhr: His Religious, Social, and Political Thought* (New York: Pilgrim Press, 1984), p. 379.

38. Reinhold Niebuhr, *Reflections on the End of an Era* (1934), p. 94. Quoted by Robert E. Fitch in Kegley, ed., *Reinhold Niebuhr*, p. 379.

39. "Pathos is that element in an historic situation which elicits pity, but neither deserves admiration nor warrants contrition." Reinhold Niebuhr, *The Irony of American History* (1952), p. vii.

40. See below, second paragraph,.

41. Kegley, ed., *Reinhold Niebuhr*, p. 303.

42. Niebuhr, *Irony of American History*, p. viii.

43. Ibid.

44. Ibid.

45. Ibid., p. 155.

46. Ibid., p. 157.

47. See chapter 2, fifth section.

48. Niebuhr, *Irony of American History*, p. 167.

49. Ibid., p. 169.

50. Reinhold Niebuhr, *Pious and Secular America* (1958), published in England under the title *The Godly and the Ungodly* (London: Faber & Faber, 1958).

51. Reinhold Niebuhr and Alan Heimert, *A Nation So Conceived: Reflections on the History of America from Its Early Visions to Its Present Power* (1963).

52. Reinhold Niebuhr and Paul E. Sigmund, *The Democratic Experience; Past and Prospects* (1969). Although the volume was published in 1969 and reveals the thought as well as the editing of its coauthor, the bulk of the book was presented at Barnard College in the lectures Niebuhr gave there in 1963.

53. Niebuhr, *Irony of American History*, p. 2.

54. Ibid.

55. Ibid., p. 3.

56. Ibid.

57. Ibid., p. 63.

58. Niebuhr and Heimert, *A Nation So Conceived*, p. 4.

59. Niebuhr and Sigmund, *Democratic Experience*, p. vi.

60. Reinhold Niebuhr, "The Negro Minority and Its Fate in a Self-righteous Nation," *Social Action/Social Progress*, 35/59 (Oct. 1968), 53–64. As chapter 2 indicates, Niebuhr had been engaged in the struggle for racial justice since his ministry in Detroit, and he had written articles and chapters on the problem decades before it was recognized as a major issue. The above article is a particularly good example of the type of writing to which Niebuhr subjected other American social problems. The publication of the essay in a book of essays would restore a balance to his writing on American history which may indeed be needed.

61. Niebuhr, *Irony of American History*, p. 73. The emphasis is mine.

62. "The Reinhold Niebuhr Audio Tape Collection," Union Theological Seminary in Virginia, 1979, nos. 63 and 64.

63. Fox, *Reinhold Niebuhr*, p. 248.
64. Ibid., p. 251.
65. Merkley, *Reinhold Niebuhr: A Political Account*, p. 201.
66. June Bingham, *Courage to Change: An Introduction to the Life and Thought of Reinhold Niebuhr* (New York: Charles Scribner's Sons, 1961), p. 318.

8

The Aging Liberal and Christian Realism

1952–1960

NIEBUHR'S INFLUENCE grew while his physical strength declined in the 1950s. Of course, his friend and admirer Adlai Stevenson lost the presidential race. The forces behind the amiable General Dwight D. Eisenhower dominated the period. Niebuhr, who enjoyed many associations with Columbia University, from which Eisenhower moved to assume the presidency of the United States, is reported to have enjoyed the Columbia philosopher's quip, "Our university's loss is also our nation's loss." Another friend and often opponent of Niebuhr's, John Foster Dulles, resigned from the Board of Directors of Union Theological Seminary when he accepted the post of Secretary of State. The conflicts between Niebuhr and Dulles, as represented in Niebuhr's polemics, became stronger with Dulles presiding over foreign policy from Korea to Dien Bien Phu and Suez. Though Niebuhr had served in various capacities in the State Department under Dean Acheson, there is no record of John Foster Dulles's requesting such help. Niebuhr and Dulles's foreign policy collaboration and face-to-face debates on international relations had been under the auspices of the churches.

Niebuhr's stroke and resulting paralysis slowed him down and made him dependent on others. His travel was severely restricted and he never was able to fulfill his lecturing tour of Japan or return to his dream of visiting India. His letters to friends reflect his frustrations with the limitations and pain of the illness that plagued him for the rest of his life. But there were compensations. By 1953 he could return to his teaching. His influence continued to grow in church and academic circles. Stevenson could not win, but he carried his influence into the campaigns. His theological perspective was dominant in liberal Protestantism in America. It became his fate for some of his ideas to be accepted and merged with other streams of philosophy, which were sometimes compatible and sometimes not. This was true of seminarians as well as intellectual secular and public figures. Some students followed his thought almost entirely and were regarded as Niebuhrians by students who absorbed less of his influence. Others merged his influence in their lives with that of professors of differing schools of thought.

Paul Merkley wrote of this post-stroke period:

> But while the quantity of the work declines—and while much of the fire of earlier writings is gone, there are some marginal gains. . . . He was driven to a new economy in the definition of his themes and the elaboration of his arguments.[1]

Merkley then contradicts himself on the missing "fire" by complaining about Niebuhr's harsh polemics against communism. Other examples of post-1952 "fire" are evident in the development of his causes and writings in this period. Merkley was also wrong on "the quantity of the work." In 1951, Niebuhr published 53 occasional pieces; in 1952, 60 pieces; in 1953, 84 pieces; and in 1954, 99 pieces. Similarly, the actual count of his books during the decades of his teaching career remained basically unchanged: five in the 1930s, six in the 1940s, and five in the 1950s. Actually, if one includes his books of essays by editors, the 1950s were the most productive decade. His influence through his writing had grown since the late 1940s. He had become a star intellectual, and people turned to his writing because of a recognition of its importance. He would no longer rally academics, students, worshipers, or political people to his causes by powerful oratory. Now, after the stroke, his power resided in his previously established reputation and work and in his refinement of and further writing in that tradition. Christian realism was a reforming tradition drawn from the Social Gospel movement, the reforming populism of Robert La Follette, Woodrow Wilson's reform program, and an appreciation of the hard realities of twentieth-century America. The New Deal had won many of its reforms, and the programs of the Americans for Democratic Action attempted to continue them. Robert M. Lovett had used the term *Christian Realist* to describe Niebuhr in a book review in 1934;[2] by

1941, John C. Bennett published a book entitled *Christian Realism*,[3] which outlined the emerging social thought. Niebuhr's *Christian Realism and Political Problems*,[4] a collection of essays published in 1953, had helped fix the name to his type of Augustinian theological perspective. This theology undergirded his anticommunist mixed-economy welfare-oriented democratic policies represented by liberal groups including the Liberal Party and Americans for Democratic Action.

Augustine

The influence of Augustine had grown on Niebuhr, starting with his reflections in Detroit. Ursula's encouragement of this theme of his thought bore more fruit in *The Nature and Destiny of Man*.

The lectures on Augustine had been among the strongest in his History of Christian Ethics course, and he refined a Columbia lecture on Augustine to take a central place in *Christian Realism and Political Problems* in 1953. Augustine fit: a civilization had just been racked by a civil war, and it faced another resolute foe. Christianity subdued in Eastern Europe was threatened by war and secularism in its Western homes. Niebuhr as an ethicist for the empire appreciated Augustine's sense of publicly responsible Christianity and his use of love and natural law. For Niebuhr, Augustine was the first Christian realist. He had reservations about aspects of Augustine's teaching on love and deeper reservations about Augustine's political theory. His reservations about Augustine's relevance to democratic governments would deepen in his last book, but they were present in 1953. The Augustinian theology was the context for Niebuhr's pragmatism and liberalism. He wrote:

> Modern "realists" know the power of collective self-interest as Augustine did; but they do not understand its blindness. Modern pragmatists understood the irrelevance of fixed and detailed norms; but they do not understand that love must take the place as the final norm for these inadequate norms. Modern liberal Christians know that love is the final norm for man; but they fall into sentimentality because they fail to measure the power and persistence of self-love. Thus Augustine, whatever may be the defects of his approach to political reality, and whatever may be the dangers of a too slavish devotion to his insights, nevertheless proves himself a more reliable guide than any known thinker.[5]

Wilhelm Pauck's review showed that Niebuhr's thought circled around the same themes without exactly repeating himself in his many writings. He saw Niebuhr using his dialectical skill to probe the pretensions of humanity out of his sure faith in the mercy of God. He avoided systematics that would deaden his argument, and Pauck found people ready to read or listen to Niebuhr again and again on the same themes as he presented them freshly. The historian's praise for Niebuhr's treatment of Augustine was emphasized:

> In his treatment of "Augustine's Political Ethics," Dr. Niebuhr proves himself, in my opinion, as a sound historical interpreter. In very brief compass he succeeds in clarifying the complete thought of Augustine without simplifying it.[6]

His later writings would not directly attack liberalism, but they still criticized optimistic idealism. His Augustinian-Reformation theological base could be seen.

Pragmatism

In retrospect, Niebuhr's debt to pragmatism can be seen throughout his writing. His attacks on liberalism had obscured the pragmatic quality of his thought, and it had been particularly hidden by Marxist and Christian dogma. The philosophy of William James had been important to Niebuhr as a young student,[7] and Niebuhr's methodological presuppositions continued to reveal the influence of James. In the 1930s, Niebuhr cooperated with and argued against John Dewey. In the 1940s, he came to appreciate the pragmatic liberalism of President Roosevelt. In the 1950s, he explicitly advocated Christian pragmatism.

Niebuhr's pragmatism is characterized by a rejection of all ideologically consistent political schemes. History is full of novelty, and the stuff of political life cannot be put into neat generalizations. Attempts to state principles of politics on divine, natural, or rational grounds have all been undermined by the relativizing forces of history. Every institution of government should, in Niebuhr's opinion, be regarded pragmatically; the social critic or philosopher should always be aware that an institution which served well in the past may be outdated and require modification. Institutions of government are to be examined, not only in the light of Marxist, liberal, or Christian canons but with regard to their usefulness for individual lives in a particular situation. This pragmatism forces the teacher of social ethics to refrain from expounding the moral law for political life and inclines the teacher to study how tentative regulative principles of morality function in history. Though occasionally Niebuhr would protest against the use of any principles in judging politics, his more consistent position is that principled judgments and action on the basis of such judgments are essential. For example, he attacked Barth's "extreme pragmatism, which disavows all moral principles"[8] at the time of the Hungarian revolution of 1956.

William James

Unfortunately, Niebuhr did not provide a precise record of his debt to William James. His intellectual autobiographies all indicate his move toward pragmatism, but they do not discuss James. The question of influence is inevitably a difficult one to answer satisfactorily, though one quotation provides a clue. "I stand in the William James tradition. He was both an empiricist and a religious man, and his faith was both the consequence and the presupposition of his pragmatism."[9] Four aspects of Niebuhr's thought reveal sufficient similarities with William James's definition of pragmatism to regard him as a pragmatist even if the exact degree of dependence on James is indeterminable. His thought is strikingly similar to that of James in social ethics, epistemology, and apologetics. His avoidance of optimism and pessimism in the expectations of improvement in man's political life is also foreshadowed in James's meliorism.

In social ethics, Niebuhr follows pragmatism. He regards some form of pragmatism or utilitarianism as the only way of making moral judgments about social and political questions. Both means and ends are judged pragmatically, and any conflict between the two is also weighed pragmatically: that is, a judgment is reached in terms of the concrete interests involved. He recorded his commitment to pragmatism in social-ethical theory in bold terms:

> When viewing a historic situation all moralists become pragmatists and utilitarians. Some general good, some summum bonum, "the greatest good of the greatest number" or "the most inclusive harmony of all vital capacities" is set up as the criterion of the morality of specific actions and each action is judged with reference to its relation to the ultimate goal.
>
> The choice of instruments and immediate objectives which fall between motive and ultimate objective raises issues which are pragmatic to such a degree that they may be said to be more political than they are ethical.[10]

Niebuhr's ethic is not simply William James's ethic. It preserves a dualistic note inherited from Augustine and Luther that is not important to James. It is also informed by a vision of Christian perfectionism by which James's ethic was untroubled. In the practical conclusions reached, it tended to be more consistently "tough-minded" than was the ethic of William James.

The prestige of Paul Tillich has supported the view that Niebuhr had no epistemology. Tillich began an essay entitled "Reinhold Niebuhr's Doctrine of Knowledge" with the assertion, "The difficulty of writing about Niebuhr's epistemology lies in the fact that there is no such epistemology. Niebuhr does not ask, 'How can I know?' "[11] Tillich then asserts that the omitted factor reappears in disguised form. He argues that Niebuhr's lack of epistemology is the source of his criticism of ontology. The remainder of the article criticizes Niebuhr for refusing to accept Tillich's ontology. Niebuhr's thought does appear weak when judged by the canons of Tillich's ontology. Skepticism regarding Tillich's ontology, however, is not the same as the lack of all epistemology. Niebuhr never wrote a formal essay on epistemology, but he considered the problem at length in three books[12] and in several essays on related subjects. Tillich's refusal to acknowledge Niebuhr's consideration of the epistemological question was caused partly by his desire to reveal Niebuhr's lack of ontology but also by the strangeness to Tillich's thought of Niebuhr's epistemology. Niebuhr stood in the empirical tradition of William James, which was anathema to German idealism.

Niebuhr combines a high degree of skepticism about claims of metaphysical or religious knowledge with a frank acceptance of the achievements of the sciences. Knowledge consists of an awareness of coherences in life. These coherences are more easily attainable in realms unqualified by human freedom and human self-interest. The skepticism about metaphysical or religious knowledge combines with his doctrine of the free but self-interested self to make him a critic of attempts to establish a "scientific morality." On the other hand, he welcomed the refinements in social research that were moving toward greater accuracy in predicting the political behavior of man.[13]

Niebuhr shares the modern world's confidence that the sciences will continue to produce new knowledge in their respective spheres. He finds the subject-and-object dilemma in epistemology rationally unanswerable, but he assumes that there is an ultimate congruity.[14] He assumes a large degree of coherence in a basically ordered but unfinished world.[15]

> The whole of reality is characterized by a basic coherence. Things and events are in a vast web of relationships and are known through their

relations. Perceptual knowledge is possible only within a framework of conceptual images, which in some sense conform to the structures in which reality is organized. The world is organized or it could not exist; if it is to be known, it must be known through its sequences, coherences, [causalities] and essences.[16]

If asked, "How do you know?" Niebuhr would answer by describing the process of verifying the idea. The process of verification would involve the coherence of the idea with other ideas, logic, or the observable world.

It is natural to test the conformity to the particular coherence in which it seems to belong. We are skeptical about ghosts, for instance, because they do not conform to the characteristics of historical reality as we know it.[17]

Niebuhr's position, so far presented, is in harmony with the following statement by William James: "Truth for us is simply a collective name for verification-processes. . . . Truth is *made*, just as health, wealth and strength are made, in the course of experience."[18]

Niebuhr confirmed[19] that the following quote from James represents his approach to the epistemological question.

It matters not to an empiricist from what quarter an hypothesis may come to him: he may have acquired it by fair means or by foul; passion may have whispered or accident suggested it; but if the total drift of thinking continues to confirm it, that is what he means by its being true.[20]

Like James, Niebuhr assumes that most intellectual achievements represent modification of previously held ideas.[21] Niebuhr characteristically works through a problem in political thought by assembling the various answers to the problem, checking each possibility, and accepting one that is verified in the sense of cohering to other needed ideas and experience.

One level of Niebuhr's Christian apology is very close to that of James. They both abandoned traditional natural theology because of dissatisfaction with arguments for the existence of God and an antagonism toward rational systems, which they thought prematurely closed a developing world.

Both apologists recognized an area of life that was beyond the reach of empirical studies. Neither had a bias toward rejecting theological statements as meaningless. Both personally possessed lively religious convictions. James's formula sums up one level of their agreement on apology:

> If theological ideas prove to have a value for concrete life, they will be true, for pragmatism, in the sense of being good for so much. For how much more they are true, will depend entirely on their relations to other truths that also have to be acknowledged.[22]

Niebuhr made use of this form of pragmatic apology for theological ideas when he pointed toward the quality of the Christian's life as verification of the Christian insight. "The only way of validating such a faith is to bear witness to it in life."[23] The use of the argument of pragmatic utility for religious beliefs is shown in quotations from three of his works:

> This is a final enigma of human existence for which there is no answer except by faith and hope; for all answers transcend the categories of human reason. Yet without these answers human life is threatened with skepticism and nihilism on the one hand; and with fanaticism and pride on the other.[24]

> Since supreme omnipotence and perfect holiness are incompatible attributes, there is a note of rational absurdity in all religion, which more rational types of theologies attempt to eliminate. But they cannot succeed without sacrificing a measure of religious vitality.[25]

> Life has a center and source of meaning beyond the natural and social sequences which may be rationally discerned. This divine source and center must be discerned by faith because it is enveloped in mystery, though being the basis of meaning. So discerned, it yields a frame of meaning in which human freedom is real and valid and not merely tragic or illusory.[26]

The argument from the utility of a theological conception is one important level of Niebuhr's apologetic and one he seems to have taken from William James, though it was available elsewhere.

A fourth similarity in the thought of Niebuhr and James is the hopeful pragmatism to which the former came in the postwar years. One need not conclude that Niebuhr had once been a pessimist to recognize a more hopeful note in his analysis of the self and society in his last writings. He did not adopt Spengler and Unamuno as his disillusionment with liberalism grew, but he was influenced by them. He found the provisional pessimism of Marxism helpful in qualifying the idealism of the social revolutionary. His theology had insisted that the Christian message was heard best in a world aware of the tragic quality of history. His final thought, that of a Christian informed by liberalism and pragmatism, was close to the position described by James as meliorism.[27] He could see that some of the conditions of a healthy political order were already present, but so were forces resisting health. The political philosophy of liberalism could be affirmed and the values of liberty, equality, and fraternity pursued, but the struggle was not over, nor was the outcome secure. As in James, pragmatism and liberalism interacted to produce a sober, goal-oriented philosophy, which could lay claim to a middle position between optimism and pessimism. Niebuhr's meliorism, however, was closer than that of James to the latter's category of "tough-minded" political thought. Niebuhr retained a larger degree of eschatological perspective than did James, and he also was more inclined than James to emphasize the inevitable corruption of political community. This higher degree of "tough-mindedness" was one of the chief differences between Niebuhr and John Dewey, the most famous exponent of pragmatism after James.

John Dewey

Niebuhr attacked Dewey's thought repeatedly,[28] and the followers of Dewey have not been reticent in counterattacking.[29] This interest in the basic disagreements between Niebuhr and Dewey should not obscure their common debt to William James or the similarities of their thought. They both considered the context in reaching a decision on political policy. They joined in opposing the great systems of philosophical rationalism. Both represented their thought as developing rather than defending a system. Neither thinker gave a completely naturalistic account of man, for both knew that man was continuous and discontinuous with nature.[30]

There is sufficient reason to regard the Niebuhr-Dewey controversy of the 1930s as an intramural affair. Both men were liberals who owed much to William James and pragmatism. Both were associated, during the Depression, with a variety of causes and a collection of ideas loosely described as socialist in inspiration.[31] The intramural character of the debate (Dewey taught at Columbia) increased its importance in the minds of many residents of Morningside Heights, as institutional interests and departmental concerns could not easily be separated from some of the arguments.

Niebuhr's quarrel with Dewey was not primarily a theological one. In fact, Niebuhr reviewed Dewey's *A Common Faith* in rather positive terms. Dewey's form of naturalism was not attacked from a more orthodox Christian perspective. The one note of mild criticism in the review, which might be interpreted as complimentary, was that Dewey did not suspect how close his creed was to the teaching of prophetic religion.[32]

Niebuhr's attack upon Dewey focused on what creative social intelligence could be expected to accomplish.[33] Both Niebuhr and Dewey admitted that the social order has always been dominated by force. Dewey hoped that the new social sciences could change the way society was administered. Niebuhr hoped for a radical realignment of the balance of power in society, but he did not expect reason to control force.

> Professor Dewey has a touching faith in the possibility of achieving the same results in the field of social relations which intelligence achieved in the mastery of nature. The fact that man constitutionally corrupts his purest visions of disinterested justice in his actual actions seems never to occur to him.[34]

Arthur Schlesinger, Jr., has used the following categories to delineate the differences between the two thinkers:

> In the case of Dewey, it should be said that his disdain for the New Deal and his commitment to socialization proceeded naturally enough from his disregard for power in society and from his faith in human rationality and scientific planning; but for Niebuhr, who was realistic about man and who wanted to equilibrate power in society, the commitment to socialization was both the price of indifference to the achievements of piecemeal reform and a symptom of despair. Where Dewey spurned the New Deal because of his optimism about man and his belief in science, Niebuhr seemed to spurn it because of his pessimism about man and his belief in catastrophe.[35]

Schlesinger came close to understanding their common rejection of the New Deal, but the differences are much more subtle; the polarities of optimism and pessimism will not stand serious scrutiny any better than Niebuhr's own treatment of Dewey as a "child of light." Nor can it be argued convincingly that Dewey disregarded power in society while Niebuhr was indifferent to piecemeal reform. Throughout the decade of the 1930s, Niebuhr wrote editorial after editorial for reform, fought for unpopular reform causes, and gave himself to left-wing political activity. Certainly he hoped, under Marxist influence, for a radical transformation of American society, but his hope did not lead him, as it did more consistent Marxists, to oppose reforms for the sake of increasing class polarization. Niebuhr himself did not criticize Dewey for disregarding power but rather for relying too heavily on the possibility of conflicting claims being adjusted through discussion, democracy, and education.[36] Morton White's observation, in the context of criticizing Niebuhr's thought, is closer to the full breadth of the two social philosophers than is Schlesinger: "All we have here is the recognition that men are somewhere between the serpent and the dove, and while Niebuhr puts us closer to the serpent, Dewey puts us closer to the dove."[37]

Dewey and Niebuhr concurred during the Depression on the need for a third political party to lead the country into socialism. Both expected radical changes in the economic and social structure of the country and thought the changes would come through revolution, if not achieved by democratic reform. Their deep differences were seen in their criticism of Marxist radicals. Niebuhr criticized them for romantic illusions concerning the possibility of eliminating force from human affairs. Dewey criticized them for lacking a rigorous social science. In their appreciation of democracy the same fundamental difference could be seen. Niebuhr regarded democracy as the best governmental system for the adjustment of power; Dewey praised democracy for enabling social ideals to be tested by experience, making possible the selection of the most rational policy.

Niebuhr's central criticism of Dewey was drawn from Marxist sources; later it was to be based on Christian doctrine. Dewey's faith in "creative social intelligence" did not take adequate account of how social science was subject to misuse by self-interested men. Social science was easily converted to ideological uses by those less interested in truth than in pursuing their own ends. Niebuhr was left unimpressed by the analogy of the success of science in nature to possible success in human affairs. Dewey emphasized the continuity of humanity, nature, and society.

> The intelligent acknowledgment of the continuity of nature, humanity, and society will alone secure a growth of morals which will be serious without being fanatical, aspiring without sentimentality, adapted to reality without conventionality, sensible without taking the form of calculation of profits, idealistic without being romantic.[38]

Niebuhr emphasized the discontinuity between history and nature. It was precisely in freedom over patterns of nature that human distinctive qualities resided. The study of history was not subject to the same means of inquiry that had proven so fruitful in the study of nature. Niebuhr's charge that the social sciences were not developed to the same extent as the natural sciences was irrefutable. He regarded the theory, that this qualitative difference between the two areas of study was caused by a "cultural lag" that would be overcome, as the "pathos of liberalism." The social crisis was not due to a lack of research and education but to the clash of self-interested groups. These groups adopted whatever social science was available to the justification of their own purposes. He admitted the need for reason in planning social action, but he regarded Dewey's estimate of the hopes for rational arbitration of social conflict as overly optimistic.[39] He could agree with Dewey that reason was a practical instrument for solving problems, but he thought that reason was a fragile instrument used to justify particular interests.

Niebuhr never wrote extensively on Dewey's approach to international politics. However, the gap between their understanding of international affairs was as great as any difference between them. Niebuhr was particularly opposed to schemes for world government or the outlawing of war. Dewey revealed a robust confidence in the outlawing of war.[40] He believed that the "people" of America had a particularly significant role to play in dismantling the war institution. His analysis focused on the reasonableness and utility of outlawing wars and providing alternative means of settling international disputes. His theory lacked any feel for the Hobbesian state of anarchy that prompted nations to seek desperately their own security. Dewey's political analysis did not indicate the dynamic evils of Hitlerism and Stalinism, although both were already rather conspicuous.

Niebuhr charged that the failure of educators to realize the seriousness of the mid-1930 social crisis was partly due to the comfort and security of their essentially middle class position. Similarly, in his opinion, the tendency of the educator to see the solution of the social crisis in the training given to the expert reflected a certain class bias. Liberal hopes that the evolving intelligence of the general community would lead to reform were refuted by the nonexistence of such a community. Society was composed of competing classes, and the perspective of each class was limited by its own economic interest.[41]

Dewey's political model, like Plato's, subordinated class conflict to the needs of education. Class antagonisms could be overcome by rational adjustment, and the rational adjustment of these antagonisms required educational reform. Educational reform and political reform are related and interdependent in both Plato and Dewey. Niebuhr protested against the tendency to obscure the perennial problems of politics under the vocabulary of education. His criticism of Dewey's discussion of politics in educational terms and his use of theological vocabulary for the discussion of politics gave an unfortunate obscurantist cast to his critique. Niebuhr regarded Dewey's tendency to develop "a political theory in the form of a philosophy of education,"[42] and his hopes for resolving political problems through science as attempts to escape from the realm of politics. Niebuhr remained skeptical of all attempts to eliminate political conflicts through some program of increasing social science, but the original source of this skepticism was his Marxist tendency to regard the social sciences as easy prey to ideological perversions. This polemic against reducing politics to science became one of the defining characteristics of the realist school.

Christian Pragmatism

In debt to William James and in dialogue with John Dewey, Niebuhr developed a new form of pragmatism by combining it with Christian theology. In an important article, he argued that pragmatism was the new direction in the field of Christian, political, and social ethics.[43] The acceptance of pragmatism meant the dissolution of the traditional dogmas of both the left and the right. Christian pragmatism meant, to Niebuhr, a recognition of the complexity of the issues of economics and politics, a commitment to justice, and an acceptance of a sense of responsibility for political life.

The synthesis of pragmatism and theology relativized all political ideals by criticizing them from the perspective of theological absolutes. The theological absolutes, however, were sufficiently transcendent to prevent their interference with the promotion of the highest degree of justice possible in a given situation. All absolutes could be corrupted, and the Christian absolutes had been corrupted repeatedly; but properly used they provided ultimate intellectual defenses against tyranny, anarchy, and nihilism. The absolutes that the theological tradition offered were the authority of God, the moral law revealed as the law of love in Christ, the dignity of person, and the reverence for the "orders" of community life.

Pragmatism prides itself upon its openness to helpful contributions from other philosophies. Particularly in the area of political philosophy, pragmatism is open to influences from other bodies of thought. For James, Dewey, and Niebuhr, liberalism informed their pragmatism. Niebuhr's exultation over pragmatism's dissolution of the dogmas of the left and the right is partly intrinsic to pragmatism, partly a new confidence in liberalism, and partly a Christian nonchalance about particular social and political dogmas. The Christian influences in Niebuhr's pragmatism were often subtle and stemmed from his theologically grounded doctrine of humanity.

Liberalism

Niebuhr's liberalism in politics is rooted deeply in his theology. The connections between his theology and his liberal politics is nowhere seen more clearly than in a brief article entitled "Freedom," written for a theological dictionary. In that article he argued that humanity has belatedly come to realize the need for shaping its institutions of order so as to secure the greatest freedom. Freedom is rooted in human nature; it is freedom more than any other quality that distinguishes humanity from nature.

> The community must give the person a social freedom which corresponds to the essential freedom of nature, and which enables expression of hopes and ambitions and engagement in interests and vitalities which are not immediately relevant to the collective purposes of the community, but which in the long run enrich the culture and leaven the lump of the community's collective will and purpose.[44]

The connection of liberty-producing political institutions and the freedom of human nature is a bold step, one which many theologians and political philosophers have refused to take. The linkage is an indication of the theological roots of Niebuhr's political liberalism.

The Practice of Liberalism

Niebuhr's admiration for Franklin D. Roosevelt grew after 1940. His respect increased as he saw Roosevelt beguile a conservative and isolationist nation into adopting programs of social welfare and international responsibility. His commitment to what Niebuhr understood to be liberal ideals was clear, as was his commitment to resolute and successful political action.

Niebuhr wrote that Roosevelt had learned from Wilson's errors and that his commitment of the United States to a continuing role of world responsibility marked a new level of maturity in American foreign policy.[45] He recognized that Roosevelt operated within the framework necessitated by the pride and power of the great nations. The concessions were not regarded as simple expediency but a wise recognition of the limits the sovereignty of nations placed upon international politics.

Niebuhr's praise for Roosevelt's foreign policy balanced tribute to his political vision and to his command of pragmatic politics. The Lend-Lease Act, which drew the United States deeper into the European conflict, was particularly praised by Niebuhr as an example of political sagacity. "Roosevelt was no systematic political thinker; but he saw the main issue clearly and acted upon his convictions with as much consistency as the confused state of American public opinion would allow."[46]

Niebuhr judged political ideas in terms of their results. The verification of political theory in terms of its products revealed his deep pragmatism, even though he often introduced such judgments with the words of one of his favorite texts, "By their fruits ye shall know them." The achievements of the Roosevelt era forced Niebuhr to admit that liberalism, shorn of its illusions and pragmatically oriented, had greater resources than he had anticipated. Roosevelt became the symbol of pragmatic liberalism for Niebuhr.

Niebuhr has said that he heartily approved of being interpreted as a liberal and, as evidence of his liberal politics, pointed to his role in founding Americans for Democratic Action.[47] He helped merge the Union for Democratic Action into the broader Americans for Democratic Action and presided with Elmer Davis over the new organization's first conference in Washington, D.C., in 1947. He continued to serve actively as a leader until his illness in 1952 forced him to curtail his activities. Niebuhr was influential in the early hard line that ADA took against Communist policy and in insisting that the United States play a responsible role in resisting communism. In penning the first draft of an ADA statement on foreign policy, he wrote:

> The foreign policy of the United States is determined by the responsibilities which we have acquired as the most powerful nation in the free world and by the necessity of exercising our responsibilities in the continual contest between the world-wide tyranny of communism.[48]

Niebuhr viewed ADA as a tool for implementing Roosevelt's pragmatic liberalism on the domestic front and opposing the spread of Marxism on the international front while avoiding the errors of idealism. Niebuhr's identification with liberalism in the form of Americans for Democratic Action is clear in a letter written in 1954 to David C. Williams:

> It's thrilling to belong to an organization which began its existence with a challenge to communism from the liberal standpoint, and is now

leading the liberal forces in this nation in resisting the corruption of McCarthyism.[49]

Ten years after ADA's founding, Niebuhr still thought of its two central presuppositions as representative of the achievements of Franklin D. Roosevelt: first, liberalism had to be realistic in international politics; second, the balances within a democratic society needed continual refining to ensure that higher degrees of justice be attained.[50] Gradually, Niebuhr's polemics against liberalism became more discriminating and his harsh criticism was directed toward idealism and optimism. This shift reflected both his increased awareness of his own liberalism and an inclination to define liberalism differently.

The Theory of Liberalism

Niebuhr's critique of liberalism served as a healthy antidote to utopianism. In his later years, he often emphasized that his attack upon liberalism was exaggerated and overstated. Earlier discussion of Niebuhr's definition of liberalism emphasized that his real interest was to attack various expressions of facile optimism.[51] The reason Niebuhr could, in his later years, describe himself as a liberal is that he had never rejected the major part of liberalism, and the aspect of liberalism that he attacked was not an integral one.

Daniel Williams, while concurring with Niebuhr's attack on utopianism, believes that Niebuhr's method of isolating single traits led him to state his criticism of liberalism in an exaggerated manner, obscuring some of the truth represented by liberalism.[52] Niebuhr's reply to Williams ascribes his inexact definition of liberalism as caused by defining "liberalism too consistently in terms of its American versions."[53]

Niebuhr does not escape criticism by claiming that the liberals he was attacking were American. For liberalism as a political philosophy in the New World was freed of some of the very optimism that characterized liberalism on the continent of its birth. Certainly there have been a sufficient number of dreamers in America, and many of these gave expression to their hopes in the Social Gospel. But the mainstream of American political thought has revealed a pragmatic or realist shape. The liberalism of the Adamses and Madison was tempered by a realism not too different from Niebuhr's.[54] Enlightenment optimism was present but not prevalent in the founders of the American republic. John Adams's rejection of Condorcet illustrates the contrast between the optimism of some French democrats and the sobriety of the American democrats.

> Thus Condorcet was untroubled. Instead of bemoaning the fact that the Americans were Blackstonian historians, he proudly welcomed them into the fraternity of the illuminated. American constitutionalism, he said, "had not grown, but was planned"; it "took no force from the weight of centuries but was put together mechanically in a few years." When John Adams read this comment, he spouted two words on the margin of the page: "Fool! Fool!"[55]

The liberalism of the New World was not so self-consciously bourgeois as that of the old because the middle class had not had to break feudal patterns, nor was it on the defensive against conservatism and radicalism. The Enlightenment "heaven on earth" received minor support in the United States, but as the grievances of the New World were less anguished than those of the old, the political leaders could set about improving and ensuring some satisfactions on earth.

The comfort and the sobriety of the country's founding fathers were not unrelated. The impending millennium of Enlightenment political thought had its American supporters, but they were not in the majority, nor did they have the power to act on their vision. Louis Hartz's study of the influence of liberalism in America emphasizes the differences between European and American liberalism, and chief among these differences is the failure of optimism to dominate American liberalism.

> Thus the American liberals, instead of being forced to pull the Christian heaven down to earth, were glad to let it remain where it was. They did not need to make a religion out of the revolution because religion was already revolutionary.[56]

The study to this point has discussed Niebuhr and liberalism within the terms of his definition of it, which assumed optimism as the necessary and central ingredient. Niebuhr has admitted that this understanding of liberalism is defective. An alternative understanding reveals the continuity of Niebuhr's political philosophy with liberalism.

Beginning with Niebuhr's own description of liberalism as being in its broadest sense synonymous with the democratic protest against feudal society, several of the central ideas of liberalism as a political philosophy can be delineated. "The ideas at the heart of the liberal faith . . . are ideas of freedom and also ideas about the conditions, political and social, of making freedom secure."[57] These ideas arose out of older ideas and institutions, but in the seventeenth, eighteenth, and nineteenth centuries they were elaborated in the manner regarded as liberal. The word *liberal*, in the sense of a body of political ideas, is of relatively recent origin, gaining currency in the last century. The ideas of freedom that are characteristic of liberalism are connected with the rise of the modern state, the expansion of commerce and industry, the rise of the city, and the dissolution of the medieval religious consensus.

The idea of natural law had a long history, but the change from the emphasis on natural law to that of natural rights was a characteristically seventeenth-century shift. Locke moved the idea of natural rights to the center of political thought. The idea of natural rights was based on certain illusions: radical individualism, the myth of the state of nature, and the myth of a social contract. But the insistence that humanity had certain rights survived the criticism of those illusions. These rights were to be guarded against the encroachment of the state, which in liberal thought was both necessary and dangerous. The rights claimed by Locke for all against the state were available to only a few, and Locke, as Mill after him, did not possess clear ideas of how the rights he claimed for the aristocrats could be extended to all. Socialist attempts to extend Locke's natural rights do not necessarily imply a rejection of the idea of freedom that Locke held. The elaboration and application of the seventeenth century's ideas of freedom has resulted in both Whigs and socialists adopting liberal concepts of freedom. The Whigs retain more of Locke's aristocratic bias, while the liberal socialists improve on Locke by attempting to realize the rights he demanded by social planning. The rights claimed by liberalism were the right of spiritual privacy, the right of resistance to established authority, the right to limit the authority of a government over its citizens, the right to criticize the government in speech and in the press, the right to a just opportunity to secure material possessions, and the right to personal liberty insofar as it did not infringe upon the welfare of others in society. While not all liberals would agree with such a statement of liberal demands, it does represent the essentials of the liberal creed. The list does not enter into the claims and counterclaims of the political economists, for the term *liberal* can with some justification be associated with directly opposing claims in economics. In political philosophy, however, the term does have a general structure that can be defined, theorists who can be regarded as liberal,[58] and governments in which the incarnation of liberalism can be seen. Understanding liberalism as a collection of ideas about human freedom and the limitation of government to secure those freedoms does not necessarily imply any dependence on a vision of moral progress in history. Many liberals did believe in historical progress, but some did not. Many believers in historical progress were not liberals in the political-philosophical use of the term. The idea of historical progress has its own history and needs to be analyzed in its own terms.

Niebuhr eventually disassociated liberalism from utopianism and admitted that his reactions to utopianism had been extreme.

> My second account of a gradual revision of my originally held opinions must deal, of course, with my rather violent, and sometimes extravagant, reaction to what I defined as the "utopianism," i.e., the illusory idealist and individualist character, of a Protestant and bourgeois culture before the world depression and two world wars.[59]

His later writings would not directly attack liberalism, but they still criticized optimistic idealism. His Augustinian-Reformation theological base could be seen as he worked out his preference in political philosophy for John Milton over John Locke and James Madison over Thomas Jefferson.

The Self and the Dramas of History

If June Bingham's account of Niebuhr's pneumoencephalogram following his stroke is to be taken literally, he came off the operating table with notes for his next book. In any case he was soon at work, and the work was on the more internal aspects of humanity. He reasoned about the self, and eventually the title of the essay "The Self and the Dramas of History" was given to the whole book.[60] It is obvious that three other books of his carry basically the same title; *Moral Man and Immoral Society*, *The Nature and Destiny of Man*, and *Man's Nature and His Communities* all focus on the one hand on human nature and on the other on social-political reality. *The Self* had its uniqueness in focusing on internal dialogues. Niebuhr attributed much of his inspiration to Martin Buber's *I and Thou*. A friend of the Niebuhrs', W. H. Auden, had dedicated his volume *Nones* to the Niebuhrs, and he also was in conversation with both Ursula and Reinhold about the internal dialogues of the self.

The first seventy pages are new material. Here in very short chapters, perhaps reflecting the short period Niebuhr now had each day for work, he meditated on the self. The self was more than mind or body, for him, but intimately related to each.

The self was the unique facility of the human being to think about and enter into dialogue with both of the other faculties. He accepted the designation of spirit for it when reflecting on Charles Lindbergh's story of struggling with body and mind on his solo flight. Though the twelve short chapters are probably clearer on what the self is not than on what it is, it would seem to be the organizing center of the human being, which holds dialogues with others, reflects, initiates action, and remembers in its own way. The biblical picture of the self is as a free, responsible, embodied person in the community. The self's relationships are with its self, other selves, and ultimately God.

The remaining two thirds of the book reworked themes he had developed elsewhere. The second part focused on the Hebrew and Hellenic contributions to understanding history and the human role in it.

The third part does not seem to fit the pattern of any book. It consists of five chapters, or about two fifths of the book, on the religious meaning of technical society, democratic government, poverty, world community, and individual versus communal interpretations. In each case the analysis is traced through historical reflections on various theories. The analytical reader asks, "What is going on?" The book proves to be another book of essays. Niebuhr was an excellent essayist more than he was a builder of large books. The essays of the closing section are the topics of the practical half of Christian Ethics 495–496 or 497–498, which he taught from 1955 to 1968 in one form or another. They also cover the topics of state and property from his basic course "Theological Foundations of Christian Ethics," Christian Ethics 221. The essays represent the way he taught seminary social ethics. The analysis does not get away from the biblical and church historical concepts but traces the history of the ideas offered to resolve the issues in Western cultures. Niebuhr's way of doing social ethics, which was to trace the relative insights of natural reason in the light of biblical faith and church history's development of that faith, dominates the chapters.

The book reflects the cold war in its abiding sense of the dangers of nuclear war and the communist threat of totalitarianism. He thinks labor unions and welfare-state measures have made the promises of communism irrelevant in the Western world. He anticipates the third world's increasing attraction to communism. Yet even at his most pessimistic, Niebuhr still entertained hopes that communism might disintegrate. The dogma of communism seemed to him intellectually weak. Also, he did not anticipate that communism could survive pluralism. "In the long run, the Russian-dominated alliance is therefore likely to disintegrate."[61] While he regretted communism's attractiveness to the poorer countries of the world, he worried more about the United States. The danger was that the United States in its illusions would act belligerently rather than prudently. Patient coexistence with the threatening communist powers was required. The United States was neither as innocent nor as powerful as it regarded itself. The best that could be hoped for was some contributions toward a "tolerable world community." His broad advice was for technical and financial aid to the third world, patient resistance to communism, and realistic ideological competition with communism.

Theological Foundations of Christian Ethics

After the 1955 publication of *The Self and the Dramas of History*, Niebuhr's writings emphasize politics and history. The theological side of his work was primarily carried on in his class lectures. He had given courses on Christian anthropology and theology of history since the preparation of the Gifford Lectures. During the war in 1941, he had begun a new course of two semesters in Christian Ethics 31-32, "The Foundation and Application of Christian Ethical Principles." This course evolved and in the 1950s it was entitled "Theological Foundations of Christian Ethics," usually numbered CE 221; sometimes it appeared as CE 222.[62] Often John C. Bennett would take the second semester, applying Christian ethics to practical problems. In Niebuhr's class notes, the course moves from method considerations, through the doctrine of God, Christ, love, and natural law, to practical issues. It was given the last time by Niebuhr in 1956. The course consisted of five major sections. The first was introductory and taken over from a previous course in philosophy of religion. It was on the relationship of ethics to metaphysics and metaphysics to theology.

Unreflective answers to the question "What should I do?" were of two types. One might rely on either scriptural or customary authority. Moving to reflective answers on ethics involved the question "What must I be?" or "What are the requirements of essential human nature?" He then surveyed answers from existentialism, sociology, evolutionary naturalism, classical ethics, and the Western philosophies of Hegel, Kant, and Marx. All these when analyzed by Niebuhr expressed ultimate assumptions. He also reviewed definitions of "the structure of human existence" by Erich Fromm, John Dewey, and Karen Horney. His inquiry about the relationship of morals and ultimate presuppositions found that some moral standards were present with a variety of faith presuppositions, while other moral standards depended on particular faith presuppositions. Some ultimate presuppositions could be changed on the basis of new evidence. But of course deep commitment to certain presuppositions would affect the "capacity to find the evidence."

The second section of the course on theological presuppositions of Christian ethics was on God as creator, sovereign, judge, and redeemer. Niebuhr's ethics have often been regarded as derived from his anthropology, but these course notes reveal another Niebuhr. If James Gustafson had known about this course, he would have proposed a more nuanced comment on Niebuhr. Niebuhr's ethics here display a theist commitment which would have pleased Gustafson. In his next section, though, Niebuhr moved on to the revolution in Christ, which carried his approach beyond Gustafson. Gustafson had said, "Reinhold Niebuhr's account of the nature of man determines to a considerable extent his view of ethics and the recommendations he makes for action."[63] The idea of creation in Niebuhr's thought was to portray humanity as dependent on a mysterious source of creation. The creator was transcendent of the creation as in the doctrine of the creation from nothing. Nature was not sacred but created; it could be exploited. The world is good, but not God. Nature itself still had discord and dissonances and was characterized by struggle. Harmony was for eschatological fulfillment. Niebuhr distinguished radically between natural evil and human evil and, following the biblical authors, focused on human evil.

The sovereignty of God is expressed in "providence, judgment, and redemption." The moral standards of the Bible are often related to "the character of the transcendent God." Standards are set which are not met whether they are "the justice demanded by the first covenant, or the law of Christ in the second covenant."[64] The prophetic demands for "universality and absoluteness" in morality are anchored in human dependence on the creator God. So biblical ethics have both transcendent and sociologically relevant aspects. Natural law seems to be a way of relating the world governed by God's providence to a world community "governed by divine reason." Humans participate in this reason to a degree, and hence the possibility of natural law.

Yet history does not meet the standards of ultimate judgment. Redemption is always required. The whole history of relating divine judgment to the history and experience of communities has remained incomplete. The sovereignty of God as judge shows that all are involved in guilt, that those who are called by God are under a special judgment, and that those who have power are especially guilty. Still, in the Bible, justice is not exactly defined. It is supported for "the weak against the strong." It has an immediate or existential character. It serves as a proximate norm for the affairs of people, and it needs to be made relevant to each historical period. Judgment comes in conscience, in historical forces, and in biblical faith in unique providential acts.

The incompleteness of judgment and the ambiguities of history lead to expectations of messianic resolution. The redemptive power of suffering is anticipated in the Old Testament and becomes the means of reinterpreting the messiah in the New Testament.

In the New Testament, for Niebuhr, Christ is the message, not a moral example, nor is the New Testament a moral rule book. In Christ, God reconciled the world. Mysteries of the divine were clarified, "particularly the mystery of his justice and mercy." Incarnation's importance was atonement. The church becomes a covenant community as the social, ethical "byproduct" of the gospel. God's mercy resolves the ambiguities of history. The acceptance of the revelation by faith violated reason. The acceptance is an existential encounter of the self with God through this new symbolization of what God has been accomplishing. In this acceptance and the reality of the new community, certain legalisms, righteousness definitions, and nationalisms are refuted. In some ways messianism as the fruit of prophetism was refuted; in other ways, it was fulfilled.

In the third section of the course, Niebuhr worked on the ethical implication of the two natures of Christ from the Nicene Creed. He found beyond the metaphysics a meaning of a divine overcoming of sin with the implication of an ethic of reconciliation and responsibility. He discussed the divine nature and the word, human nature and eschatology, the double nature of love as proclamation and eschatology, the character of God in history, and forgiveness, grace, and power.[65] Within this framework he traced different Christian strategies of relating ultimate love to the world; he looked at Catholic, Lutheran, Calvinist, sectarian, and Social Gospel answers.

The analysis of the norm of love included the topics of the love of

Christ, second Adam, forgiveness, original innocence, sin and freedom, perfection of Christ, and the indeterminate character of perfection as well as freedom. The love of Christ was a more directly relevant norm for personal life and a less directly relevant norm for collective life. The love commandment received an analysis in several lectures moving through Aristotle, Plato, Augustine, Kierkegaard, Luther, Rauschenbusch, Harry Stack Sullivan, Fromm, Buber, Brunner, Anders Nygren, and D'Arcy. In these lectures, Niebuhr worked on love as mutual love and love as eros, as well as love as agape.[66] He preferred the conceptions of natural love from classical thought over some modern tendencies to reduce the meaning of love to sociological or psychological categories. He regarded natural love as incomplete and needing agape, or grace. Agape could be expressed as sacrificial love possible by grace but not as a duty. Common grace provided endless possibilities for love in human affairs. Second, it could be expressed as "forgiving love in emulation of God." Mutual human relatedness needed forgiving love. Also, agape was present as a sense of obligation, as law.

After analyzing love, he shifted into the fourth and fifth sections of the course. In the fourth part, the relationships of love to the relative standards of natural law were worked out. Love had eclipsed law, but in the Calvinist tradition in which he stood in ethics, law had a use within love. Laws or principles of the relative historically particular type were needed to guide individual conscience and social programs. Reason intuited these guiding principles and subjected them to critical analysis. In their prudent and skillful application they were doing historically the work of love. Justice became "an instrument of love." To apply such an ethic required that legalism be avoided or corrected. The difficulty of avoiding biblical legalism in the history of Christianity has been amply demonstrated. Still, biblical norms are to be taken seriously and used with love and natural law principles.

When Niebuhr declined to submit an essay for a volume on Joseph Fletcher's situational ethics, he expressed his confidence in Paul Ramsey's ability to adequately criticize Fletcher's tendency toward "Barthian antinomianism."[67] He specifically praised Ramsey for his combination of agape and natural law ethics. This, in fact, was the way Niebuhr worked. Ramsey's description of Niebuhr's method as a "Christ-transforming natural law"[68] ethic was accurate. Niebuhr called the section on norms "The Proximate Norms of Christian Ethics," and the relationship of proximate norms or relative natural law to ultimate norms was the special relationship of justice to love. In the final section of the course, under the title "Norms for Institutions (Relative Natural Law)," he discussed Christian norms and expectations for government, economy, and family. These long sections on the practical application of his method are similar to discussions of these subjects in many other places. Their importance in appreciating the whole of Reinhold Niebuhr's work is that here the full Christian theological meaning of using agape as the bridge to reasoning about practical moral problems is very clear. Agape does not stand alone; it is a theological virtue and requires placement in the theological context for its power and meaning to be seen.

Empires in Struggle

Niebuhr's major new work in this last decade of active teaching was *The Structure of Nations and Empires*.[69] J. Robert Oppenheimer had asked him to take a chair in history at the Institute for Advanced Studies in Princeton. Union Theological Seminary asked him to postpone until 1958 and granted him a sabbatical for most of the year. Ursula joined him in Princeton and commuted back to her responsibilities at Barnard College. He expressed his gratitude to the seminary for granting a sabbatical only two years before his retirement in 1960 at the age of 68. His letters from Princeton indicate his insecurity at trying such a monumental task, given the state of his health and the vastness of the subject. He had written many essays on international policies and theoretical reflection on international relations. But here he was trying to encompass the sweep of much of human history to search for patterns and lessons for the conduct of the American empire. A whole community of academics read parts or all of his manuscript and advised him on it. The ones who are well known included Arthur Schlesinger, Jr., Will Herberg, Daniel D. Williams, John C. Bennett, Kenneth Thompson, Hans J. Morgenthau, Llewellyn Woodward, and George F. Kennan. Several of them encouraged him to proceed when his energy was running low and when he felt discouraged. In his preface he particularly thanked Ursula for "taking a year's leave from her teaching post at Barnard College" and helping revise "the manuscript chapter by chapter."[70]

The two immediate political impulses to the book were the militancy of Khrushchev in suppressing the Hungarian liberalizing movement and the West's failure to oust Nasser from Suez in 1956. His previous writing on Suez and on Russian and American foreign policies flow together in the new book. He wants, by studying the phenomena of empire, to help the United States accept its hegemonic role and its imperial competition with the Soviet Union. He feared that liberal democratic traditions with appeals to universalism and the United Nations were insufficient to guide the United States in its responsibilities. Given the goal of equipping the United States with a realistic liberalism adequate for foreign policy, he proceeds to analyze questions of political philosophy, different imperial histories, the issues of imperialism, and Soviet imperialism, and then in conclusion he returns to the cold war.[71]

He urged patience in the managing of the conflict. He did not believe Russian despotism would last forever, and he saw it being eroded by educational opportunities and criticisms from conscience.[72] He did not expect its demise in the near future, but he anticipated a return to more traditional patterns of imperial competition rather than those of a militant ideology. In the wake of the Russian space achievements and few signs of economic weakening in 1958, he could not foresee the collapse of Eurocommunism; still, he was hopeful about its decline. He criticized the overly rigid ideological clamor of the West, which often made Washington, D.C., seem less open to pluralism in the world than its Moscow rival. He did not expect the deterrent to be eliminated, but he did think the cold war could be relaxed and that communism would decline. The West's role was not to pretend to solve the problem but to avoid utopian remedies, to work out trade relations, and to realize its common fate with its foe under nuclear terror.[73]

On completion of his sabbatical of writing, Niebuhr returned to Union. He added to his course offerings the substance of his research and reflection for two years until his retirement. The course was listed in the catalog as Christian Ethics 274:

> The course will consider the relationship of the Christian Church to empires and nations; the peculiar history of the rise of America to the position of hegemony in the Western world; the contest with communism and the moral perplexities of a nuclear age.[74]

On the syllabus for Christian Ethics 274 the title was given as "Dominion in Nations and Empires." The titles of the topics covered in the lectures correspond almost exactly to the chapter titles of the book.

Richard Fox dismissed *The Structure of Nations and Empires* as "an amorphous heap of data and generalizations." He indicated that of the political scientists receiving it, only "Arnold Wolfers bothered to acknowledge it."[75] Charles Brown, looking at the evidence a little more carefully, found favorable reviews by several political scientists, including Arnold Wolfers, Samuel P. Huntington, Robert Strauss-Hupe, Kenneth Thompson, and Hans J. Morgenthau.[76] Paul Merkley, whose interest in the more radical phases of Niebuhr's politics led him to engage in careful research, unearthing much new material on the early periods, seems not to have read *The Structure of Nations and Empires*. He dismissed the later work of Niebuhr, and this philosophy of the cold war appears not to be referenced in Merkley's discussion of Niebuhr on imperialism.[77] The same casual reading of the Niebuhr literature also led him into common but unfortunate errors as to Niebuhr's judgments, influence, and position on the Vietnam War. Kenneth Thompson has commented that Richard Fox has no particular competence in international politics and that the book is, in fact, the volume of Niebuhr's most often assigned to students by political scientists.

Niebuhr's retirement coincided with the ending of the Eisenhower era and the accession to power of John F. Kennedy and the Harvard liberals, who knew of Niebuhr's work. Niebuhr promoted Hubert Humphrey until his defeat at the convention and then switched his support to Kennedy. Intellectuals around Kennedy had coveted Niebuhr's support for months. Niebuhr was reluctant to support Kennedy because of a perceived lack of moral character in the young Senator. Under the prodding of Arthur Schlesinger, Jr., he did help clear the way for Liberal Party support of Kennedy, introducing him at the Liberal Party's dinner. Later he assisted in the election by attacking the Billy Graham–Norman Vincent Peale attempt to reject Kennedy because of his Catholic loyalties. On arriving at Union Theological Seminary in the fall of 1960, he got involved in the campaign to dislodge anti-Catholic criticism from Kennedy's candidacy. By the time of the election, virtually the whole seminary supported Kennedy against Nixon.

NOTES

1. Paul Merkley, *Reinhold Niebuhr: A Political Account* (Montreal: McGill–Queens University Press, 1975), pp. 201–202.

2. Robert M. Lovett, "The Christian Realist," *The New Republic* 78 (May 2, 1934), 288.

3. John C. Bennett, *Christian Realism* (New York: Charles Scribner's Sons, 1941).

4. Reinhold Niebuhr, *Christian Realism and Political Problems* (1953).

5. Ibid., p. 146.

6. Wilhelm Pauck, "Essays in Theology and Politics," *Christianity and Society* 19 (Winter 1953–54), 24–25.

7. In a letter to Samuel Press in 1914, Niebuhr mentioned that he had found William James's *The Varieties of Religious Experience* and *The Will to Believe* "very good"; June Bingham, *Courage to Change: An Introduction to the Life and Thought of Reinhold Niebuhr* (New York: Charles Scribner's Sons, 1961), p. 85. The following discussion of pragmatism and liberalism is an edited version of my *Reinhold Niebuhr: Prophet to Politicians* (Nashville: Abingdon Press, 1972), pp. 145–163.

8. D. B. Robertson, ed., *Essays in Applied Christianity* (1959), p. 186.

9. Quoted in Bingham, *Courage to Change*, p. 224.

10. Harry R. Davis and Robert C. Good, eds., *Reinhold Niebuhr on Politics* (1960), p. 200.

11. Charles W. Kegley, ed., *Reinhold Niebuhr: His Religious, Social, and Political Thought* (New York: Pilgrim Press, 1984), p. 90.

12. Reinhold Niebuhr, *Discerning the Signs of the Times* (1946), *Christian Realism and Political Problems* (1953), and *Pious and Secular America* (1958).

13. Niebuhr, *Pious and Secular America*, p. 7.

14. Niebuhr, *Christian Realism*, p. 176.

15. Niebuhr's trust in the coherence of the world and man's ability to create models adequate to portray these coherences is most applicable in the natural sciences, in the human sciences dependent on biology and chemistry, and in the areas of social sciences amenable to statistics and predictions of probability. The emphasis on coherence is radically qualified, and the mystery of man's existence is emphasized in the tradition of Pascal to provide a basis for dealing with unique events, necessary rational contradictions, the failure to provide one scheme of meaning for all the structures of human life, and human freedom. See *Christian Realism*, pp. 176–179.

16. Ibid., p. 175.

17. Ibid., pp. 175–176.

18. William James, *Pragmatism: A New Name for Some Old Ways of Thinking* (New York: Longmans, Green & Co., 1907), p. 218.

19. Statement by Reinhold Niebuhr, personal interview, March 24, 1967.

20. William James, *The Will to Believe* (New York: Longmans, Green & Co., 1896), p. 17.

21. Ibid., pp. 188–189.

22. James, *Pragmatism*, p. 73.

23. Niebuhr, *Pious and Secular America*, p. 142.

24. Reinhold Niebuhr, *The Nature and Destiny of Man* (1943), vol. 2, p. 149.

25. Reinhold Niebuhr, *Moral Man and Immoral Society* (1932), p. 53.

26. Reinhold Niebuhr, *The Irony of American History* (1952), p. 168.

27. James, *Pragmatism*, p. 20.

28. See Niebuhr's *Moral Man*, pp. xiii, 35, 212; *An Interpretation of Christian Ethics* (1935), pp. 207–208; *The Children of Light and the Children of Darkness* (1944), p. 129; and *Faith and History* (1949), pp. 67, 68, 83, 95, 156.

29. Sidney Hook, "Social Change and Original Sin: Answer to Niebuhr," *The New Leader* 24 (Nov. 8, 1941), 5–7, and "The New Failure of Nerve," *Partisan Review* 10 (Jan.–Feb. 1943), 2–23; George A. Coe and Reinhold Niebuhr, "Coe vs. Niebuhr," *The Christian Century* 50 (Mar. 15, 1933), 362–364; Morton White, *Social Thought in America: The Revolt Against Formalism* (New York: Viking Press, 1949), pp. 247–267, 277–279.

30. See Roger L. Shinn, "Some Notes on Reinhold Niebuhr's Use of Philosophy" (unpublished paper for the Society for Theological Discussion, [n.d.], p. 2.

31. John Dewey was chairman and Reinhold Niebuhr was on the executive committee of the League for Independent Political Action founded in 1929.

32. Reinhold Niebuhr, "A Footnote on Religion," *The Nation* 139 (Sept. 26, 1934), 358–359.

33. See final paragraphs of this section.

34. Niebuhr, *Nature and Destiny*, vol. 1, p. 110.

35. Kegley, ed., *Reinhold Niebuhr*, p. 141.

36. Reinhold Niebuhr, "The Pathos of Liberalism," *The Nation* 141 (Sept. 11, 1935), 303–304.

37. White, *Social Thought in America*, p. 255.

38. John Dewey, *Human Nature and Conduct* (New York: Modern Library, 1930), p. 13.

39. Dewey guarded himself against charges of optimism by admitting the difficulties of applying intelligence to social problems but advocating the attempt in the face of no acceptable alternative. "There is no need to dwell upon the enormous obstacles that stand in the way of extending from its limited field to the larger field of human relations the control of organized intelligence, operating through the release of individual powers and capabilities. There is the weight of past history on the side of those who are pessimistic about the possibility of achieving this humanly desirable and humanly necessary task. I do not predict that the extension will ever be effectively actualized. . . . The failure of other methods and the desperateness of the present situation will be a spur to some to do their best to make the extension actual." John Dewey, "Authority and Resistance to Social Change," *School and Society* 44 (Oct. 10, 1936), 466.

40. John Dewey, "Foreword," in Charles Clayton Morrison, *The Outlawry of War* (Chicago: Willett, Clark & Colby, 1927), pp. vii–xxv.

41. Niebuhr, *Moral Man*, pp. 212–215.

42. Daniel J. Boorstin, *The Genius of American Politics* (Chicago: University of Chicago Press, 1943), p. 159.

43. Reinhold Niebuhr, "Theology and Political Thought in the Western World," *The Ecumenical Review* 9 (Apr. 1957), 253, 262.

44. Marvin Halverson, ed., *A Handbook of Christian Theology* (New York: World Publishing Co., 1958), p. 141.

45. Reinhold Niebuhr, "The Death of the President," *Christianity and Crisis* 5 (Apr. 30, 1945), p. 4.

46. Ibid., p. 5.

47. Statement by Reinhold Niebuhr, personal interview, Jan. 6, 1967.

48. Reinhold Niebuhr, "Draft of Americans for Democratic Action Statement on Foreign Policy," Nov. 30, 1955. Reinhold Niebuhr Papers (MSS in the Library of Congress, Washington, D.C.), Container 1.

49. Personal letter to David C. Williams, Niebuhr Papers, Container 1.

50. Reinhold Niebuhr, "Greeting Message for Tenth Anniversary Convention Journal of ADA," Niebuhr Papers, Container 1.

51. See Ronald H. Stone, Reinhold Niebuhr: Prophet to Politicians, pp. 37–40.

52. Kegley, ed., Reinhold Niebuhr, p. 273.

53. Ibid., p. 517.

54. Niebuhr's volume on democratic political theory suffers from his exaggeration of the historic dependence of democratic theory on optimistic estimates of man. Niebuhr's judgment that "the excessively optimistic estimates of human nature and of human history with which the democratic credo has been historically associated are a source of peril to a democratic society" is supported in The Children of Light and the Children of Darkness by reference to the history of political ideas. However, the volume ignores the contributions to democratic theory of Harrington, Montesquieu, and Madison. One may agree with Niebuhr's conclusion that a high degree of optimism is dangerous without agreeing that American democracy has historically been dependent upon such optimism. Niebuhr, Children of Light, p. xii.

55. Louis Hartz, The Liberal Tradition in America (New York: Harcourt, Brace & Co., 1955), p. 49.

56. Ibid., p. 41.

57. John P. Plamenatz, Readings from Liberal Writers (London: George Allen & Unwin, 1965), p. 14.

58. The claim that political theorists may be identified as liberal does not imply that such theorists are only liberals. "No liberal is only a liberal; for even in his public life, there are other sides to him which sometimes conflict with his liberalism." Ibid., p. 37. The assertion that Niebuhr is a liberal is accurate given the understanding of "liberal" discussed here. However, the factors of his pragmatism, his particular version of Christian theology, his history of political activity, and his particular political context are needed to describe his political philosophy.

59. Reinhold Niebuhr, Man's Nature and His Communities (1965), p. 21.

60. Reinhold Niebuhr, The Self and the Dramas of History (1955).

61. Ibid., p. 208.

62. "Christian Ethics 221: Theological Foundations of Christian Ethics," Niebuhr Papers, Container 46.

63. James Gustafson, Ethics from a Theocentric Perspective (Chicago: University of Chicago Press, 1981), p. 118.

64. "Christian Ethics 221."

65. Ibid.

66. Ibid.

67. Letter from Reinhold Niebuhr to Paul Ramsey, n.d. Copy in the author's possession.

68. Paul Ramsey, Nine Modern Moralists (Englewood Cliffs; N.J.: Prentice-Hall, 1962), p. 7.

69. Reinhold Niebuhr, *The Structure of Nations and Empires* (1959).

70. Ibid., p. x.

71. The reader interested in the detail of Niebuhr's thought on international relations is referred to the reprint of my previous book, *Reinhold Niebuhr: Prophet to Politicians* (Lanham Md.: University Press of America, 1981).

72. Niebuhr, *Structure of Nations*, p. 284.

73. Ibid., p. 282.

74. *Union Theological Seminary Catalogue*, 1958–59, 1959–60. The course would be continued after Niebuhr's retirement by John C. Bennett in his own manner. In 1968–69, I joined Bennett in teaching it, and I returned to Union to teach it in 1971–72. It has continued at Pittsburgh Theological Seminary, first as "Moral Issues in International Politics" and then as "Church and Society in International Perspective," taught by me for years and then, in his own style, by Gonzalo Castillo-Cardenas, also a Union Theological Seminary graduate.

75. Richard Fox, *Reinhold Niebuhr: A Biography* (New York: Pantheon Books, 1985), p. 269.

76. Charles Brown, *Reinhold Niebuhr and His Age* (Philadelphia: Trinity Press International, 1992).

77. Merkley, *Reinhold Niebuhr*. Despite Merkley's discussion of Niebuhr on empire and the cold war, there seems to be no evidence of his having read Niebuhr's major work on empire according to the text, index, and footnotes.

9

The Last Years
1961–1971

NIEBUHR'S RETIREMENT years coincided with the early enthusi-
asms of the Kennedy presidency and the fall into problems of racial
conflict, war, and poverty threatening the society. President Johnson, the consummate if irresponsible politician, would lose his wars
against poverty and the revolutionary Vietnamese. In disgrace, the
liberal Democrats would lose the presidency to Nixon, forcing Niebuhr again into opposition. He would die before seeing a populist
Democrat claim the Niebuhr banner for part of his thought and lose
the leadership of the country to the right wing of the Republican
Party. For Niebuhr himself, they were years of physical pain and
declining strength. The physical problems promoted depression,
against which he had to rally his energies. Visits from friends, the
devotion of family, essays and books to write, and causes to encourage from the sideline brought joy. Though his thought and part-time
teaching ranged over many subjects, his major contributions can be
seen in reflections on race relations, international relations, political
economy, and democracy. He retired from Union in 1960 at the required age of sixty-eight. He offered one course at Union in 1961,
moved on to teach at Harvard in 1962, and back to Morningside
Heights to Barnard College in 1963. During 1964–1968 he returned
to Union to offer a seminar in social ethics, first at the seminary and
then in his apartment on Riverside Drive, overlooking the Hudson
River.

Race Relations

The Christian contribution to improving race relations in the 1960s was symbolized by Martin Luther King, Jr.,'s leadership. As a theological student, King had studied Niebuhr's writings and written papers on his thought.[1] His appreciation of Niebuhr's strategies and his own understanding of his differences with Niebuhr bore fruit throughout his leadership from 1954 to 1968. The two men recognized each other as allies. Niebuhr, who had participated in inviting King to Riverside Church to speak on April 4, 1967, against the Vietnam War, wrote the foreword to the publication of King's address. He attempted to clarify two issues.

> We quite appreciate that some of the civil rights leaders have disassociated themselves from Dr. King's opposition to the Vietnam War, in part because of fear that the civil rights movement itself will be confused by this opposition view. Dr. King knows this to be a hazard. But after all he is one of the great religious leaders of our time and he has a right to speak on any issue which concerns mankind. These two causes are interrelated not by reason of Dr. King's championing of them. Both causes must be pursued. Let us simply say that Dr. King has the right and a duty, as both a religious and civil rights leader, to express his concern in these days about such a major human problem as the Vietnam War.
>
> The second concern is about Dr. King's position on nonviolent resistance to evil. Many of the journals and the public have confused his position with absolute pacifism, which they reject. I think, as a rather dedicated anti-pacifist, that Dr. King's conception of the nonviolent resistance to evil is a real contribution to our civil, moral and political life.
>
> We hope therefore that this volume will have a wide reading among thoughtful persons of our churches, of our schools, and of the entire land.[2]

Niebuhr's own writing, which continually attacked the ravages of racism on two fronts, politics and economics, increasingly linked the tragedy of Vietnam to the failure of African Americans to advance.[3] In "A Question of Priorities" he linked the demise of President Johnson's antipoverty programs directly to the war. From poverty, misery, and disillusionment, mixed with signs of hope from the civil rights struggle, Niebuhr thought, the riots emerged.

The distance of Martin Luther King, Jr., from Niebuhr involves his African American experience, his continued loyalty to the tradition of liberal Boston personalism, and his tendency to use eschatology more as a spur to social action than as a limiting concept against social utopianism. However, their deep mutual respect and their alliance in the fight against racism and the Vietnam War brought them together. Andrew Young made the point in a testimonial dinner for John C. Bennett:

> I want to begin by saying that there was always a misunderstanding of what Martin Luther King was about. I remember one night when somebody came at him with some of the philosophical presuppositions of strict Gandhian nonviolence, and he responded about three o'clock in the morning with the most brilliant lecture I had ever heard on *The Nature and Destiny of Man*, Reinhold Niebuhr, and the thinking of John Bennett and *Christianity and Crisis*. He reminded us that he had done his Ph.D. thesis on Paul Tillich, and you realized how everything he did was formulated much more out of a sense of Christian realism and out of the historic black reality of the Christian Church in the Southern part of the United States than I think the press ever really understood.
>
> We always tried to make nonviolence something that was very idealistic and ethereal and for the saints to live by, and never really understood as Dr. Niebuhr said, as far back as *Moral Man and Immoral Society*, that nonviolent power and economic withdrawal would be the means that the black community might eventually use to gain justice.[4]

King deepened his social thought in the struggle, but his "realistic pacifism" is very close to Niebuhr's Christian realistic advocacy of nonviolent resistance. Niebuhr supported King's struggle and was jubilant over his victories. Much of what he had hoped for in 1932 was realized by King in the 1950s and 1960s. The structure of King's ethic hung on love, justice, and power, as did Niebuhr's; the differences between them faded as Niebuhr referred to King as the outstanding Protestant leader of his day, white or black. In Niebuhr's estimation, King combined idealism and realism appropriately; in Niebuhr, King found concepts that made sense of the heartrending struggle of the civil rights movement.

Niebuhr supported students and faculty from Union Theological Seminary in their direct action in the civil rights movement, saddened that his own physical condition prevented him from more active participation.

The linking of King and Niebuhr has continued in seminary classes across the nation. One example has been a social ethics course specifically on King and Niebuhr at Pittsburgh Theological Seminary. Preston Williams of the Harvard Divinity School has referred to Martin Luther King, Jr., as a "Christian realist." Peter Paris of Princeton Theological Seminary relies on Niebuhr's thought and joins it with King in his classes at Princeton. He reminded listeners at an executive committee meeting of the Society of Christian Ethics that Jesse Jackson's original Operation Breadbasket was a direct application of Niebuhr's thought, learned in graduate theological education, to the ghetto of Chicago.

A week after the bombing of the Sunday school of the Sixteenth Street Baptist Church in Birmingham on September 15, 1963, James Baldwin and Niebuhr engaged in a broadcast dialogue sponsored by the Protestant Council of the City of New York.[5] Baldwin and Niebuhr were in substantial agreement. Niebuhr confessed to reading almost everything Baldwin had written, but Baldwin did not return the compliment. Their most significant disagreement was on King's relationship to the church. Baldwin saw King using the church as "a tool"; Niebuhr saw the African American church awakening to its potential and providing the leadership in alliance with secular forces for the civil rights revolution. Niebuhr also held to nonviolent pressure as the way for a minority to force change. Baldwin encouraged the use of violence.

Niebuhr's realism led him to expect "slow erosion of racial prejudice."[6] He welcomed the courts' attempts to desegregate the schools, but he expected community pressures to delay the process.

He understood the Supreme Court's decision in Brown v. Board of Education of Topeka as reflecting the rising social consciousness of the country on human rights, but he expected local communities to find ways of evading the court's mandate.[7] Almost four decades after the 1954 decision, community resistance in the North as well as the South supports his analysis of the deep-rootedness of prejudice and the creative but limited role of law in changing mores.

His critique of the lack of creative action in the community was especially sharp regarding the church. The church's universal mission was falsified while it remained more segregated than theaters, public accommodations, and athletics. The local control of Protestant churches rendered them less able to desegregate than Roman Catholic churches. Neither law nor religion could overcome the bigotry of the nation, but still he saw progress being made, although slowly.

His last major essay on race[8] located the slowness to integrate in the idealism of the country, which obscured the roots of prejudice in human sin. Both its secular and religious idealism contributed to a self-righteousness that did not understand the fury of oppressed minorities. He concurred with the report of the National Advisory Commission on Civil Disorders, which located the sources of the rage of the riots of

1966–1968 in the poverty, poor housing, and unemployment of African Americans in the United States. The "helplessness of the black minority is due to a complacent self-satisfaction about our American democracy."[9] He traced this self-satisfaction from the country's founding documents to the current complacency about African American deprivation. Only a total national response could deal with the race-related poverty that was the national shame.

The churches had failed to transcend the barriers of race in their own life, and also they had not criticized the country's idealistic complacency concerning "the horrible injustices to its Negro minority."[10] As he called for a program to combat racism, he urged the church to witness to transcendence across racial lines with various organizational steps. He pleaded for programs that at that time had possibilities of legislative implementation—a negative income tax, scholarship programs, antipoverty programs—and endorsed the commission's recommendations for new national priorities in the new administration.

However, Niebuhr's plea in 1968 for new priorities regarding race were to be ignored, as his endorsement of Hubert Humphrey for the presidency was rejected by liberal admirer and conservative opponent alike. With Humphrey's defeat, policies of benign neglect were implemented, the African American community could not organize around leadership to replace the assassinated Dr. King, and the beneficent intentions of the Carter administration could not overcome the inflation and unemployment that ravaged the African American community. The failure continues.

Niebuhr's strategies for countering racism from 1925 to 1971 included moral teaching, education, economic boycott, study commissions, civil rights legislation, cooperative economic organization, antipoverty legislation, church action, writing, rallies, and demonstrations. The black church partly overcame its otherworldly piety and led the action; here and there the white churches responded creatively; still, integration of the churches moves ahead slowly. The reuniting of Niebuhr's strategies with religious imagination appropriate for the 1990s remains the task of the churches.

Peacemaking and Realism

Reinhold Niebuhr's many debates with Christian pacifists and his polemics against idealists in politics obscured his commitment to the search for peace. His fate is not too different from that of Hans Morgenthau, whose passion for peace is seen in the title of his famous text, *Politics Among Nations: The Struggle for Power and Peace.* Power was central to international politics for both Niebuhr and Morgenthau, but their goal was peace. Both vigorously opposed the war in Vietnam. The other direct use of U.S. military force abroad during Niebuhr's later years was President Johnson's intervention in the Dominican Republic, and Niebuhr opposed that in print also.[11]

The major critique of Niebuhr's public policy positions concerns his thought regarding the cold war. Probably only consistent pacifists would decry his support of U.S. participation in World Wars I and II. Opinion divides around support for the U.S. position in the Korean War. Walter LaFeber regards Niebuhr as one of the main systematic thinkers who contributed to the philosophy of the American cold warriors. His *America, Russia, and the Cold War* attributes immense influence to Niebuhr in shaping the American thinking about the cold war.

A fellow theologian, John M. Swomley, Jr., accuses Niebuhr of providing "the religious rationale for the military foreign policy that created the contemporary American empire and the policy of global intervention culminating in the war in Vietnam."[12] Building on the insight of Charles West, he suggests that Christian realism served an ideological role in justifying American empire. The record shows that Niebuhr consciously provided rationale for competition with the Soviet Union while he explicitly attacked the Vietnam policy. As we have seen, one of his most famous essays, "The King's Chapel and the King's Court," explicitly attacked the attempt by the Nixon administration to religiously legitimize its policies.[13]

Niebuhr had hoped during World War II for postwar cooperation among the victors, but tensions between the Soviet Union and the Western allies convinced him during the war that both sides would try to advance their own interests. The collapse of the wartime alliance led him to regard the Soviet Union as a dangerous opponent. Its creed and policies led him to believe that it was important to rally the United States to assume responsibility after the war and to oppose the presumed ambitions of the Soviet Union. The role of Niebuhr in leading American liberals to oppose communism is well known. As he had provided arguments for the opposition to Nazism before and during World War II, he supported opposing communism.

Some Christian authors on the left have been outraged by Niebuhr's critique of communism and his contributions to realist political theory. From the advantage of hindsight, it seems Niebuhr was basically correct. Communism needed to be opposed patiently and resolutely. Cornel West is particularly critical of Niebuhr's thought on this point. He does not like his support of Israel either. West objects, but he does not really show Niebuhr to be mistaken.[14] Niebuhr's comments on the problems with communism seem to be in line with what voices liberating themselves from communism have been saying in 1988–1991.

It really is not a critique to say Niebuhr was European and North American in orientation; he never claimed to be anything else. He perceived the competitive existence of the United States and the Soviet Union as necessary to maintaining peace. "There cannot be war between us without mutual annihilation. There must not be war."[15] He envisaged the competition extending for decades or even longer. There could be no resolution through war, but neither partner in the competition could be expected to surrender its respective myths and ideologies. Wise diplomacy was the most important element in maintaining an uneasy partnership in preventing nuclear war. He had no great confidence in education, cultural exchanges, religious impulses, or disarmament plans to eliminate the competition of two continental empires competing for influence and interests in the world. This view of the world, essentially of two nuclear-armed scorpions locked in a small bottle, was not a world he would have wished for but it was what he perceived. It was also a world subject to the winds of revolutionary demands flowing through undeveloped areas, and a world made more dangerous and unified by technological development.

He warned of the danger of U.S. overreliance on military power. The tendency to build defense pacts in Asia revealed little understanding of the political complexities there. Military force could be effective in crises, but without political forces of cohesion, military force could accomplish little. Overreliance on military power was a temptation to a nation as wealthy as ours, but it could contribute to our political embarrassment. Military force for Niebuhr was a means of last resort, but the American temptation was to use meat-ax diplomacy where subtlety was called for. The understanding of the needs of a population required wise statecraft, not primarily military power.[16]

In the winter of 1953–54, and again in the spring of 1954, he was urging France to give up its defense of colonialism in Indochina to grant those countries their independence. In the summer of 1954 he again wrote how it would have been tragic to involve U.S. forces on the side of the Vietnamese losers against the communists.[17] Cautionary warnings against military involvement continued into the 1960s, until

Niebuhr was forced to oppose sharply the Johnson administration's war.

The real risk of preserving the nuclear stalemate rested in the political sphere. He noted that technical miscalculation might bring about the nuclear catastrophe, but his primary concern was in political miscalculation. A defeat in some vital area of competition might tempt one side or the other to resort in hysteria to nuclear weapons. This I think was the central reason for his continued reference to the "balance of power" in the post–World War II situation. He often described it as a "nuclear umbrella"; competition could go on, but it must be limited so as not to threaten the vital interests of the other party. Of course, it was not balance of power in any prenuclear meaning of the term but an arrangement, ironically stumbled into, that was not securing peace in any deep sense but was at least avoiding nuclear holocaust.

He rejected the notion of "winning the cold war," and I do not think he ever entertained the idea of "rolling back communism" as John Foster Dulles had dreamed of briefly. Without war and without hysteria, he counseled the United States to meet the Soviet challenge.

> World peace requires that the dynamic of this strange political movement be contained, its ambition to control the world be frustrated, and its revolutionary ardors be tamed by firm and patient resistance.[18]

Niebuhr regarded the complex and threatening postwar world as requiring prudence and political shrewdness. Was he merely commenting on the world in these numerous editorials, articles, and books on empire, power, and American history, or was he seeking a political effect? I think he was very political in his writing. He wrote in a major essay on the theory of international politics, "If power is identical with authority, it follows that the climate of a culture or its 'ideology,' which sanctions a particular type of authority, is really the ultimate source of power."[19]

Niebuhr knew that the facts did not interpret themselves. The complexities of the international world had to be reduced to be understood and put into perspective to become politically relevant. He did not write much about method in either theology or international politics. But what he wrote about myth, symbol, and ideology shows he knew that in their articulation resided power. The articulation was itself a creative act even as it remained loyal, to the best of one's ability, to the materials being discussed. Millions of events were occurring in the

world, but he would write, "Thus modern history is fated to be governed by the contrasting myths of the two superpowers."[20] He knew
that these myths were not easily changed and that he was powerless to
affect the mythology or perspective of the Soviet Union. He set out to
affect the mythology and perspective of the United States in its understanding of the Soviet Union. So his critics who accuse him of presenting an ideology for U.S. participation in the cold war are correct. The
perspective he presented, however, was one of a precarious partnership between the two countries in preserving nuclear peace while
struggling elsewhere. The struggle Niebuhr envisaged was primarily
ideological. Finally, authority rested on a governing group's ability not
only to ensure order but to deliver or promise a tolerably just society.

In the ideological struggle, he felt that the United States with its ties
to previously colonial powers and its own problems of race and social
justice was at a temporary disadvantage in the developing world. However, the creed and the actual accomplishments of Marxism were so
badly flawed he believed that patient resistance would eventually encourage other governments to find their own solutions without suc-
cumbing to alliances with communist powers.

Technological aid and economic aid were among the major contributions the United States could make to the health of developing
nations. In 1962 he regarded the ability to provide funds for aid as
"the litmus test of the capacity of a democracy to survive in the
contest."[21]

Elsewhere, I have criticized Niebuhr's overly optimistic expectations
for the Alliance for Progress.[22] It is unfortunate that his critic, John M.
Swomley, Jr., takes part of the paragraph in which he is arguing for a
strong interventionist policy in Latin America in the terms of the Alliance for Progress as evidence of the advocacy of imperial self-interest
and neglects to mention that his use of economic power was for attempted land reform and education.[23] For the sake of changes in the
oligarchic practices of Latin America, Niebuhr urged intervention,
overriding liberal reservations about anti-imperialism. To him, the
United States was an empire in a struggle. Critics often seem to find
fault with Niebuhr, as if he were responsible either for the empire or
the struggle. Certainly his views shaped perspectives on the empire and
the struggles, but they are rooted in reality as well as perspective. A
sympathetic reading of Reinhold Niebuhr's writing finds him urging a
cautious policy of statecraft, the upbuilding of the developing world,
a nuclear partnership, a decrease in American reliance on military

power, outright rejection of U.S. policy in Vietnam, and a struggle to criticize and replace the political leadership responsible for it.

Competitive coexistence in Niebuhr's perspective called for ideological debate. Hence, while he tried to clarify and reform American ideology by interpreting its religious and secular elements, he severely criticized the pretensions and illusions of Marxism. This criticism of Marxism can be seen as fueling the cold war. However, in Niebuhr's perspective, it was exactly the ideological debate that needed to be carried on in order to follow Senator Fulbright's idea of not trying "to redress ideological deficiencies with military power."[24] He feared the military-industrial complex, criticized its dominance of the U.S. economy, and resisted journalistically some of its demands for new systems.[25]

Doves in the peace movement will probably never be at ease with Niebuhr. Statecraft would seek to broaden national interest to a wise view of the broader world interest and attempt to reconcile the two, he said, but force remained a means of last resort. Hawks could never be content with Niebuhr either. In World War II he had argued against unconditional surrender, attacked the policies of massive bombing of German cities, sponsored German refugees and German political groups in the United States working for moderation in the treatment of Germany, and helped defeat the Morgenthau plan for reducing postwar Germany to a pastoral economy. With Augustine, he believed peace to be among the highest achievements, but to preserve it required a mixture of means, including political authority, which relied on both agreement and force.

On questions of disarmament, then, he was not a dreamer. He had witnessed the difficulty of disarmament plans in the early twentieth century. The ban on nuclear testing he regarded as a great achievement, as he thought negotiations to stop the antiballistic-missile race were a gain. The nonproliferation treaty seemed to him of dubious worth because it represented the satiation of the "haves" and the repression of the "have nots."[26] Community had to precede disarmament or, at least, accompany it in its formation. The formation of that community was significantly begun in the work of UNESCO, which he served as a U.S. delegate, but finally it required the moderation of the revolutionary ardor of communism, the development of the third world, and wise statecraft on the part of the Atlantic Alliance. So there was no guarantee of peace.

The building of community as seen in the work of UNESCO was

flawed. The flaws revealed the spiritual nature of contemporary humanity. Modern humanity had to find ways of continuing to build community across international borders and of avoiding discouragement when it failed to complete the task. His comment on UNESCO stands as his attitude toward the building of a world community.

> Here is an organization which seeks to realize the impossible: a world community. It must not regard this end as a simple possibility; but neither can it dismiss the task as an impossibility. It stands, therefore, constantly at the final limit of the human situation where the possible and the impossible are curiously intermingled and where it is difficult to distinguish between God's and our possibilities.[27]

Beyond Religious Socialism

The practical problems of auto workers in Detroit inspired Niebuhr's interest in political economy and led him to criticize the moral pretensions of the Ford Motor Company in the 1920s. The needs of rural sharecroppers led him to experiment with a cooperative means of economic organization. The plight of the unemployed in the Depression inspired his constant work for economic reform in the 1930s. He approached economic issues as a Christian social ethicist, and his writing on economic matters often dealt with the history of Christian ethics in relationship to the rights of property or the various forms of social organization. In analyzing wages paid to the workers at Ford Motor Company or in formulating and raising a budget for the Delta Cooperative Farm, he became very specific. A tendency to abstraction, however, often led him to contrast Karl Marx's thought with Adam Smith's and not to enter into much detail in the intermediate realm of economic theory where crucial issues were being fought.

John C. Bennett, Arthur Schlesinger, Jr., and Kenneth Thompson have all analyzed Niebuhr's relationship to socialism. There is little to be added.[28] The practical origin of his interest in economics helps to explain the infrequency of his post-1940s work on economics. He became interested in economics to advance the cause of the workers, and with the victories of labor during the New Deal his interest in economics declined. Labor's winning the right to organize and bargain was a fundamental victory that changed the country. With this victory, the socialist option lost its power. In a tribute to Norman Thomas he could not refrain from pointing out the irrelevance of socialist faith to the American scene. Though he had broken with socialism as a party

243

movement over its foreign policy, the reason for dismissing socialism after the war was hidden in the tribute: "The organization of unorganized workers changed the social and moral climate of American industry more than the nationalization of the means of production could ever have done."[29] He had worked hard for socialism, and his commitments to many aspects of its intended reforms continued. His developing theological work led him to develop his own form of Christian pragmatism on economic issues. He remained sympathetic to socialist critiques of American culture. He recognized in the 1950s the extent to which business passions contributed to a banalization of American culture and left pockets of poverty in the country. But against his friend and former socialist ally, Eduard Heimann, he defended Christian pragmatism in the absence of persuasive arguments that some other inclusive theoretic system could better analyze American ills or propose remedies.[30]

The failure of religious socialism and political socialism in the United States left Niebuhr without a developed alternative policy. He never returned to the analysis of economic reality with the same energy that he had exhibited as a socialist. In dealing with the remaining pockets of poverty, he favored New Deal type policies in the Kennedy and Johnson administrations and regarded the old laissez-faire capitalism as dead. He still regarded a policy of government activism as necessary to correct the inequities of the race problem.

To refer to the American system in 1964 as "free enterprise" was to render a mythical account that obscured the realities of the mixed economy.[31] Though no longer favoring nationalization of industry, Niebuhr wanted a recognition of the government-management-labor alliance. A progressive income tax, a tax on estates, government regulation, and government planning regarding the economy had been partly won through the New Deal, and near the end of his life, with a Republican administration accepting most of the New Deal gains and advocating a negative income tax, he did not fear a return to laissez-faire economics. Generally his postwar writing on economic thought reflects the same pattern. The United States had been blessed by the wealth of a continent to rise to affluence. The affluence had obscured the need for social reform and allowed the creed of Adam Smith to live longer in the United States than in Europe. But experience refuted both Smith and his alternative, Marx, and the United States had tolerably corrected its injustices while avoiding the perils of the collective power of the Marxist state. Strong governmental leadership was still necessary to correct disproportionate economic power. His practical concerns were represented by the two organizations he was instrumental in forming, the Liberal Party and Americans for Democratic Action.

His references to a tolerable justice being achieved in the United States referred to the legitimization of labor power and did not sanction complacency in the struggle to win economic rights for those excluded. He assumed the ongoing interventionist policy of the government to limit freedom in the marketplace for the sake of justice. Liberty and equality were both regulative principles; neither was to be absolute. He feared the military-industrial complex and was not optimistic about limiting its influence in the economy or on government.

On economic matters, only general guidelines of moral advice for the late twentieth century can be derived. First, economic policy must be guided by the political process practiced aggressively and democratically for the benefit of the have-nots. In his own time these were the workers, the minorities, and the developing peoples of the third world. He assumed rather than advocated that the American middle class would protect its own interest, and he hoped that through the political process this interest would be generously adjusted to wider interests. Nostalgia for laissez-faire capitalism was to be expected, but it was largely irrelevant to the agenda of the technological nations of the developed world. Mixed economies were the best adjustment to Western history and needs, and governmental processes to eliminate the effects of poverty and protect against undue centralization of economic power were required.

The return of a modified laissez-faire direction in economic thinking since his death, the curtailing of the government's regulatory powers, and the tilting of government policies to favor the privileged have tempted some to use Niebuhr, and particularly his critique of socialism, as ideological justification for these directions. Nothing could be further from his intentions. In revising his thinking, he made it clear that his conception of human nature was intended to reinforce progressive movements in the society.[32]

Democratic Experience
on the World Scene

Niebuhr continued in his retirement to reflect upon the problems that had exercised him in his teaching career, and in 1969 he published another book on politics.[33] At Harvard in 1961–62, he taught a course jointly with Paul E. Sigmund, analyzing democracy as a theory and system of government and discussing its future in the developing nations of the world. He gave the same course himself at Barnard in 1963; and these class notes yielded the book, *The Democratic Experience: Past and Prospects.* The genesis of the book was in the early 1960s during the bloom of the promises of the Kennedy era. It was conceived and planned before the intractability of the race problem was conceived as clearly as it was in the late 1960s. The malaise caused by the Vietnam War had not yet spread to erode the confidence of the citizens of the United States in their country's purposes. Paul Sigmund, working with Niebuhr's outline and general concepts, completed the book when Niebuhr's poor health kept him from finishing it. Sigmund's influence and style are more noticeable in Part II, on the developing nations, than in Part I, on democracy in the West. Sigmund's contributions made it possible to reflect on the specifics of recent events in the developing nations of Asia, Latin America, and Africa. The particulars of the origin of this book are relevant, as they explain some of its weaknesses when examined in the context of the year of its publication. The date of the lectures—1961–62—also means that *Man's Nature and His Communities,* published in 1965, represents Niebuhr's reflections at a later point than *The Democratic Experience,* although it was published in 1969.

The book brings together many themes of Niebuhr's earlier thought on democratic politics. Its purpose is both to support the concept of democracy for those countries that possess its prerequisites and to argue that democracy cannot be superimposed on societies that lack the conditions of democracy. The authors describe their position as a "pessimistic faith in the democratic idea."[34] They admit the dangers and problems of democratic government to be sizable, but they find alternative forms of government less attractive. Communist utopians and democratic utopians both are judged to be productive of illusions which threatened man's ability to regulate his common life. The exposure of utopian illusions and the attempts to understand the inevitable tensions between the individual man and his communities are similar to the thrust of Niebuhr's other volume on democratic theory, *The Children of Light and the Children of Darkness.*

Niebuhr treats the claims of Marxists and democrats alike when they speak of freedom from fear or absolute egalitarianism. He trusts that democrats will be safer and wiser in avoiding political slogans while seeing the dangers of Marxist utopianism. The title of his first chapter, "Democracy and Communism: Two Utopian Ideologies," overstates his case. There are large elements of sober political thought in both systems. Marx had some utopian notions, and Niebuhr has some eschatological ones, but neither Marx nor Niebuhr can be dismissed as utopian or otherworldly. People live by visions as well as by systems of production, and both Marx and Niebuhr knew it when they were not polemicizing against the illusions of others. Niebuhr is correct that both Franklin D. Roosevelt and Karl Marx had some utopian elements in their perspectives, but to obscure their respective pragmatic and empirical elements is to attack straw opponents. The analyst of democracy must certainly subject the government to the most sober and realistic examination possible. Niebuhr recognized the element of vision as a perennial feature of American life, and he could have reflected longer on why this was so. Is it true that most societies have some utopian expressions, which give, to greater or lesser degrees, some legitimation to the reality that exists? Is the role of a utopian vision as a mythological support for social change or revolution always a negative element? He wrote, "Some deep current in the American tradition must undoubtedly account for the persistence of this note in our national life."[35] The observation raises the possibility that a political system must have mythological support. The issue may not be the need to destroy utopian illusions but to analyze them for their usefulness in promoting desired values.

Democracy is a term with many possible meanings, and the authors of the volume do not pin it down to any precise definition. They use it to cover various forms of the republican organization of government, constitutional monarchies, and to encompass the governments of France, the United Kingdom, Japan, India, the United States, Mexico, and others. It is often used synonymously with their term "free government," which one can define at least functionally. A free government is one outside the communist orbit that presupposes national unity, protects individual rights, and has independent institutions, competitive elections, and enough political equilibrium to begin to meet issues of social justice.[36] The book is written against a cold war background, which contrasts democracy and communism as if they were polar concepts, the one incarnated in the United States and the other in the Soviet Union.[37] The use of the same term for so many different governments gives the term *democracy* an equivocal character. The equivocation is necessary if the term is to be used to trace the emergence of present patterns of government from the contingencies of European history. In the modern world the term is not used by the authors equivocally as much as analogously. There are analogies between the contemporary forms of government discussed that justify the use of a common term at a very general level of discussion. The equivocation occurs when the same term is applied to the entire governmental experience of Britain, France, and the United States, from 1800 to 1969.

The authors discuss the contributions of predemocratic Europe to the conditions necessary for the emergence of democracy. Three factors are thought to be necessary prerequisites for democracy: (1) a unity of the nation that will hold despite conflicting subnational group interests; (2) humanism expressed in terms of individual rights and values; and (3) a balance of power that permits the development of a tolerable level of social justice.[38]

Their analysis of the situations in the world led them to a mixed prognosis for the future of democracy. Democracy was expected to remain more of an ideal than a reality. Authoritarianism seemed destined to continue to hold sway in communist states. Though they expected democratic leaders and particular historical contingencies to allow for democratic growth in some of the developing nations, a more common phenomenon would be, they predicted, cycles of alternating democracies and dictatorships.[39] They were not pessimistic about democracy in Western Europe and North America, but its future in the rest of the world was an embattled one.

The book has three major weaknesses: omission of the problems that racism, imperialism, and militarism created for the United States. As the problem of racism has been referred to before,[40] the criticism here is reserved to the interrelated issues of imperialism and militarism.

The authors spoke of an impending crisis in Latin America, but their hopes that it could be avoided were clear.[41] This optimism was based on political parties such as Chile's Christian Democrats, events in Venezuela and Colombia, and U.S. support for democracy in Latin America. The authors' support for the Alliance for Progress and their rejection of Castroite solutions distinguish them from the left, which would regard the United States as "the principal obstacle to the establishment of meaningful democracy in Latin America."[42]

It is possible to agree with the authors that a judgment on the influence of the United States on Latin-American democracy is a mixed one[43] and still deplore the pattern of U.S. exploitation in Latin

America. The dangers of revolutions in Latin America may have hidden the dangers of imperialism from these scholars. The alternatives of democracy and communism that provide the polar concepts for the book disguise the problems confronting Latin America. In many countries, as the authors recognize, democracy has been imposed on a feudal system blended with laissez-faire economic structures. The exhaustion of Marxism in Europe and the failure of revolutionary movements to gain power in Latin America provide another opportunity for a birth of democracy in Latin America. The World Council of Churches has wisely used the term *responsible society* instead of democracy as a goal for social development in the third world. With its connotations of state direction, pluralism, civil liberties, and resistance to foreign exploitation, a responsible society may be a better goal for Latin America than cold war democracy. Dom Helder Câmara, the former head of the Roman Catholic archdiocese of Olinda and Recife in northeastern Brazil, has pointed out the dangers of anticommunism in Latin America.

> All around me—in my diocese, in my country, in the whole of Latin America—I see millions of people who are ill and underfed, who live in miserable shacks and who have no opportunity to improve their lot. They suffer the consequences of an extremism—a massive, hysterical anticommunism which reaches such a point of blindness and hate that, in some instances at least, it seems to be (and may God forgive me if I pass judgment) a new form of industry. Any new idea or any suggestion aimed at improving the condition of the poor is instantly and efficiently labeled "communism." This attitude leads to deadlocks that in turn lead to repression, despair and terrorism.[44]

Brazil is as good an example as any in Latin America to point out that U.S. influence has been retrogressive, even though the case is not as extreme as in Guatemala, the Dominican Republic, Haiti, or Cuba. The United States did not hesitate to express its desire for changes in the government of Brazil. In 1964, U.S. displeasure with the leftist-leaning President João Goulart was a precipitating factor in the right-wing military coup d'état that drove him from office. The United States responded to the changes in the governing structure of Brazil with a four-hundred-million-dollar loan beyond the funds previously programmed for the Alliance for Progress.

Soon after assuming office, President Humberto de Alencar Castelo Branco was pressured by U.S. Ambassador Lincoln Gordon and John J. McCloy of Hanna Mining to expedite Hanna's interests in Brazil, which were under litigation in Brazil's Federal Court of Appeals. Various warnings from U.S. officials like Thomas Mann encouraged the government to conclude that U.S. help was not unconnected with rulings on the Hanna interests. Leftist gains in the elections of October 1965 were annulled by decree and Brazil's Supreme Court was packed. In less than a year the new court ruled as the United States wished.[45]

The merging of U.S. economic interests and political pressures in Brazil points to the need for a more complex model of political life in Brazil than the authors provided. The political future of Brazil is inseparable from its relations with the colossus of the north, and more attention to the economic influence of the United States must be given in studies of the prospects for democratic government in Latin America.

The second criticism of the volume, that it failed to wrestle with the danger to American society of increasing militarism, is based on both a general omission of the problem and its specific disavowal. "The result of this subordination of military power to civil authority was to eliminate the military oligarchy as an important part of the power structure in free societies."[46] The neglect of the growing military influence on American institutions was due partly to the fact that in 1961, when the course was first given, or even in 1963, when the course was last given, the problem was not as apparent as it was by 1969, when the book finally appeared. This interpretation is partly supported by statements about the danger of the military that Niebuhr made elsewhere. For example, in an interview published in 1969 he responded to a question regarding the realistic possibility of stopping the development of the antiballistic missile system then under debate in the Senate with a far-reaching skepticism about the military:

> Well, I don't know. I'm not enough of an expert on all the details. I think that the dominance of the military, whether in the ABM system or in the Viet Nam War, is nearly overwhelming. I think that Ike was quite right at the end of his term when he warned against what he called the military-industrial complex. After all, we've got a budget of which 50 percent goes to the military, and military expenses account for many of the high production rates that reduce unemployment and so forth.
> So these are fantastic problems that American technological society faces. . . . The question is, "What will the President do in relationship to the Joint Chiefs of Staff?"[47]

Further evidence that Niebuhr too was becoming increasingly alarmed over the expansion of the military is his response to my criticism of his book on this problem. He wrote, "You are right; in the light of Viet Nam my confidence in the subjection of military to political authority is too simple."[48]

Niebuhr's political philosophy is not endangered by the evidence that the offices of the Pentagon had come to dominate "the largest network of submanagement and industrial resources in the world."[49] The threat to the continuation of democracy as he understands it is increased, however, by the escalation of military influence.

The combined problems of racism, imperialism, and militarism force a less sanguine picture of democracy than the volume provides. Niebuhr's preference for democracy is not invalidated; his faith in it was after all a pessimistic faith; he found it less objectionable than other forms of government. Since his death, his confidence in democracy has been validated as, in various meanings, it became the rallying cry for progressives against authoritarianism. The book needs revisions, but it is far wiser than it appeared to the generation of romantic revolutionaries of the 1960s and 1970s. As others write their books on the prospects of democracy on the world scene, the new economic realities will be one of the major variables from the earlier Niebuhr-Sigmund attempt.

Concluding Seminars

Upon retirement, Niebuhr had continued in 1960–61 to teach his advanced seminar for seniors and graduate students in Room 1042, a rather worn locale across from the bookstore. In 1961–62, he went to Harvard and lectured to classes of over 500 students on what would eventually become the volume on democracy with Paul Sigmund. In the fall of 1962, he took the course to Princeton, to classes only a little smaller. His correspondence includes comments in which he regards the Harvard students as sharper than the Princeton students. In the spring of 1963, he concluded teaching the course on the prospects of democracy in the world in lectures at Barnard. I sat in on those lectures at Barnard and began a series of conversations that would continue until his death. In 1963–64, he gave the seminar in ethics again at Union, and he continued it in his home on Riverside Drive from 1964 through 1968. Sometimes ill health prevented him from meeting the seminar, and other department members would substitute; students have mentioned substitutions by Henry Clark, Roger Shinn, Paul Abrecht, and José Miguez-Bonino. Niebuhr had hoped to give it one more time in 1969, but health, finances, and other general considerations led him to give up the Riverside Drive apartment and not return for the spring semester of 1969. In 1968 and 1969, we worked together on publishing an essay on race relations in *Social Action*, a book of essays, *Faith and Politics*, and an interview in *Christianity and Crisis*.[50] In 1969, when I suggested a Festschrift for his eightieth birthday, he declined as was his tendency on grounds of humility, but then added that he did not expect to live to eighty.

The best record of the seminar is his own personally typed notes from the last time he gave it in the spring of 1968.[51] He stated the problem of Christian thought in developing a social ethic. Social ethics required discriminate standards of justice for competitive groups. Biblical ethics tended to provide messianic answers, absolute standards, and ultimates of love. He then explored, from a survey of church history, how the eschatological expectations and absolutes had been related to the compromises and relativities of church social teaching. Strengths and weaknesses of church teaching were developed from the major thinkers and movements of church history. Particular emphasis was placed on concepts of justice in natural law and the origins and place of regulative principles of equality and liberty. Then he surveyed how he worked out social ethics in international relations, economics, national societies, race relations, and the morality of family and sexual relations. Though he had worked on these materials in the classroom since coming to Union in 1928, he could still in 1968 make most sessions fresh and provocative.

Niebuhr was nervous about the class, and at the end even the one-hour period could exhaust him. Other times, occasionally, he would sit around after the presentation and discussion and join in refreshments, which Ursula served. About half the seminar consisted of his presentations and discussion, and the other half would be sharing one of the student papers, class discussion of the topic, and Niebuhr's comments on the paper. His ever agile mind and compulsions would sometimes cause him to interrupt a slow or pedantic student to help the class grasp the essential points. Usually, however, he was patient, finding something significant in even rather inane comments. Sometimes, when a student paper would set itself against Niebuhr's reputed position, he would surprise his young attacker by agreeing. Even a paper defending Kierkegaard, as a source of Christian social wisdom to which Niebuhr should have been more generous, would receive a comment as to how much Niebuhr appreciated the paper and that his critic would be surprised to learn how much he agreed with the criticisms. Of course, next week the flaws in Kierkegaard might form part of Niebuhr's introductory comments. He loved to debate, and he would let the students lead him away from the syllabus to examine current social issues. On occasion when graduate students pressed the attack, as for example on his traditional Christian sexual morality, he would permit extra sessions of the seminar to focus on the issue as long as he deemed it beneficial.

Students were permitted a great deal of latitude in their papers. The topics and bibliographies were usually cleared with the graduate teaching assistant, and Niebuhr was informed as to the subjects. In 1964, for example, papers were presented on Hans Morgenthau's political ethics, Kierkegaard's *Works of Love* for Christian social ethics, the meaning of "responsibility," the doctrine of love, American liberty and law, just war thinking and nuclear weapons, business ethics, problems of Indian democracy, a critique of Niebuhr's *Faith and History,* age of secularism, Darwinian social thought, love and self-seeking, and the ethics of Bonhoeffer and Barth in Paul Lehmann's thought. After each brief presentation, Niebuhr would comment and then discussion followed.[52] I took the seminar as a student one year and assisted him in it for two years while studying for a Ph.D. at Columbia University. I always regarded the seminar as the learning equivalent of all the rest of the graduate courses I was taking at the time. Roger Shinn, who had taken the seminar years earlier, arranged for me to assist Niebuhr in the course.[53] Shinn's own comments about the impact of Niebuhr's teaching, from an earlier period, summarize the results for many who came under his influence:

> His courses were the most exciting, provocative, and intellectually stimulating of any I ever took. I sometimes fought him. He won most of the fights; I, in my own opinion, won a few. No other teacher ever left my mind so buzzing with insights, so discontent with my prior ideas. . . .
> For a generation of scholars Reinhold Niebuhr virtually defined the field of Christian ethics in North American theological education; when I decided to make a career teaching in that field, it was the field that he had defined. Whatever differences of opinion and accent we had, they were on the turf that he had mapped. . . . Niebuhr, more than any other person outside my family, had influenced my life and thinking.[54]

A few of the students from the seminar would regularly escort Niebuhr on his hour-long walks on Riverside Drive. These times were filled with discussions of politics, theology, sexual ethics, and the content of the seminar. He served as a revered friend to the students. His natural grace and warmth made him easier to talk to than many of the other professors. On those walks he also would provide counsel to the students about their own social action involvements. He advised students on a sit-in at the South African embassy, on lobbying for civil rights legislation, and on a witness for civil rights legislation before the Lincoln monument. He also talked about the bank campaign to begin to dissociate U.S. capital and industry from apartheid. In 1968, he quietly encouraged some Union students to go ahead and work for the Rockefeller campaign for the presidency. For a while, his letters to Will Scarlett document that he would consider voting Republican for the first time in his life if Rockefeller could evolve a plan to stop the Vietnam War. The Nixon convention victory and Humphrey's emergence as the Democratic nominee, of course, ended that unusual speculation.

Final Revisions

Niebuhr had revised his thought throughout his teaching career. Students had learned that he would not necessarily be held to or defend a position he had taken in an earlier book. In the early 1960s, he was revising his reflections for the last time. He proposed several versions for his last book. He had learned from his critics and continually from the dialogue at Union Theological Seminary. His vast organizational work, many friendships, public meetings, think-tank associations, and political connections all provided input. The individual mind blended this material with the additional information harvested from continual study.

The book *Man's Nature and His Communities* reflected some of the discussions of Niebuhr's last seminars, and it was included among the readings for the seminar in 1967 and 1968. It was written while he was still hoping President Johnson could find a way out of Vietnam that would maintain some U.S. prestige and not weaken America's competition with communism. It was finished before he openly broke with President Johnson over the conduct of the war and began supporting alternative leadership. It was in the midst of the civil rights revolution and slightly before the massive student protests. It is more a book of Niebuhr's mature revisions than it is a commentary on the 1960s, which can be derived from his many essays in the period.

Arthur Schlesinger, Jr.,'s essay on Niebuhr's political philosophy indicated that a new synthesis had been achieved in Niebuhr's thought in the postwar period.

> The penetrating critic of the Social Gospel and of pragmatism, he ended up, in a sense, the powerful reinterpreter and champion of both. It was the triumph of his own remarkable analysis that it took what was valuable in each, rescued each by defining for each the limits of validity, and, in the end, gave the essential purposes of both new power and new vitality.[55]

There were aspects of Niebuhr's thought that were not yet clear in 1956 when Schlesinger announced the synthesis. He could not anticipate how far the new development in Niebuhr's thought would revise previous opinions. The failure was not Schlesinger's, it was an inevitable result of a characteristic of Niebuhr's writing. His brother Richard noted the difficulty of understanding Reinhold Niebuhr because of his hidden presuppositions. "Reinie's thought appears to me to be like a great iceberg of which three-fourths or more is beneath the surface and in which what's expressly said depends on something that is not made explicit."[56]

The publication of *Man's Nature and His Communities* in 1965 brought together the various strands of revision that had been taking place in Niebuhr's political philosophy since the war. The book reveals more clearly than any other work the presuppositions of his political philosophy that were guiding his occasional and theoretical writings on international politics. It recants previous polemics against liberalism and reflects the reliance on liberalism and pragmatism that characterize his work. The long essay on political idealism and realism is his solution to the problem he regarded as the most important in political philosophy. It relates liberal principles of social morality to the factors in politics that inhibit the realization of those ideals in an attempt to resolve the problem he had wrestled with since his earliest writing.

The significance of the work for an interpretation of Niebuhr's thought is best expressed in the "Introduction" to the volume.

> This volume of essays on various aspects of man's individual and social existence is intended to serve two purposes: Namely, to summarize, and to revise previously held opinions. . . .
> The systematic essays are intended to "revise" previously held opinions only in the sense that they seek to give a systematic account of the revisions which have taken place in the author's mind in a whole lifetime of study and of writing books too frequently.[57]

The Egoistic Self

The differences between the analysis of man's nature in *Man's Nature and His Communities* and *The Nature and Destiny of Man* are due primarily to the disappearance of the theological vocabulary. The themes of *The Nature and Destiny of Man* (the image of God, sin, *justitia originalis*, the biblical doctrine of grace, the Kingdom of God, the Parousia, the last judgment, and the resurrection) are not the themes of *Man's Nature and His Communities*. Human nature is still the subject of analysis and the focus is still on the political animal, but the style has changed. Though *The Nature and Destiny of Man* is important as a work in the philosophy of history or political philosophy, it is clearly within the theological circle. Its argument is frankly apologetic; the reader who agrees is inclined to move into the theological circle. In contrast, *Man's Nature and His Communities* translates a theologically inspired view of humanity into nontheological terms. The argument does not lead a sympathetic reader into the theological circle. Some theological insights are confirmed through empirical studies, but the reader is not given the impression that the conclusions require theology.

Man's Nature and His Communities represents, in part, Niebuhr's attempt to revise his description of the human situation in light of the criticism of his Gifford Lectures. He conceded that the attempt to revive the vocabulary of original sin had been an error. It had not been possible to free original sin from connotations that were anathema to the presuppositions of liberal culture. Looking back on the effort, he wrote that "these labors of modern interpretation of traditional religious symbols proved vain."[58] Criticism of his theological language by political philosophers who were in substantial agreement with his understanding of humanity had influenced him to describe the human situation in a more secular style.[59] His growing respect for Erik Erikson's thought is represented by the adoption of some of the language of ego-psychology for the description of the human situation. The differences between *The Nature and Destiny of Man* and *Man's Nature and His Communities* is partly one of intellectual evolution and partly simply a change in style. Throughout his career Niebuhr could write articles in either a secular or a theological mode. The pieces in *Christianity and Society* and *Christianity and Crisis* are characterized by a much more frequent usage of theological terms than articles he wrote concurrently for *The Nation* and *The New Leader*.

As early as 1956, Niebuhr's reply to William J. Wolf's critique of his doctrine of man had indicated dissatisfaction with aspects of his own thought. He admitted that his formulas of "equality of sin and inequality of guilt" and "redeemed in principle but not in fact" were unsatisfactory.[60] He never did satisfactorily meet the issues (within theological symbolism) that these formulas were designed to answer. In *Man's Nature and His Communities,* he again wrestled with the issue, but without the theological symbolism.

Niebuhr's move away from the theological symbolism of *The Nature and Destiny of Man* led to a misunderstanding with Paul Tillich. Tillich reported to a colloquium in honor of Reinhold Niebuhr on October 20, 1961, that Niebuhr had recently admitted, after years of debate, he now agreed with Tillich's description of the human situation, although there still remained differences between them.

> A week ago we had a wonderful talk in Cambridge for one to two hours, and he said to me quite spontaneously, "I have accepted your point of view in this respect. We cannot use any longer the language of the tradition if we want to communicate anything to the people of our time." As an example, he gave me his use of the words *sin,* and especially *original sin,* in his book. . . . The words *original sin* shouldn't be used at all. He accepted—if I understood him rightly—something like *universal estrangement* instead of the term *original* or *hereditary sin.*[61]

In reply to Tillich's address, Niebuhr confirmed the former's report about their agreement that traditional theological symbolism was often irrelevant, but he disagreed with Tillich's translation of the tradition into ontological terms.

> He accurately reports the conversations we had at Harvard before the Colloquium, in which I confessed that I had made a mistake in hurling the traditional symbols of Christian realism—the fall and the original sin—in the teeth of modern culture when I sought to criticize the undue optimism of the culture. Both these symbols, though historically significant, are subject to misunderstanding in a secular culture. . . . I still think that Paul Tillich's translation of these symbols into the ontological terms *essential* and *existential* man is too Plotinian in that it implies, if not asserts, that the whole temporal process is a corruption of the eternal. Thereby one precious Biblical concept, embodied in the idea of the goodness of creation, may be obscured. I would now rather translate these historic symbols into descriptive, rather than ontological, terms.[62]

The hint provided here, that a further attempt at a description of the human predicament would be made, was fulfilled in *Man's Nature and His Communities.*

Niebuhr's translation of the historic symbols into descriptive terms

(1) retains the emphasis upon freedom of his earlier writing, (2) expresses sin as overly consistent self-seeking, (3) interprets love as self-giving, and (4) discusses grace as the gift of security. The self is subject to impulses toward both self-seeking and self-giving. These impulses are expressed in all relationships. True human fulfillment is found when one generously gives oneself to a cause or to another self, but such self-giving presupposes that the self is not desperately seeking its own security. The self is never consistently freed from seeking its own security, but if it can presuppose security it can relate creatively to others. The impulse toward self-giving is the basis of morality, but morality itself cannot give the self the capacity to relate to others. That capacity comes only as a gift. The capacity is given originally by the family, which nurtures and protects the person. But even as the family promotes self-giving by nurturing the relatively secure person, it promotes self-seeking by promoting the family's good at the expense of, or at least at the neglect of, the good of other families. All personal lives and all achievements of human community reflect this double impulse toward self-giving and self-seeking.

Niebuhr thinks this description of the human condition is consistent with the aphorism of Jesus, "He who finds his life will lose it, and he who loses his life for my sake will find it" (Matt. 10:39, RSV).[63] Orthodox doctrine, both Catholic and Protestant, has obscured the insight by distinguishing too sharply between common and saving grace. It has thereby encouraged a view of righteousness within the community which the "long history of religious self-righteousness" refutes.[64] It has also erred in thinking that self-regard could be suppressed. The perpetual paradox that the human self is both self-giving and self-striving has been hidden. The self fulfills itself by being inclined away from preoccupation with the self by various forms of social pressures and responsibilities.[65]

Niebuhr's analysis continued his battle against claims for the perfection of either the individual or society. It was subject to those charges, leveled at him throughout his career, that it did not emphasize strongly enough the sanctification of the individual, the uniqueness of the church, and the possibilities of human achievement in society. The changes could not imply, however, that Niebuhr had not examined these possibilities. He had examined them in the light of his understanding of history, and he had found the claims unsupportable.

The sober estimate of humanity, however, was now set in the context of liberalism. The emphasis upon the continuity between the religious and the secular, or saving grace and common grace, and the openness to psychology indicated the revised direction of his thought. Rather than asserting the greater intellectual adequacy of Christian theology, he was insisting upon complementing theological insights with other methodologies. The Christian realist liberal was expressed in the final revisions.

Loyalty to Judaism

Niebuhr's final published work in his lifetime was brought out by Louis Finkelstein, the President of Jewish Theological Seminary.[66] The faculty of Jewish Theological Seminary included, among many admirers of Niebuhr, his close friend Abraham Heschel, who would join in the memorial service for Reinhold Niebuhr at Riverside Church. These final actions from the leadership of the Jewish community culminated a long relationship of friendship and alliance with the prophetic aspects of contemporary Judaism.

The roots of his appreciation of Judaism reached back to Samuel Press's courses on Amos at Eden Seminary. But it had been the friendship with Fred Butzel on the mayor's race relations committee in Detroit that translated the prophetic spirit of Judaism into contemporary life. A pattern developed of close friendship and alliances with Jews in struggling for social justice. Some of the friends were religious, like rabbis Stephen Wise and Abraham Heschel. Others, such as Felix Frankfurter, were more secular while continuing the prophetic spirit.

In this final essay, Niebuhr analyzed the common heritage and the differences among Protestantism, Catholicism, and Judaism. Their common agenda was to interpret the relationship of the transcendent to humanity and to present a morality to govern relationships among neighbors. He saw the traditional religions as surviving contemporary secularism and, in religious symbol and morality, providing a structure for human life. Much of the argument of the essay is also found in his final book *Man's Nature and His Communities.* He writes more as the philosopher of religion analyzing symbols than as the self-conscious Christian theologian.

The differences with Judaism are found in their differing responses to the messianic hopes of Judaism and to the messianic foundations of Christianity. He posed the issue as he frequently did, with a favorite quote from Martin Buber, the late great Jewish philosopher who once described the issue of messianism which divides Jews and Christians in an address to Dutch clergymen.

"To the Christian, the Jew is a stubborn fellow who, in an unredeemed world, is still waiting for the Messiah. To the Jew, the Christian is a heedless fellow who affirms, in an unredeemed world, that redemption has somehow or other taken place." Buber's astute description of the non-negotiable Christological issue derives, naturally, from a Jewish viewpoint.[67]

For Niebuhr the Christian interpretation of the Messiah is as suffering servant, whether this is from Jesus himself or the early church. The church's piety is Christ-centered and is not dependent on either legendary materials about miraculous births or physical resurrections. In Jesus as the Christ is found the reconciliation of God and humanity in forgiveness, and this is more true than hopes for a messianic age in history. He does not expect Jews to agree; Christ will remain the stumbling block. Judaism is an authentic religion, and though individual Jews for whom Judaism fails may become Christians, Niebuhr rejected active mission toward Jews. The differences in ethics for Niebuhr also reflect the different approaches to messianic claims. For Christians, the new law of Matthew reflected that the new age had begun; for Judaism the Torah would only be transcended when the messianic age arrived. Between Judaism and Christianity, Christ remained the non-negotiable symbol.

Between Protestantism and Catholicism, which agreed on the fundamentals of faith, the papacy was the non-negotiable religious symbol. The claims of religious authority of the papacy were idolatrous to Protestants. Roman Catholicism depended on papal authority in religious matters for its unity. Protestantism was driven to disunity rather than centralize religious authority. Niebuhr's writings in the late 1960s welcomed the increasing freedom found in post–Vatican II Catholicism. Clearly he regarded papal monarchy as close to the essence of Roman Catholicism and did not expect to see it eclipsed.

In their struggles to express the reality of the relationship of the human being to God and to find a responsible morality for the late twentieth century, the three faiths were united and moving toward universality. In their historical development of religious symbols to express the universal, they were particular and divisive. Tolerance, coexistence, and cooperation could be expected and were necessary counters to secularism. Unity was not anticipated.

While preparing his final volume on the revisions of his thought, Niebuhr had meditated on his relationship to Judaism.

> I am Christian but since all of my political activity left of center has been conducted in partnership with Jews, I have an increasing respect for the Jewish capacity for civic righteousness. Its source is a mystery to me in the sense that some of my Jewish friends find it in the tradition of the Hebrew Torah, some in the prophetic tradition (where I would be inclined to find it); and some merely ascribe it to the critical perspective which the minority status gives the Jews. I am reminded of an incident in Detroit, in which the social conscience of a wonderful Episcopal bishop, the late Charles Williams, was involved. Bishop Williams was the leader of a small group of dissidents from the "Detroit establishment" of pre–New Deal days in which the word of Henry Ford was law and gospel. A young parson sought the bishop's aid in organizing a "Christian Layman's League." He said the main purpose of the league was to enforce Sunday closing of all businesses rigorously. "I thought so," said the bishop. "When it comes to the weightier matters of the law, there are only three Christians in Detroit, and two of them are Jews."[68]

Niebuhr reflected on the sources of the social righteousness he perceived among Jews. He thought that perhaps it should be attributed to the prophetic tradition. He noted that many of the most religious Jews attributed it to the Torah. Butzel, however, attributed the passion for social righteousness to their minority status, which resulted in suspicion of the establishment and compassion for other minorities. Niebuhr never resolved the issue in his own mind, but he noted that Butzel's genius was responsible for the beginning of "my long love affair with the Jewish people."[69] His respect for the Jews had led him in an early article to contrast their concern for social justice with the relative impotence of German-Americans in supporting any progressive causes. The superiority of Jewish social sensitivity to most Protestant social consciousness was to remain a theme throughout Niebuhr's teaching and writing. The urban pastorate of Detroit was essential in developing Niebuhr's own social sensitivity and his realism, and part of that mixture was his debt to Jewish friends.

Niebuhr followed the rise of anti-Semitism in Germany in the 1920s and 1930s, reporting on it in church journals. In a visit to Europe in 1933, he had entered into an argument with his German family's anti-Semitic pastor, disrupting his aunt's dinner. It was on this trip that he conveyed the invitation for Paul Tillich to come to Union Theological Seminary.

Tillich and Niebuhr, as allies, tried to rouse Americans to the horrors of German anti-Semitism in the 1930s. They formed Christian organizations to aid Jews, and Niebuhr served on the executive committee of the Christian Council on Palestine, a pro-Jewish-homeland organization. On its behalf, he testified to the Anglo-American Committee of Inquiry on Palestine in 1946. He argued that the Jews had a right to a secure homeland and that the logical place was in Palestine. The group as a group had a right to survival. He assumed it would be in a Palestinian state under UN trusteeship with a Jewish minority. Any resettlement of populations would involve compensation.

Niebuhr, along with Tillich, came to a position that may be regarded as Christian Zionism. They passionately believed in the need for U.S. support for a secure homeland for the Jews, and they believed Palestine to be the best and historically determined site. They accepted Israel as fact in 1948. He continued to write on developments in Israel and on its wars. His comments revealed his respect for Israel and his general disrespect for Arab politics. Both his commitment to democracy and to welfare mixed economies inclined him to support the Israeli developments.

For Niebuhr, Israel was primarily a refuge for the victims of the Holocaust. He regarded it as a responsibility of the United States to protect Israel for reasons of moral responsibility and for reasons of national interest. He wrote, before the 1956 Israel-Egypt War:

> Our nation has a special interest in the preservation of the state of Israel. That interest is not only dictated by national interest in a state devoted to Western democracy and surrounded by Islamic nations in various stages of feudal decay, but is also dictated by humane considerations. For the state of Israel is, whatever its limitations, a heartening adventure in nationhood. It has gathered the Jews of all nations, the remnants of the victims of Hitlerism and other forms of nationalistic persecution and given them of their own. Whatever our political or religious positions may be, it is not possible to withhold admiration, sympathy, and respect for such an achievement.[70]

Israel was not for Niebuhr the fulfillment of any biblical prophecy. It was a result of the Holocaust and it was justified as a refuge. In writing on the strange mixture of secular and religious forces in the modern world, he regarded the emergence of Israel "as a kind of penance of the world for the awful atrocities committed against the Jews."[71] He noted that injury was done to the Arabs, but still he wrote, "Many Christians are pro-Zionist in the sense that they believe a homeless people require a homeland."[72] Justice still required, in Niebuhr's understanding, further work on behalf of the Palestinians.

Ursula Niebuhr has continued the pro-Israel work she shared with Reinhold. Many of his students have also continued the work of Christian-Jewish reconciliation. Rabbi Heschel traveled in a station wagon with his wife, daughter, a colleague of Niebuhr's, and his teaching assistant up to Stockbridge for Niebuhr's funeral on June 4. Heschel used the words Niebuhr had used from Job in announcing his father's death[73] in the memorial service.

> The Lord has given, the Lord has taken,
> Praised be the name of the Lord.
> My flesh and my heart may fail,
> But God is the strength of my heart.
> He is my portion forever.

Later that Friday, wanting to avoid travel on the approaching Sabbath, Heschel hurried back to New York City.

Last Months

In the closing months of his life, Reinhold prepared for death. Friends continued to visit and to receive his encouragement and love. He complained of his pain and of his inability to contribute more to the fight against the Vietnam War. But he sprinkled his struggles against illness, war, cruel politics, and racism with his Christian confessions.

A few years earlier, before the Vietnam War was Americanized and escalated, Reinhold Niebuhr had been awarded the Presidential Medal of Freedom. Now, near the end, Ehrlichman was gathering FBI investigations of him in the White House after his stinging attack on the false use of piety in the White House chapel to sanction the war and imperial presidential pretensions. Niebuhr was criticizing both the utopianism and drift into violence of the students of the radical left and their establishment elders, who in their pride had led them there. His critiques of the new left and his perennial critiques of Marxism and utopianism assured that many Christian activists would never be satisfied with his thought.

His view of Soviet communism led many to call him a theologian of the cold war. In retrospect, his view of Soviet communism seems appropriate; he was more profound, perhaps, but no more polemical than the Eastern Europeans who overthrew it in 1989–1991. His recommended policies of patient resistance, ideological critique, self-correction, and aid to the developing world in the face of communism seem in broad outline wise.

No one could succeed to his mantle. However, many took pieces of his thought and carried his influence throughout the country in various academic appointments, political campaigns and offices, journals, and books. He knew this in his last days and was grateful, while remaining humble about his own contribution.

Ursula continued to care for him, to nurse him, to love him, and, near the end, to read to him. She has written that perhaps Reinhold was a little naive about family, expecting it to be more loving than it was. In her love he certainly found much of the devotion and sacrifice he attributed to families at their best.

She read from various sources to him, including Robert Coles's underground conversations with Daniel Berrigan.[74] She would monitor visitors, who were of all different levels of skill in calling on the infirm, so that Niebuhr could get the most out of each visit without overly tiring himself.

He had entered the hospital, after being weakened by pneumonia, with a pulmonary embolism. I did not see him in those last months. His son, Christopher, has written that he was sent home in April as he was too weak for treatment. He then would have days in which he recovered strength and days when he weakened.[75]

Near the end of April he responded to a letter I had written him from the Washington, D.C., jail.

YALE HILL
STOCKBRIDGE, MASSACHUSETTS 01262

April 27, 1971

Dear Ron,

Thank you so much for your letter about your prison experience. And your lobbying in Washington against this futile war. I am proud of that common editorial in the four papers, Protestant and Catholic. And even more proud of your non-violent demonstration, even though a minor law ordained your jailing. I am glad you found my *Reflections at the End of an Era* relevant. We are indeed at the end of an era of national innocence. Let us hope that we have arrived at the age of maturity. My book, incidentally, was too much influenced by the Marxist Apocalypse.

In my illness and weakness, I can only take part in the day's events through friends like you. My affectionate regards to you. God bless you.

He died peacefully at home on June 1, 1971. Students and friends around the country phoned each other and wept.

NOTES

1. See Kenneth L. Smith and Ira G. Zepp, *Search for the Beloved Community* (Valley Forge, Pa.: Judson Press, 1974); John J. Ansbro, *Martin Luther King, Jr.: The Making of a Mind* (Maryknoll, N.Y.: Orbis Books, 1982); and Taylor Branch, *Parting the Waters* (New York: Simon & Schuster, 1988).

2. "A Foreword by Dr. Reinhold Niebuhr" in *Dr. Martin Luther King, Jr., Dr. John C. Bennett, Dr. Henry Steel Commager, Rabbi Abraham Heschel Speak on the War in Vietnam* (New York: Clergy and Laymen Concerned About Vietnam, 1967), p. 3.

3. See "A Question of Priorities," *The New Leader* 51 (Jan. 15, 1968), 9–11, and "The Negro Minority and Its Fate in a Self-righteous Nation," *Social Action/Social Progress* 35/59 (Sept./Oct. 1968), 53–64.

4. *Christianity and Crisis* 31 (May 3, 1971), 80. Quoted in Smith and Zepp, *Search*, p. 72.

5. Thomas Kilgore, Reinhold Niebuhr, James Baldwin, "The Meaning of the Tragedy in Birmingham" (New York: Protestant Council of the City of New York, Sept. 22, 1963). Copy in the author's possession provided by Christopher Niebuhr.

6. Reinhold Niebuhr, *Pious and Secular America* (1958), p. 82. The remainder of the discussion of race, peacemaking, and socialism is an edited version of my article "The Contribution of Reinhold Niebuhr to the Late Twentieth Century" in Charles W. Kegley, ed., *Reinhold Niebuhr: His Religious, Social, and Political Thought* (New York: Pilgrim Press, 1984), pp. 66–77. Reprinted by permission.

7. The most significant research into Niebuhr's judgments about the Supreme Court is incorporated into the essay on the long correspondence between Frankfurter and Niebuhr by Daniel Rice, "Felix Frankfurter and Reinhold Niebuhr: 1940–1964," in *The Journal of Law and Religion* (1983), 325–

426. Detailed comments on local community atrocities against the civil rights movement are found in the foreword Niebuhr was asked to write for a volume on the crimes against blacks and civil rights advocates: "Foreword," *Mississippi Black Paper* (New York: Random House, 1965).

8. Reinhold Niebuhr, "The Negro Minority," pp. 53–64.

9. Ibid., p. 55.

10. Ibid.

11. "Caribbean Blunder," *Christianity and Crisis* 25, no. 9 (May 31, 1965), 113–114.

12. John M. Swomley, Jr., *American Empire: The Political Ethics of Twentieth Century Conquest* (London: Macmillan Co., 1970), p. 34.

13. See chapter 7, note 22.

14. Cornel West, *Prophetic Fragments* (Grand Rapids: W. B. Eerdmans Publishing Co., 1987), pp. 144–152.

15. "After Sputnik and Explorer," *Christianity and Crisis* 18 (Mar. 4, 1958), reprinted in Ernest W. Lefever, *The World Crisis and American Responsibility* (New York: Association Press, 1958), p. 126.

16. "The Limits of Military Power," *The New Leader* (May 30, 1955). Reprinted in Lefever, *World Crisis.*

17. See *Christianity and Society* 19 (Winter 1953–54, pp. 9–12; Spring 1954, p. 4; Special Issue 1954, p. 4).

18. Ronald H. Stone, ed., *Faith and Politics* (1968), p. 215.

19. Ibid., p. 203.

20. Ibid., p. 236.

21. Ibid., p. 218.

22. Ronald H. Stone, *Reinhold Niebuhr: Prophet to Politicians* (Nashville: Abingdon Press, 1972), pp. 207–210.

23. Swomley, *American Empire,* p. 35.

24. Ronald H. Stone, "An Interview with Reinhold Niebuhr," *Christianity and Crisis* 29 (Mar. 17, 1969), 51.

25. Ibid.

26. Ibid.

27. "Peace Through Cultural Co-operation," *Christianity and Crisis* 9 (Oct. 17, 1949). Reprinted in Lefever, *World Crisis,* pp. 111–112.

28. Paul Merkley's study, *Reinhold Niebuhr: A Political Account* (Montreal: McGill-Queens University Press, 1975), presents the most complete account of Niebuhr's incessant activity on behalf of socialist causes.

29. "Norman Thomas: Incarnate Conscience," *Christianity and Crisis* 24, no. 23 (Jan. 11, 1965), 271–272.

30. "Commentary," *Social Action* 23, no. 5 (Jan. 1957), 12–14.

31. Stone, ed., *Faith and Politics,* p. 246.

32. Reinhold Niebuhr, *Man's Nature and His Communities* (1965), pp. 24–25.

33. This discussion of democracy on the world scene is an edited version of my *Reinhold Niebuhr: Prophet to Politicians,* pp. 204–211.

34. Reinhold Niebuhr and Paul E. Sigmund, *The Democratic Experience: Past and Prospects* (1969), p. vi.

35. Ibid., p. 9.

36. Ibid., p. 92.

37. Ibid., p. 3.

38. Ibid., p. 73.

39. Ibid., p. 184.

40. See final paragraphs of chapter 7.

41. Niebuhr and Sigmund, *Democratic Experience*, pp. 151–152.

42. Ibid., p. 146.

43. Ibid., p. 148.

44. Helder Câmara, "From Dichotomy to Integration," *The Christian Century* 86 (Dec. 10, 1969), 1574.

45. Carl Oglesby and Richard Shaull, *Containment and Change* (New York: Macmillan Co., 1967), pp. 83–97.

46. Niebuhr and Sigmund, *Democratic Experience*, p. 85.

47. Stone, "An Interview with Reinhold Niebuhr," p. 51.

48. Letter to Ronald H. Stone (May 27, 1969), in the author's possession.

49. Seymour Melman, "How to Cut the Military Budget by $54 Billion," *Commonweal* 91 (Nov. 28, 1969), 274. See also Seymour Melman, *Our Depleted Society* (New York: Dell Publishing Co., 1965).

50. "The Negro Minority and Its Fate in a Self-righteous Nation," *Social Action/Social Progress* 35/59 (Oct. 1968), 53–64; *Faith and Politics* (New York: George Braziller, 1968); "An Interview with Reinhold Niebuhr" *Christianity and Crisis* 29 (Mar. 17, 1969).

51. "Seminar in Ethics," Reinhold Niebuhr Papers (MSS in the Library of Congress, Washington, D.C.), Container 56.

52. Seminar notes from 1964 in the author's possession.

53. Roger Shinn wrote to me in Oxford, England, when I was contemplating staying in Oxford for a second year to complete an advanced degree in philosophy. At the time, the offered prospect of captaining the Oxford University boxing team the next year was also attractive. The opportunity to assist Niebuhr drew me from Oxford back to New York. I have not regretted the choice.

54. Roger L. Shinn, response to questionnaire, in the author's possession.

55. Kegley, ed., *Reinhold Niebuhr*, p. 324.

56. H. Richard Niebuhr, "Reinhold Niebuhr's Interpretation of History," Niebuhr Papers, Container 17.

57. Niebuhr, *Man's Nature*, p. 15. There are several different versions of the book's preface, indicating various versions of the book were considered.

58. Ibid., p. 24.

59. Ibid.

60. Kegley, ed., *Reinhold Niebuhr*, p. 513.

61. Harold R. Landon, ed., *Reinhold Niebuhr: A Prophetic Voice in Our Time. Essays in Tribute by Paul Tillich, John C. Bennett and Hans J. Morgenthau* (New York: Seabury Press, 1963), pp. 34–35.

62. Ibid., p. 120.

63. E.g., Niebuhr, *Man's Nature*, p. 106.

64. Ibid., p. 111.

65. Ibid., p. 125.

66. "Mission and Opportunity: Religion in a Pluralistic Culture," in Louis

Finkelstein, ed., *Social Responsibility in an Age of Revolution* (New York: Jewish Theological Seminary, 1971), pp. 177–211.

67. Ibid., p. 191.

68. Unpublished draft of "Introduction," *Man's Nature and His Communities,* Niebuhr Papers, pp. 1–2, Container 40.

69. Niebuhr, *Man's Nature,* p. 18.

70. "New Hopes for Peace in the Middle East," *Christianity and Crisis* 16 (May 28, 1956), 65.

71. Niebuhr, *Pious and Secular America,* p. 109.

72. Ibid.

73. Richard Fox, *Reinhold Niebuhr: A Biography* (New York: Pantheon Books, 1985), p. 293.

74. Robert Coles, *The Geography of Faith* (Boston: Beacon Press, 1971).

75. Letter from Christopher Niebuhr to Cynthia Thompson. Copy in the author's possession.

Appendix

November 15, 1990

Dear Graduate of Union Theological Seminary:

Will you share your reflection on Reinhold Niebuhr with me? I am writing a volume entitled *Professor Reinhold Niebuhr*. It is a short intellectual biography with a focus on his vocation as a teacher of Christian social ethics at the seminary. I want to gain insight as to his impact on students and on their vocations. My hypothesis is that his role as a teacher was more central to his life than previous studies have revealed.

In particular will you share any information you can with me on the following questions:

What courses (approximate titles and dates) did you take with Reinhold Niebuhr?

Did you ever receive counsel from Reinhold Niebuhr? (Approximate year of conversation and subjects under discussion.)

In what ways have you felt the influence of Reinhold Niebuhr in your vocation?

What was your sense of Reinhold Niebuhr's dedication to and influence at Union?

Do you have any comments on Reinhold Niebuhr's relationship with Harry Ward, John C. Bennett, Henry Coffin, Henry Pitney van Dusen, or Paul Tillich? Any stories?

In retrospect, how would you evaluate or grade Reinhold Niebuhr's courses you took?

What attitude do you think your fellow students had toward Reinhold Niebuhr? What attitude did you have?

Did Reinhold Niebuhr ever advise you on Christian social action? What topic?

Any other stories you think readers of *Professor Reinhold Niebuhr* would enjoy?

Would you have referred to him as "Reinie" in conversation with others? In addressing him?

He often used the criterion of "relevance." Did his courses seem relevant to the society of the time? Did they seem relevant to your ongoing work in society?

Please sign your name here, granting permission for me to use your answers and to quote you in *Professor Reinhold Niebuhr*.

    Name

    Address

    Dates at Union

Thank you for your help. I think our collective wisdom about our teacher will provide a helpful picture of his vocation. I, of course, await your answers and judgments. If you wish to withhold permission for any part of your answers to be published, just indicate on the form which parts you would prefer to be kept confidential.

Thank you for your kind help.

Sincerely yours,

Ronald H. Stone

Union '63, '68

Works by
Reinhold Niebuhr

BOOKS

1927 *Does Civilization Need Religion? A Study in the Social Resources and Limitations of Religion in Modern Life.* New York: Macmillan Co.

1929 *Leaves from the Notebook of a Tamed Cynic.* New York: Willett, Clark & Colby.

1932 *The Contribution of Religion to Social Work.* New York: Columbia University Press.

Moral Man and Immoral Society: A Study in Ethics and Politics. New York: Charles Scribner's Sons.

1934 *Reflections on the End of an Era.* New York: Charles Scribner's Sons.

1935 *An Interpretation of Christian Ethics.* New York: Harper & Brothers.

1937 *Beyond Tragedy: Essays on the Christian Interpretation of History.* New York: Charles Scribner's Sons.

1940 *Christianity and Power Politics.* New York: Charles Scribner's Sons.

1941 *The Nature and Destiny of Man: A Christian Interpretation*, 2 vols.
1943 New York: Charles Scribner's Sons.

1944 *The Children of Light and the Children of Darkness: A Vindication of Democracy and a Critique of Its Traditional Defense.* New York: Charles Scribner's Sons.

1946 *Discerning the Signs of the Times: Sermons for Today and Tomorrow.* New York: Charles Scribner's Sons.

1949 *Faith and History: A Comparison of Christian and Modern Views of History.* New York: Charles Scribner's Sons.

1952 *The Irony of American History.* New York: Charles Scribner's Sons.

1953   *Christian Realism and Political Problems.* New York: Charles Scribner's Sons.
1955   *The Self and the Dramas of History.* New York: Charles Scribner's Sons.
1958   *Pious and Secular America.* New York: Charles Scribner's Sons.
1959   *The Structure of Nations and Empires: A Study of the Recurring Patterns and Problems of the Political Order in Relation to the Unique Problems of the Nuclear Age.* New York: Charles Scribner's Sons.
1963   (With Alan Heimert) *A Nation So Conceived: Reflections on the History of America from Its Early Visions to Its Present Power.* New York: Charles Scribner's Sons.
1965   *Man's Nature and His Communities.* New York: Charles Scribner's Sons.
1969   (With Paul E. Sigmund) *The Democratic Experience: Past and Prospects.* New York: Frederick A. Praeger.

COLLECTED ESSAYS

1957   (Ed. by D. B. Robertson) *Love and Justice: Selections from the Shorter Writings of Reinhold Niebuhr.* Philadelphia: Westminster Press.
1958   (Ed. by Ernest W. Lefever) *The World Crisis and American Responsibility.* New York: Association Press.
1959   (Ed. by D. B. Robertson) *Essays in Applied Christianity.* New York: Meridian Books.
1960   (Ed. by Harry R. Davis and Robert C. Good) *Reinhold Niebuhr on Politics.* New York: Charles Scribner's Sons.
1968   (Ed. by Ronald H. Stone) *Faith and Politics: A Commentary on Religious, Social and Political Thought in a Technological Age.* New York: George Braziller.
1974   (Ed. by Ursula M. Niebuhr) *Justice and Mercy.* New York: Harper & Row.
1977   (Ed. by William G. Chrystal) *Young Reinhold Niebuhr: His Early Writings—1911-1931.* St. Louis: Eden Publishing House.
1986   (Ed. by Robert McAfee Brown) *The Essential Reinhold Niebuhr.* New Haven, Conn.: Yale University Press.
1988   (Ed. by Larry Rasmussen) *Reinhold Niebuhr: Theologian of Public Life.* London: William Collins.

LETTERS

1991   (Ed. by Ursula M. Niebuhr) *Remembering Reinhold Niebuhr: Letters of Reinhold and Ursula M. Niebuhr.* New York: HarperCollins.

Index

INDEX

INDEX

Switzerland, 3
Swomley, John W., Jr., 238, 241

Taft, William Howard, 6
Teheran Conference, 154, 160
Thomas Aquinas, 69, 70, 94
Thomas, George F., 141
Thomas, Norman, 54, 84, 111, 113, 243
Thompson, Kenneth, 165, 228, 243
third world, 221
Tillich, Paul, 56, 74, 115, 116, 123, 124, 142, 149, 185, 207, 257, 261, 262
Torah, 260, 261
Treaty of Versailles, 100, 155
Trinity, 45
Triple Alliance, 47
Triple Entente, 47
Troeltsch, Ernst, 41, 48, 49, 51, 57, 64, 69, 106; *The Social Teaching of the Christian Churches,* 48
Truman, Harry, 183

Unamuno, Miguel de, 41, 195
Union for Democratic Action, 128
Union Theological Seminary, xiii, xiv, 2, 18, 42, 49, 53, 54, 67, 76, 82, 84, 113, 122, 143, 153, 173, 177, 185, 226, 227, 233, 252, 254, 261
United Church of Christ, 177
United Kingdom, 247
United Nations, 130, 173
United Nations Educational Scientific Cultural Organization, 158, 181, 242, 243
University of Chicago, 197
University of Iowa, 39
University of Kansas, 39
University of Missouri, 39
Utah, 4, 5
utilitarianism, 206

utopianism, 104, 141, 196, 217, 220, 246, 247

"Validity of Religious Experience and the Certainty of Religious Knowledge, The," 13
van Dusen, Henry Pitney, 130
Vernon, William T., 32
Versailles Conference, 28
Vietnam War, 184, 191, 234, 238, 239, 242, 246, 249, 250, 251, 254, 263
Vrooman, Carl, 6, 15

War Department, 128
War Welfare Commission, 28, 36
Ward, Harry F., 19, 54, 55, 57, 61, 84, 110, 131
Washington, D.C., 2, 264
Weber, Max, 41, 49, 72, 135, 190
West, Charles C., 60, 61, 162
West, Cornel, 239
Western civilization, 41, 46, 47, 95, 97, 98, 127, 134
White Citizens Council, 113, 114
White, Morton, 211
Whitehead, Alfred North, 14, 41, 43, 136, 189
Williams, Charles, 32, 261
Williams, Daniel D., 217, 226
Williams, Preston, 235
Williams, Roger, 73
Wilson, Woodrow, 6, 15, 26, 28, 39, 203, 205
Wilsonian liberalism, 46
Winchester Cathedral, 81, 178
Wise, Stephen, 259
Wolf, William J., 256
Wolfers, Arnold, 227, 228
World Council of Churches, 7, 197
world government, 157–158, 213
World Tomorrow, The, 53, 117, 122

283